HOME!

A Bioregional Reader

Edited by
**Van Andruss, Christopher Plant, Judith Plant
and Eleanor Wright**

Foreword by Stephanie Mills

NEW SOCIETY PUBLISHERS

Philadelphia, PA

Santa Cruz, CA

Gabriola Island, BC

DEDICATION

For Fred, and for children everywhere.

Inquiries regarding requests to reprint all or part of *Home! A Bioregional Reader* should be addressed to:
New Society Publishers,
4527 Springfield Avenue, Philadelphia PA, USA 19143
or
P.O. Box 189, Gabriola Island BC, Canada V0R 1X0.

ISBN USA 0-86571-188-7 Paperback .
ISBN USA 0-86571-187-9 Hardcover
ISBN Canada 1-55092-007-3 Paperback
ISBN Canada 1-55092-006-5 Hardcover

Cover art by Carl Chaplin, "Walk For The Environment, 1989."
Cover design by Barbara Hirshkowitz.

Book design & typesetting by *New Society Publishers Canada*. Electrical energy produced by a seven inch turgo wheel on the creek.

To order directly from the publishers, add $1.75 to the price for the first copy, $.50 cents each additional. Send check or money order to:
New Society Publishers,
P.O. Box 582, Santa Cruz CA, USA 95061
or
P.O. Box 189, Gabriola Island BC, Canada V0R 1X0.

New Society Publishers is a project of the New Society Educational Foundation, a non-profit, tax-exempt public foundation in the U.S.A.. Opinions expressed in this book do not necessarily represent positions of the New Society Educational Foundation.

Table of Contents

ACKNOWLEDGMENTS

Grateful thanks go to all authors of this book for freely and generously contributing their works. Many have labored in the field for over a decade, bringing a bioregional philosophy to public consciousness. Not only have they racked their brains formulating an original set of ideas; they have also contrived their expressions in such ways as to be plain and communicable.

Inspiration came from the North American Bioregional Congresses and especially those thinkers and friends along the West Coast who counselled and encouraged us—Bill Aal, Freeman House and Seth Zuckerman. Loving thanks go to Judy Goldhaft and Peter Berg, who continue to act as a rich source of information and artfulness in the bioregional movement.

Our thanks also to Ellen Sawislak and David Albert, the only publishers we know of who make house-calls up wild mountain trails; to Carl Chaplin for the cover art, originally the poster for Vancouver's first "Walk For The Environment;" to Sheila Foley for her painstaking help in identifying graphics for the book; to our community who kept things going while the editors pored over papers; and to the folks at the Hat Creek Gathering who, over the years, brought home to us the real possibility of bioregional cultures.

Finally, thanks to Robin for her patience.

✳

Grateful acknowledgement is made for permission to reprint previously published and copyrighted articles and material from the following sources:

"The Value of a New Word: Bioregionalism" by Geraldine Payton. First published in *Columbiana*, Summer 1988. Reprinted by permission granted by author and publisher, *Columbiana Magazine. Journal of the Intermountain Northwest*, Chesaw Rt, Box 83F, Oroville, WA 98844.

"Living By Life: Some Bioregional Theory and Practice" by Jim Dodge. First published in *Co-Evolution Quarterly*, Winter, 1981. Reprinted by permission from the author and *Whole Earth Review*, 27 Gate Five Road, Sausalito, CA 94965.

"Topography of the Bioregional Movement" by Sheila Rose Purcell. First published in *Raise the Stakes*, No. 8, Fall 1983. Reprinted by permission from the author and Planet Drum Foundation, Box 31251, San Francisco, Shasta Bioregion, CA 94131.

"More Than Just Saving What's Left" by Peter Berg. First published in *Raise the Stakes*, No. 8, Fall 1983. Reprinted by permission from the author and Planet Drum Foundation.

Excerpts from "Regenerate Culture!" an interview with Gary Snyder in *The New Catalyst*, Spring 1986. Reprinted by permission of the publisher, *The New Catalyst Quarterly*, Box 189, Gabriola Island, BC V0R 1X0, Canada.

"Bioregional Perspectives" by Gary Snyder. Excerpt from *The Practice of the Wild*, San Francisco: North Point, 1990. Copyright 1990 by Gary Snyder. Reprinted by permission from the author and North Point Press.

"Revaluing Home: Feminism and Bioregionalism" by Judith Plant. First published in *The New Catalyst #2*, Jan/Feb 1986. Reprinted by permission from the author and *The New Catalyst Quarterly*.

"In Pockets of Resistance: The Back-to-the-Land Movement Matures" by Christopher Plant. First published in *Kanada: Ein Express Reisehandbuch*, Ed. Maria Feltes and Thomas Feltes. Germany: Mundo Verlag, 1989. English translation reprinted by permission of the author.

"Paradigm Shift" by Kirkpatrick Sale. First published in *Dwellers in the Land*, San Francisco: Sierra Club Books, 1985. Reprinted by permission from author and publisher.

"Where you at? A Bioregional Quiz" compiled by Leonard Charles, Jim Dodge, Lynn Milliman, Victoria Stockley. First published in *Co-Evolution Quarterly*, Winter, 1981. Reprinted by permission from *Whole Earth Review*.

Excerpts from "The Bioregional Vision," an interview with Kirkpatrick Sale in *The New Catalyst*, Spring 1987. Reprinted by permission of the publisher, *The New Catalyst Quarterly*.

"Don't Move" by Gary Snyder first appeared in *Upriver, Downriver*, No. 10, 1987. Reprinted by permission from author and publisher, *Upriver Downriver*, P.O. Box 849, Arcata, CA 95521.

"Reinhabiting California" by Peter Berg and Raymond F. Dasmann. First published in *Reinhabiting a Separate Country. A Bioregional Anthology of Northern California*. Ed. Peter Berg. San Francisco: Planet Drum Foundation, 1978. Reprinted by permission from authors and Planet Drum Foundation.

"Future Primitive" by Jeremiah Gorsline and L. Freeman House. First published in "North Pacific Rim Alive," Bundle #3, 1974. Reprinted by permission granted by authors and Planet Drum Foundation.

Excerpts from "Living Here" by Frisco Bay Mussel Group. First published by Planet Drum Foundation, San Franciso, 1977. Reprinted by permission from authors and publisher.

"At Home in L.A." by Sue Nelson is excerpted from a prose poem entitled "Land & the People 1989" delivered at the panel on Green Cities at the 1989 U.S. Green Gathering in Eugene, Oregon. Reprinted by permission of the author.

"Mish Meditation" appears by permission of its author, Lance Scott.

"Speaking in the Haida Way" by Gwaganad (Diane Brown). First published by *Ruebsaat's Magazine*, 685 W. 19th Avenue, Vancouver, BC V5Z 1W9. Reprinted by permission from author and publisher.

"The Earth" by Baden Powell, was first published in *Reinhabiting a Separate Country. A Bioregional Anthology of Northern California*, San Francisco: Planet Drum Foundation, 1978. Reprinted by permission of author and publisher.

Excerpts from "Home" by Luanne Armstrong were first published in *The New Catalyst* No. 15, Fall 1989. Reprinted by permission from the author and publisher, *The New Catalyst Quarterly*.

"The Hudson River Valley: A Bioregional Story" by Thomas Berry. Excerpts from *The Dream of the Earth*, San Francisco: Sierra Club Books, 1988. Copyright 1988 by Thomas Berry. Reprinted by permission from author and publisher.

"The Salmon Circle," by Fraser Lang and "The Salmon Dance" by Alison Lang first appeared in *NABC III Proceedings*. Reprinted by permission of the authors.

Excerpts from *Micro-Cosmos: Four Billion Years of Microbial Evolution* by Lynn Margulis and Dorian Sagan. Copyright 1986 by Lynn Margulis and Dorian Sagan. New York: Summit Books, a division of Simon & Schuster, Inc. Reprinted by permission of authors and publisher.

"From a Mechanical to an Ecological Worldview" by Nancy Jack Todd and John Todd. Excerpts from *Bioshelters, Ocean Arks, City*

Farming: Ecology as the Basis of Design. San Francisco: Sierra Club Books, 1984. Reprinted by permission of authors and publisher.

"Culture is the Missing Link" by Van Andruss and Eleanor Wright. First published in *The Catalist*, April-May 1984. Reprinted by permission of authors.

"Totem Salmon" by L. Freeman House. First published in "North Pacific Rim Alive" Bundle No. 3 by Planet Drum Foundation, San Francisco: 1974. Reprinted by permission of author and publisher.

"How Humans Adapt" by Kelly Booth. First published in *The Catalist*, April-May 1984. Reprinted by permission of author.

"Home is Here" and "The Parasites" by Wilfred Pelletier and Ted Poole. Excerpted from *No Foreign Land: The Biography of a North American Indian*, by Wilfred Pelletier and Ted Poole. Toronto: Random House of Canada Limited, 1973. Reprinted by permission of Pantheon Books, a division of Random House.

"Searching for Common Ground: Ecofeminism and Bioregionalism" by Judith Plant. First published in *The New Catalyst*, No. 10, Winter 1987/1988. Reprinted by permission of the author and the publisher.

"Community—Meeting our Deepest Needs" by Helen Forsey. Excerpted from *Healing the Wounds: The Promise of Ecofeminism*, ed. Judith Plant. Philadelphia & Santa Cruz: New Society Publishers, 1989. Reprinted by permission of the author and publisher.

"Bioregion as Community: The Kansas Experience" by Gary & Julie Coates. Excerpted from an article first published in *Co- Evolution Quarterly*, Winter 1981. Reprinted by permission of authors and publisher.

"Bioregionalism/Western Culture/Women" by Marnie Muller. First published in *Raise the Stakes*, No. 10, Summer 1984. Reprinted by permission of author and publisher, Planet Drum Foundation.

"Earth Diet, Earth Culture" by William Koethke. First published in *Fifth Estate*, Spring 1987. Reprinted by permission of author and publisher, *Fifth Estate*, P.O. Box 02548, Detroit, MI 48202.

"The Council of All Beings" by Pat Fleming and Joanna Macy. Excerpted from *Thinking Like a Mountain. Towards a Council of All Beings* by John Seed, Joanna Macy, Pat Fleming, Arne Ness. Philadelphia & Santa Cruz: New Society Publishers, 1988. Reprinted by permission of authors and publisher.

"Getting Over The Distance Between Us," by Jerry Martien. Reprinted by permission of the author.

"Fantasy of a Living Future" by Starhawk. Excerpt from *Truth or Dare: Encounters with Power, Authority, and Mystery*. Copyright 1987 by Miriam Simos. Reprinted by permission of Harper & Row, Publishers, Inc.

Exerpts from "Ecotopia Emerging" by Ernest Callenbach. New York: Bantam Books, 1981. Reprinted by permission of author and publisher.

"Green City: An Introduction" by Kathryn Cholette, Ross Dobson, Kent Gerecke, Marcia Nozick, Roberta Simpson, Linda Williams. Excerpted from a presentation at the Green Cities Conference in Chicago and published in *City Magazine*, Vol. II, No.1, Summer/Fall '89. Reprinted by permission of authors and publisher, *City Magazine*, 71 Cordova Street, Winnipeg, MB R3N 0Z9, Canada.

"On Permaculture and Community" by Bill Mollison. Excerpts from *Permaculture Two: Practical Design for Town & Country in Permanent Agriculture*. Tagari Books, 1979. Reprinted by permission of author and publishers, Tagari Publications, P.O. Box 1, Tyalgum, NSW 2484, Australia.

"A Green City Program for San Francisco Bay Area Cities and Towns" by Peter Berg, Beryl Magilavy, Seth Zuckerman. First published in *A Green City Program* by Peter Berg, Beryl Magilavy, Seth Zuckerman. San Francisco: Planet Drum Books, 1989. Reprinted by permission of author and publisher, Planet Drum Books.

"To Learn the Things We Need to Know: Engaging the Particulars of the Planet's Recovery" by Freeman House. First published in *Whole Earth Review*, Winter 1989-90. Reprinted with permission from the author and *Whole Earth Review*.

"Watersheds" by David McCloskey. First published in *Coming Home: On Naming and Claiming Your Bioregion*, 1985. Reprinted by permission of author.

"Taking Steps Toward a Restoration Ethic" by Jamie Sayen. Excerpted from an article in *Earth First!*, Beltane edition, 1989. Reprinted by permission from the author and publisher, *Earth First!*, P.O. Box 7, Canton, NY 13617.

"Wilderness" and "Wilderness for Science" by Aldo Leopold. Excerpts from an essay entitled "Wilderness" in *A Sand County Almanac*. Reprinted by permission of the publisher.

"Devolutionary Notes" by Michael Zwerin. Excerpted from *Devolutionary Notes*. San Francisco: Planet Drum Foundation, 1980. Reprinted by permission of author and publisher, Planet Drum Foundation.

Excerpt from *The Breakdown of Nations* by Leopold Kohr. London & New York: Routledge & Kegan Paul, 1957. Reprinted by permission of author and publisher.

"Bioregionalism and the Green Movement" by Brian Tokar. Excerpted from *The Green Alternative: Creating an Ecological Future*. San Pedro: R & E Miles, 1987. Reprinted by permission of author and publishers.

"Growing a Life-Place Politics" by Peter Berg. First published in *Raise the Stakes*, No. 11, Summer 1986. Reprinted by permission of author and publisher, Planet Drum Foundation.

"Municipal Libertarianism" by Murray Bookchin. Excerpts from "Cities, Councils and Confederations," from *Turtle Talk: Voices for a Sustainable Future*, by Christopher & Judith Plant. Reprinted by permission of publishers.

"Spiritualism: The Highest Form of Political Consciousness. The Haudenosaunee Message to the Western World" from *Basic Call to Consciousness*, ed. *Akwesasne Notes*, Rooseveltown: New York, 1978. Reprinted by permission of publishers, *Akwesasne Notes*, Mohawk Nation via Rooseveltown, NY 13683.

"The Fourth World Declaration" by John Papworth, from *The Declaration of the First Assembly of the Fourth World*, 1980. Reprinted by permission of the author and the *Fourth World Review*, 24 Abercorn Place, London, N.W.8, England.

"Strategies for an Alternative Nation" by Bill Mollison. Excerpts from *Permaculture: A Designer's Manual*. Tagari Publications, 1988. Reprinted by permission of author and publisher, Tagari Publications.

"A Proposal of Marriage" by Michael Crofoot. Reprinted from the *Second North American Bioregional Congress Proceedings*, Hart Publishing, 1987. Reprinted by permission of author.

"LETS: The Local Employment Trading System" by Michael Linton and Thomas Greco. First published in the *Fourth World Review*, No. 26, 1988, with acknowledgements to *Whole Earth Review*. Reprinted by permission from authors and publisher, *Fourth World Review*.

"Bioregional Education" by Frank Traina. Editorial in *Pollen: Journal of Bioregional Education*, Vol. 1, No. 1, 1990. Reprinted by permission of author and publisher, Sunrock Farm, 103 Gibson Lane, Wilder, KY 41076.

"Building a Bioregional/Sustainable Alternative" by Douglas Aberley. Excerpt from "Sustaining Development in Rural British Columbia: A Bioregional Context," 1989. Reprinted by permission of author.

"Organizing a Bioregional Congress" by David Haenke. First published in the *Second North American Bioregional Congress Proceedings*, 1988. Reprinted by permission of author.

"Sexism, Racism & the Land" by Milo Guthrie. Excerpted from a report on a workshop at the Third North American Bioregional Congress, 1989. Published in the *Third North American Bioregional Congress Proceedings*, 1989. Reprinted by permission of author.

"MAGICal Reflections: All Species Representation at the Congress" by David Abram. From the MAGIC (Mischief, Animism, Geomancy, and Interspecies Communication) Committee report in the *Third North American Bioregional Congress Proceedings*, 1989. Reprinted by permission of author and publisher.

Excerpt from an interview with Jeffrey Lewis by Paul Cienfuegos and Ellen Rainwalker first appeared in the *North American Bioregional Congress III Proceedings* 1989. Reprinted by permission of author and publisher.

"Consensus" by Caroline Estes. First published in *The New Catalyst*, No.3, Spring 1986. Reprinted by permission of the author and publisher.

"Sustaining Bioregional Groups: The KAW Experience" by Caryn Mirriam-Goldberg. Excerpted from the *Third North American Bioregional Congress Proceedings*, 1989. Reprinted by permission of author.

"One Town's All-Species Day" by Chris Wells. First published in the *Third North American Bioregional Congress Proceedings*, 1989. Reprinted by permission of author.

"Welcome Home" Statement from the *First North American Bioregional Congress Proceedings*, 1984.

"Epigraph," by Gary Lawless. Reprinted by permission of the author.

FOREWORD

Stephanie Mills

We have now officially entered the Earth Day Decade, and a media-stirred multitude of citizens is asking what can be done, indeed what *they* can do, about environmental crisis.

Much of the conventional wisdom offered in response is easy and relatively superficial, ultimately unconvincing, or to put it more charitably, amounts to just preliminary conditions. An average guy or gal may do every last one of the fifty simple things to save the Earth and by the millenium, still find themselves hurtling around the sun on a dying planet.

If that is so, what *would* it mean to get serious about saving the Earth, anyway?...

...Probably a little "something more" than Green consumerism, and certainly more than lately-Green politicians.

In *Home!* you will hear the voices that are articulating the something more. It is called bioregionalism. Infused with the poetry of nature observed, bioregionalism is an intelligent and imaginative political philosophy, perhaps the only one currently affirmed by truths evident to the indwelling senses. Certainly it is unique in eschewing centralized authority, and hierarchy, in the governance it sketches.

Bioregionalism is about growing a lifeway, rather than imposing policy or fine-tuning and reforming industrial civilization's present practices in order to buy more time for what Freeman House calls "the commodity spectacle." It seeks more thorough change. For humans again to participate in, rather than mine, Earth's ecosystems, most of our lately-accustomed ways—of thought, perception, society, tenure, and livelihood—will have to be radically reshaped towards sustainability. In dozens of particular places across the continent of North America, (and doubtless elsewhere, by other names) bioregionalism is conjuring those shapes. It aims at "saving the whole by saving the parts," in Peter Berg's succinct formulation.

Bioregionalism upholds the hope of learning to live more lightly on the Earth, of developing communities integrated with their local ecosystems—creaturely associations that can carry the lifesome ethic forward through the generations.

For taking this longer view, bioregionalism is often categorized as "visionary;" and visionary is sometimes a euphemism for impractical. (This neatly overlooks the fact that what industrial civilization has deemed practical has proved everywhere to be lethal.)

So. Concede that it is visionary, even idealistic: bioregionalism cleaves to the value that free people, freely associating, informed by the biological and geological truths of their home places, will bring the best within themselves, along with the health of their lands, to full flowering. And, because the biological is unsentimental and the geological hard, bioregionalism is, equally, mundane. Reinhabitation—the work of making oneself sustainably at home—takes labor in the land and a rigorous study of natural history and all its implications.

Thanks to its holism and diversity, bioregionalism defeats making any single manifesto. Thus *Home!*, by virtue of being a collection, is an apt introduction to the varied expressions, concerns, and actions of bioregionalism. Surely there could be no likelier creators of such a reader than the editorial collective that has gathered and shaped this book. These are people who really live the bioregional ethic. Members of a larger group of homesteaders in a remote but nonetheless threatened mountain region in interior of British Columbia, they strive as a community for a high degree of self-reliance, relate with due respect to the first peoples of their region, employ consensus decision-making, exercise their citizenship in defense of the forests around them, and have contributed to the bioregional movement as a whole by their salient publishing and thoughtful participation in (and in 1988, their hospitality to) the North American Bioregional Congress.

The bioregionalist faith as it is fleshed out in these pages is that given a little push by clear ideas, local organizing, and that which can be learned from digging in the dirt, humans can and will come together to work for the restoration of life—home life—and the regeneration of its wild diversity.

It is life's earthly beauty and its daily consummations, not the cheap glamor of political or technological dominance, that draws bioregionalists on.

GROWING HOME

An Introduction

Judith Plant

"We are all longing to go home to some place we have never been—a place, half-remembered, and half-envisioned we can only catch glimpses of from time to time. Community. Somewhere, there are people to whom we can speak with passion without having the words catch in our throats. Somewhere a circle of hands will open to receive us, eyes will light up as we enter, voices will celebrate with us whenever we come into our own power. Community means strength that joins our strength to do the work that needs to be done. Arms to hold us when we falter. A circle of healing. A circle of friends. Someplace where we can be free."
— *Starhawk from* Dreaming The Dark: Magic, Sex and Politics

Home! Remembering and reclaiming the ways of our species where people and place are delicately interwoven in a web of life—human community finding its particular place within the living and dying that marks the interdependence of life in an integrated ecosystem. This is the pattern of existence that *bioregionalism* explores. For this term is about being and acting and is more than just a set of ideas. It is the practice of coming to terms with our ecological home. Each of us yearns for this experience, indeed our weakened species is crying out for this wholeness. There is no blueprint, no map of how to get there. How will we ever find our way home?

*

We have walked from the road past many fish camps. Hundreds, indeed thousands of salmon are hanging to dry, cut in the traditional way on the rocky shores of the strong river that runs through our home. Families are working together, the smell of campfires in the air, the dry wind and hot sun taking us back in time. For this practice which we are witnessing close-up for the first time, has been with these people forever. The atmosphere is celebratory, the salmon runs are the best for many years.

Standing on a huge boulder in the midst of the fast-flowing river, she dips her net in and pulls the long pole towards her, again and again. The eldest child waits, with club in hand, totally involved, honored to be out on the rocks with his mother. She is a strong person, her body created from this place, fully grown on salmon, saskatoons, deer

meat, home-grown food. The integrity of her life since birth, in this place with her people, radiates from every pore, from her smile, through her children. Soon a fish is hauled out of the water, then another and another. Quickly clubbed, the salmon are soon gathered together and we carry them back to camp where they will be cut and hung on racks to dry. As we watch the knife making perfect slices, each and every time, what comes to mind is that these people are *just being at home.*

*

We were guests that summer day at the fish camps—for many native people in this region don't really want non-native folks hanging about. This feeling is understandable. This is their work and non-native society has shown little or no respect for the salmon. In fact, the salmon are sick, they are being poisoned by the pulp mills, among other things, up and down the river. Indeed, the next run was not edible because of a huge spill of wood preservative at the river's mouth.

Totem Salmon: this species' health is a reflection of the quality of the water that runs through the land, that mingles with the air. This collection of essays inevitably speaks to this creature. For here, in the Northwest, the salmon and the people are one and this fish is our totem. Where have the salmon gone in the heavily industrialized nations? At best, they have been farmed, with antibiotics—desperate attempts to keep this symbol of health alive in an environment that cannot sustain life. As contributor after contributor suggests, when the salmon thrive, so will we.

*

So many people in the last twenty years have turned off the television, awakened, and dedicated their lives to coming to terms with the social, cultural and political legacy of modern society. It must be turned around. Folks have dug in, and in many ways are working towards a healthy and sane future for all children. During these last two decades this work has taken different forms: the peace, feminist, and back-to-the-land movements, the environmental struggles that seem endless, social justice issues, and the recognition that we must respect all of life, all are elements that are embraced by the term bioregionalism. This is why, for our little community in the mountains of the northwest, this word made so much sense: it articulated what we, and so many others, were already doing. And it has brought us together with many like-minded individuals and groups.

This naming of something that is already going on is the power of *bioregionalism*. It has given our community common ground with people in urban and rural areas all over Turtle Island (the native image of North America). Connecting our work with others, sharing experiences, finding new ideas and differences has enriched our lives exponentially. More than all of this, bioregionalism gives us roots, not just history. This way of being is a new/old idea, for knowing one's people and place is the ancient way of survival and its memory is stirred by our yearning for home.

*

As for so many people these days, whether in city neighborhoods or rural areas, our community seems to most fervently gather around watershed protection activities. Perhaps this is so because

water is absolutely fundamental to survival. More and more people, too, are becoming aware that water does not just flow from the tap, that its origins can be traced, and its quality, or lack of it, can be known. A first step in knowing home, in the bioregional sense, is to be intimately familiar with this most basic element of life. And it's a great organizing tool, for it begins to define the natural boundaries of place.

One of our protect-the-watershed schemes over the past several years has been knapweed pulling. This "noxious weed" was introduced into the bioregion several years ago, seeds transported mostly by vehicles. The typical government response is to spray it to death. We said no, we'll pull it by hand. Surprisingly, they agreed not to spray and even to pay us what it would have cost them to do the job. So, in the spring and summer, almost every Saturday, we can be seen weeding the roadsides, children, young and old, endless chattering making the work move quickly. It's often difficult to get there when the gardens are desperate for similar attention but we know that each one of us makes such a difference to the morale of the whole. And somehow, it's a great time! While the carrots might not be thinned that day, the nascent culture is surely nourished by this empowering, collective responsibility-taking.

Watershed restoration and protection is a unifying theme for bioregionalists all over Turtle Island these days. We came upon this kind of organization several years ago through a conference organized by the Slocan Valley Watershed Protection Alliance and it was here that we ran into other folks using the term "bioregionalism." Feelings of isolation fell away as we met and strategized with new friends. And these people knew people we knew in California and in northern British Columbia. Some of our folks had earlier met up with the Planet Drum people in San Francisco and their extended community who had been thinking and acting this way for years. We're family now, all for the love of water!

*

We feel "out of *their* control," as contributor Jim Dodge has said, describing bioregional self-government. Deferring to centralized authority is just what bioregionalists are resisting. In its place is the authority that rests with local people in local places who have the integrity that comes from knowing home. Home in the sense that contributor Wilfred Pelletier, an Ojibway, means when he describes the place where he is allowed to just be, wherein the greatest freedom lies. He describes community as something that is invisible from the outside, but which, from the inside, is a living organism managing itself—community as a way of life, as survival, where each sustains all; where, if the community doesn't survive, no one survives. This, in stark contrast to modern society where every aspect of life is managed, institutionalized and controlled, where people have no control over the well-being of the basics of life: the water and the air. This system that prides itself on its ultimate control of nature is, from this other perspective of people-in-control of their own communities, totally and wildly out of control. How could it be otherwise when rivers are fouled by all manner of human toxic waste, where air is unfit to breathe?

This Reader, however, is about taking the situation into our own hands. A daring statement but one, nevertheless, that rings true in the midst of chaotic human behavior that is destroying our habitat. Groups of people are assuming this responsibility, in incremental steps, and in ways that most appropriately respond to particular situations, whether it's keeping McDonalds out of the neighborhood, toxic waste incinerators out of the village, or creating shared parenting and home education collectives, or city gardening groups. All are the beginnings of controlling our lives.

*

Our community "governs" itself by meeting regularly, the same Sunday each month so everyone always knows when. This is our Council, not just for men, not just for adults. Everyone comes, with pots of food, games, toys and ideas for children's activities. It's an all day, all evening event. After visiting and lunch, the circle gathers. Children are first on the agenda. Adults take turns throughout the day doing "kid care"—it's a good time for those without children to lend a parenting hand. Sometimes the children have their own circle. All the events that need scheduling for the coming month are organized: forestry meetings, potato planting, education meetings, food co-op meetings…. Sometimes personal issues that need community involvement are brought to the group. Hours and hours can go by with thirty or so people

intently focussed on their collective lives. The experience is at once exhausting and exhilarating, befuddling and enlightening.

The women's meeting is the Friday evening before. This gathering is inevitably warm and often emotional. We are getting to know each other through these women's circles and the groundwork that is being laid here is felt to give strength to the upcoming Council. We have sat around campfires and chanted to the full moon, though we are most often in each other's houses which the men, with children in hand, have thoughtfully left. Sometimes in these circles our selves are revealed to ourselves, as layers of burdensome history is spoken. It was said by an elder, whose ashes now fertilize a fir tree, that if the women could get it together, we'd probably make it.

*

It's been a tough year. But after a day of sledding and fine food, people's faces show little sign of the struggles of the year before. We pull ourselves together, forming the annual large circle wherein we tell each other how it's been for us these past twelve months and where we see ourselves headed. It's the changing of a decade, as well as the beginning of the last decade before the century changes. Like the Worldwatch Institute, many people are using the phrase "the Turn-Around Decade" to describe their hopes and fears for the times to come. What becomes clear to us all is that, in our years together, with all the misunderstandings and problems that inevitably arise, we have grown in love for each other and for this place we call home.

And so we persist, because once involved in such community building, there is no turning back. Learning to love our places means simultaneously learning to love each other. A lifetime of involvement. In this new/old territory, a path towards home begins to show itself. The steps along the way to authentic community are as yet uncharted. Each promises possibilities we can barely fathom. This book, though by no means a chart, provides stepping stones along the trail.

"Winged Beginning," by Daniel O. Stolpe.

Part One

WHAT IS BIOREGIONALISM?

"Bioregionalism doesn't mean merely one thing; it isn't restricted to a single issue or special activity. It has become connective tissue joining the diverse parts of a growing organism." — Sheila Rose Purcell

For a theory and practice that promises to radically change the world so that we may all survive, "bioregionalism" is an unusually awkward and unappealing term at first sight. It's hardly surprising that many people have not heard of the word—even though they may be experienced practitioners of the art—and equally to be expected that, if they have heard of it, it may have left them cold. A deeper probe, however, reveals the extraordinary power of an idea that genuinely integrates numerous other powerful ideas into a common view of the world.

More than just a set of ideas, however, bioregionalism is a movement, too. And just as other social movements contain within their names a critique of present society and a direction for future change, so it is with the bioregional movement. Bioregionalism calls for human society to be more closely related to nature (hence, bio), and to be more conscious of its locale, or region, or life-place (therefore, region). For humans who exhibit the most extreme alienation from nature imaginable, and who—in North America especially—are uniquely *un*attached to particular places, bioregionalism is essentially a recognition that, today, we flounder without an adequate overall philosophy of life to guide our action toward a sane alternative. It is a proposal to ground human cultures within natural systems, to get to know one's place intimately in order to fit human communities to the Earth, not distort the Earth to our demands.

Jim Dodge's essay on the topic—"Living By Life"—is perhaps the most complete and concise explanation of the full scope of the bioregional view. He reiterates the need to understand natural systems, and to shape

2

human cultural behaviors to fit with nature—forming community *with* natural systems, not apart from them. He takes on the somewhat contentious task of describing how bioregions are defined, and calls unhesitatingly for political self-government within such bioregions. The task for bioregionalists, he says, is a dual one of resistance to further centralization and monoculture, and of renewal: creating alternative, small-scale communities and cultures, and repairing the damage already done to natural systems.

Peter Berg from Planet Drum Foundation, in San Francisco, continues this thought. In his view, bioregionalism is "more than just saving what's left," more than environmentalism, rather it is the political means for directing society toward restoring and maintaining the natural systems that ultimately support all of life. Importantly, he sees this work going on everywhere—in cities, suburbs, rural areas, and wilderness. His account of the diversity of those who might consider themselves "bioregionalists" is pursued further by Sheila Rose Purcell.

Gary Snyder elaborates upon how the boundaries of bioregions can be discerned—the boundaries of what he calls a regional "commons." Contrary to the current jurisdictional lines drawn by the state, he describes bioregional boundaries as following, for example, the presence of a key species such as Douglas fir. By identifying more closely with such species, even standing up for them at environmental hearings perhaps, we begin to take on the spirit of a place. In turn, this extra sensitivity to natural regions will inevitably begin to reshape the politics of Turtle Island.

The novelty of bioregionalism is perhaps best summed up by the idea of revaluing home: home as watershed, as community, as the sum total of the relations which sustain us—where human culture is formed. Judith Plant makes the important addition that a new view of home must include the insights of feminism as well as a radically different practice, if we are not to repeat the mistakes of the past.

One vital strand in the origin of bioregionalism was the back-to-the-land movement—the focus of Christopher Plant's article. He reaffirms the capacity of bioregionalism to unite diverse and scattered groups, giving new life and inspiration to land-based alternatives by "daring still to call forth planet-healing ideals."

The Value Of A New Word: Bioregionalism

Often people say, "Big fancy words. YUK! Words I've never heard before. YUK! I don't like them. Why can't you use plain everyday words we all know and are comfortable with?"

Looked at another way, a new word can be a gift, a gift of a new idea—a new concept, a new thought tool for understanding our world, a new vehicle for moving us ahead to where we'd like to go.

Gary Snyder has said that we should find our "*place*" and stay there 400 years! That's how long it takes to make enough observations about where we *are* to live there respectfully, in harmony with all the other members of the animal and plant community—the *bio-tic* community (there's that word *bio* again).

Here's another one: *re-inhabitation*. Maybe you've heard the word *habitat*: the life place (usually of an animal); the whole little system of life resources that an animal dwells in, and can't do without. Our ancestors spent thousands of generations learning how to live *in place*. Learning again, or remembering, how to live in place is one of the most important tasks we have before us.

Re-inhabitation, a lot of people believe, will be necessary for our long term survival. Living in mutual, respectful partnership with Planet Earth; taking care of our needs in a mutually benefitting exchange will sustain our own lives *and* the life of the planet.

BIO - REGIONAL - ISM

Bio... means all of life... *regional*... means within a physical or geographic boundary and ...*ism* is the human part; where we study how we relate with and live as part of the *Bioregion*.

— from **Columbiana**, Summer, 1988.

LIVING BY LIFE:
Some Bioregional Theory and Practice

Jim Dodge

I want to make it clear from the outset that I'm not all that sure what bioregionalism is. To my understanding, bioregionalism is an idea still in loose and amorphous formulation, and presently is more hopeful declaration than actual practice. In fact, "ideal" may be too generous: bioregionalism is more properly a notion, which is variously defined as a general idea, a belief, an opinion, an intuition, an inclination, an urge. Furthermore, as I think will prove apparent, bioregionalism is hardly a new notion; it has been the animating cultural principle through 99 percent of human history, and is at least as old as consciousness. Thus, no doubt, the urge.

My purpose here is not really to define bioregionalism—that will take care of itself in the course of things—but to mention some of the elements that I see composing the notion, and some possibilities for practice. I speak with no special privilege on the matter other than my longstanding and fairly studious regard for the subject, a regard enriched by my teachers and numerous bioregional friends. My only true qualification is that I'm fool enough to try.

"Bioregionalism" is from the Greek *bios* (life) and the French *region* (region), itself from the Latin *regia* (territory), and earlier, *regere* (to rule or govern). Etymologically, then, bioregionalism means life territory, place of life, or perhaps by reckless extension, government by life. If you can't imagine that government by life would be at least 40 billion times better than government by the Reagan administration, or Mobil Oil, or any other distant powerful monolith, then your heart is probably no bigger than a prune pit and you won't have much sympathy for what follows.

*

A central element of bioregionalism—and one that distinguishes it from similar politics of place—is the importance given to natural systems, both as the source of physical nutrition and as the body of metaphors from which our spirits draw sustenance. A natural system is a community of interdependent life, a mutual biological integration on the order of an ecosystem, for example. What constitutes this community is uncertain beyond the obvious—that it includes all interacting life forms, from the tiniest fleck of algae to human beings, as well as their biological processes. To this bare minimum, already impenetrably complex, bioregionalism adds the influences of cultural behavior, such as subsistence techniques and ceremonies. Many people further insist—sensibly, I think—that this community/ecosystem must also include the planetary processes and the larger figures of regulation: solar income, magnetism, gravity, and so forth. Bioregionalism is simply biological realism; in natural systems we find the physical truth of our being, the real obvious stuff like the need for oxygen as well as the more subtle need for moonlight, and perhaps other truths beyond those. Not surprisingly, then, bioregionalism holds that the health of natural systems is directly connected to our own physical/psychic health as individuals and as a species, and for that reason natural systems and their informing integrations deserve, if not utter veneration, at least our clearest attention and deepest respect. No matter how great our laws, technologies, or armies, we can't make the sun rise every morning nor the rain dance on the golden-back ferns.

To understand natural systems is to begin an understanding of the self, its common and particular essences—literal self-interest in its barest terms. "As above, so below," according to the old-tradition alchemists; natural systems as models of consciousness. When we destroy a river, we increase our thirst, ruin the beauty of free-flowing water, forsake the meat and spirit of the salmon, and lose a little bit of our souls.

Unfortunately, human society has also developed technologies that make it possible to lose big chunks all at once. If we make just one serious mistake with nuclear energy, for instance, our grandchildren may be born with bones like over-cooked spaghetti, or torn apart by mutant rats. Global nuclear war is suicide: the "losers" die instantly; the "winners" inherit slow radiation death and twisted chromosomes. By any sensible measure of self-interest, by any regard for life, nuclear war is abhorrent, unthinkable, and loathsomely stupid, and yet the United States and other nations spend billions to provide that possibility. It is the same mentality that pooh-poohs the growing concentration of poisons in the biosphere. It's like the farmer who was showing off his prize mule to a stranger one day when the mule suddenly fell over sideways and died. The farmer looked at the body in bewildered disbelief: "Damn," he said, "I've had this mule for 27 years and it's the first time he's ever done this." To which the stranger, being a biological realist, undoubtedly replied, "No shit."

*

While I find an amazing depth of agreement among bioregionalists on what constitutes *bios*, and on what general responsibilities attend our place in the skein of things, there is some disagreement—friendly but passionate—on what actually constitutes a distinct biological region (as opposed to arbitrary entities, like states and counties, where boundaries are established without the dimmest ecological perception, and therefore make for cultural incoherence and piecemeal environmental management). Since the very gut of bioregional thought is the integrity of natural systems and culture, with the function of culture being the mediation of the self and the ecosystem, one might think "bioregion" would be fairly tightly defined.

But I think it must be kept in mind that, to paraphrase Poe and Jack Spicer, we're dealing with the grand concord of what does not stoop to definition. There are, however, a number of ideas floating around regarding the biological criteria for a region. I'll mention some of them below, limiting the examples to Northern California.

One criterion for determining a biological region is biotic shift, a percentage change in plant/animal species composition from one place to another—that is, if 15 to 25 percent of the species where I live are different from those where you live, we occupy different biological regions. We probably also experience different climates and walk on different soils, since those differences are reflected in species composition. Nearly everyone I've talked with agrees that biotic shift is a fairly slick and accurate way to make bioregional distinctions; the argument is over the percentage, which invariably seems arbitrary. Since the change in biotic composition is usually gradual, the biotic shift criterion permits vague and permeable boundaries between regions, which I personally favor. The idea, after all, is not to replace one set of lines with another, but simply to recognize inherent biological integrities for the purpose of sensible planning and management.

Another way to biologically consider regions is by watershed. This method is generally straightforward, since drainages are clearly apparent on topographical maps. Watershed is usually taken to mean river drainage, so if you live on Cottonwood Creek you are part of the Sacramento River drainage. The problem with watersheds as bioregional criteria is that if you live in San Francisco you are also part of the Sacramento (and San Joaquin) River drainage, and that's a long way from Cottonwood Creek. Since any long drainage presents similar problems, most people who advance the watershed criterion make intradrainage distinctions (in the case of the Sacramento: headwaters, Central Valley, west slope Sierra, east slope Coast Range, and delta/bay). The west slope of the Coast Range, with its short-running rivers and strong Pacific influence, is often considered as a whole biological area, at least from the Gualala River to the Mattole River or, depending on who you're talking to, from the Russian River to the Eel River, though they aren't strictly west slope Coast Range rivers. The Klamath, Smith and Trinity drainages are often considered a single drainage system with the arguable inclusion of the Chetco

Topography Of The Bioregional Movement

There are many more ways of applying bioregional ideas, and more people and groups doing so, than most of us could have imagined a few years ago. Community groups from the Siskiyou Mountains of California and Oregon to the lower Hudson estuary in New York are spawning new publications and projects involving everyone from professionals to grassroots activists. Renewable energy practitioners, community planners, architects, and educators have begun to share a bioregional vision with forest workers, permaculture farmers, and food co-op activists. We're involved in a full-blown movement now, and it's time to see how individual threads weave through the whole tapestry.

Bioregionalism doesn't mean merely one thing; it isn't restricted to a single issue or special activity. It has become connective tissue joining the diverse parts of a growing organism. We should be aware of the unique role each of these parts plays and how each reaches beyond its particular function. Bioregionalism defines itself through that diverse and continuously evolving blend.

While talking to some groups, corresponding with others, and reading material from even more as Planet Drum's networker, I've discerned a pattern in the bioregional fabric that I would like to share. It has been useful for directing networking assistance, and it should be useful for understanding the varied aspects of our movement.

First of all, there are *Seed Individuals* whose appreciation of the places where they live hasn't been deadened by industrial civilization. They are full participants in the lives of those places. Whether old-timers or new settlers, country or city dwellers, their identity taps directly into the bioregion.

Next come *Circles of Friends* who share bioregional interests and who may collaborate on local information projects as a study group or undertake common tasks. San Francisco's Frisco Bay Mussel Group began by inviting speakers to address topics such as watersheds and native species, eventually publishing this information in a successful campaign to defeat a major water-diversion scheme.

United to Resist a Common Threat is a type of bioregional group that is organized around a specific issue. Herbicide spraying, mining, nuclear power plants, and other obstacles to the natural wholeness of local

and the Rogue.

A similar method of bioregional distinction is based upon land form. Roughly, Northern California breaks down into the Sierra, the Coast Range, the Central Valley, the Klamath Range, the southern part of the Cascade Range, and the Modoc Plateau. Considering the relationship between topography and water, it is not surprising that land form distinctions closely follow watersheds.

A different criterion for making bioregional distinctions is, awkwardly put, cultural/phenomenological: you are where you perceive you are; your turf is what you think it is, individually and collectively. Although the human sense of territory is deeply evolved and cultural/perceptual behavior certainly influences the sense of place, this view seems to me a bit anthropocentric. And though it is difficult *not* to view things in terms of human experience and values, it does seem wise to remember that human perception is notoriously prey to distortion and the strange delights of perversity. Our species hasn't done too well lately working essentially from this view; because we're ecological dominants doesn't necessarily mean we're ecological determinants. (In fairness, I should note that many friends think I'm unduly cranky on this subject.)

One of the more provocative ideas to delineate bioregions is in terms of "spirit places" or psyche-tuning power-presences, such as Mount Shasta and the Pacific Ocean. By this criterion, a bioregion is defined by the predominate psychophysical influence where you live. You have to live in its presence long enough to truly feel its force within you and that it's not mere descriptive geography.

areas have brought together numerous resistance groups. They express regional concern by opposing exploitive disruption, in forms such as herbicide task forces, valley protection groups, or watershed citizens organizations.

Offering a Positive Program is a natural accompaniment to the previous kind of groups. An organization that seeks to increase some life-enhancing quality of a place—whether by sponsoring native crafts, developing permaculture, creating a renewable energy center, or restoring native plants—is directly addressing long-term bioregional continuity.

Some groups are *Bioregional Too* while carrying out their other programs. The Creosote Collective in Tucson, Arizona, sees food production and distribution from a bioregional Sonoran Desert perspective, Tilth advocates a place-located view for sustainable agriculture in the Pacific Northwest, and both groups are planning bioregional gatherings. RAIN in Oregon and New Alchemy Institute on Cape Cod have evolved local activities to complement their wide-ranging interests in alternative technology and energy.

There are *Explicitly Bioregional* groups springing up in many places: Regional Awareness Project in San Antonio, Reinhabiting New Jersey, and Mogollon Highlands Watershed Association in Colorado, to mention only a few of a rapidly growing number. They have a specifically reinhabitory basis for consider-

ing a broad front of programs including locally generated arts and media, employment in restoring and maintaining bioregions, promoting local barter fairs, and bringing bioregional programs into the schools.

A *Bioregional Congress* so that as many groups as possible which represent life-place considerations can adopt common goals is a further manifestation of the bioregional movement. Ozarks Area Community Congress and Kansas Area Watershed have already established theirs; Great Lakes, Ohio River Basin Information Service, Interior Pacific Northwest, and New York state now are planning their first congresses.

Finally, there are beginnings of larger *Interbioregional* organizations, such as the North American Bioregional Congress and the Fourth World Assembly.

Although there is a progression of formally stated purposes in the categories that have been listed, relationships among them should be seen as mutualistic and non-hierarchical. Each is necessary and contributive, reflecting a healthy diversity that assures further growth. Our ability to eventually create a reinhabitory society will hinge on our ability to integrate all these manifestations of bioregionalism.

— **Sheila Rose Purcell,** *from* **Raise the Stakes** *No.8, Fall 1983.*

Also provocative is the notion that bioregion is a vertical phenomenon having more to do with elevation than horizontal deployment—thus a distinction between hill people and flatlanders, which in Northern California also tends to mean country and city. A person living at 2000 feet in the coast Range would have more in cultural common with a Sierra dweller at a similar altitude than with someone at sea level 20 miles away.

To briefly recapitulate, the criteria most often advanced for making bioregional distinctions are biotic shift, watershed, land form, cultural/phenomenological, spirit presence, and elevation. Taken together, as I think they should be, they give us a strong sense of where we're at and the life that enmeshes our own. Nobody I know is pushing for a quick definition anyway. Bioregionalism, what it is, occupies that point in

development (more properly, renewal) where definition is unnecessary and perhaps dangerous. Better now to let definitions emerge from practice than impose them dogmatically from the git-go.

*

A second element of bioregionalism is anarchy. I hesitate using that fine word because it's been so distorted by reactionary shitheads to scare people that its connotative associations have become bloody chaos and fiends amok, rather than political decentralization, self-determination, and a commitment to social equity. Anarchy doesn't mean out of control; it means out of *their* control. Anarchy is based upon a sense of interdependent self-reliance, the conviction that we as a community, or a tight, small-scale federation of communities, can mind our own business, and can make decisions regarding our individual and communal lives and gladly accept the responsibilities and consequences of those decisions. Further, by consolidating decision making at a local, face-to-face level without having to constantly push information through insane bureaucratic hierarchies, we can act more quickly in relation to natural systems and, since we live there, hopefully with more knowledge and care.

The United States is simply too large and complex to be responsibly governed by a decision-making body of perhaps 1000 people representing 220,000,000 Americans and a large chunk of the biosphere, especially when those 1000 decision makers can only survive by compromise and generally are forced to front for heavy economic interests (media campaigns for national office are expensive). A government where one person represents the interests of 220,000 others is absurd, considering that not all the people voted for the winning representative (or even voted) and especially considering that most of those 220,000 people are capable of representing themselves. I think people do much better, express their deeper qualities, when their actions matter. Obviously one way to make government more meaningful and responsible is to involve people directly day by day, in the processes of decision, which only seems possible if we reduce the scale of government. A bioregion seems about the right size: say close to a small state, or along the lines of the Swiss canton system or American Indian tribes.

If nothing else, bioregional government— which theoretically would express the biological and cultural realities of people-in- place—would promote the diversity of biosocial experimentation; and in diversity is stability. The present system of national government seems about to collapse under the weight of its own emptiness. Our economy is dissolving like wet sugar. Violence is epidemic. The quality of our workmanship—always the hallmark of a proud people—has deteriorated so badly that we're ashamed to classify our products as durable goods. Our minds have been homogenized by television, which keeps our egos in perpetual infancy while substituting them for a sense of self. Our information comes from progressively fewer sources, none of them notably reliable. We spend more time posturing than we do getting it on. In short, American culture has become increasingly gutless and barren in our lifetimes, and the political system little more than

a cover for an economics that ravages the planet and its people for the financial gain of very few. It seems almost a social obligation to explore alternatives. Our much-heralded standard of living hasn't done much for the quality of our daily lives; the glut of commodities, endlessly hurled at us out of the vast commodity spectacle, is just more shit on the windshield.

I don't want to imply that bioregionalism is the latest sectarian addition to the American Left, which historically has been more concerned with doctrinal purity and shafting each other than with effective practice. It's not a question of working within the system or outside the system, but simply of working, *somewhere*, to pull it off. And as I mentioned at the beginning, I'm not so sure bioregionalism even has a doctrine to be pure about—it's more a sense of direction (uphill, it seems) than the usual leftist highway to Utopia…or Ecotopia for that matter.

Just for the record, and to give some credence to the diversity of thought informing bioregionalism, I want to note some of the spirits I see at work in the early formulation of the notion: pantheists, Wobs, Reformed Marxists (that is, those who see the sun as the means of production), Diggers, libterrereans, Kropotkinites (mutual aid and coevolution), animists, alchemists (especially the old school), lefty Buddhists, Situationists (consummate analysts of the commodity spectacle), syndicalists, Provos, born-again Taoists, general outlaws, and others drawn to the decentralist banner by raw empathy.

*

A third element composing the bioregional notion is spirit. Since I can't claim any spiritual wisdom, and must admit to being virtually ignorant on the subject, I'm reluctant to offer more than the most tentative perceptions. What I think most bioregionalists hold in spiritual common is a profound regard for life—all life, not just white Americans, or humankind entire, but frogs, roses, mayflies, coyotes, lichens: all of it: the gopher snake and the gopher. For instance, we don't want to save the whales for the sweetsie-poo, lily-romantic reasons attributed to us by those who profit from their slaughter; we don't want them saved merely because they are magnificent creatures, so awesome that when you see one close from an open boat your heart roars; we want to save them for the most selfish of reasons: without them we are diminished.

In the bioregional spirit view we're all one creation, and it may seem almost simple-minded to add that there is a connection—even a necessary unity—between the natural world and the human mind (which may be just a fancy way of saying there is a connection between life and existence). Different people and groups have their own paths and practices and may describe this connection differently—profound, amusing, ineluctable, mysterious—but they all acknowledge the importance of the connection. The connection is archaic, primitive, and so obvious that it hasn't received much attention since the rise of Christian dominion and fossil-fuel industrialism. If it is a quality of archaic thought to dispute the culturally enforced dichotomy between the spiritual and the practical, I decidedly prefer the archaic view. What could possibly be of more *practical* concern than our spiritual well-being as individuals, as a species, and as members of a larger community of life? The Moral Majority certainly isn't going to take us in that direction; they're interested in business as usual, as their golden boy, James Watt, has demonstrated. We need fewer sermons and more prayers.

This sense of bioregional spirit isn't fixed to a single religious form or practice. Generally it isn't Christian-based or noticeably monotheistic, though such views aren't excluded. I think the main influences are the primitive animist/Great Spirit tradition of various Eastern and esoteric religious practices, and plain ol' paying attention. I may be stretching the accord, but I also see a shared awareness that the map is not the journey, and for that reason it is best to be alert and to respond to the opportunities presented rather than waste away wishing life would offer some worthy spiritual challenge (which it does, constantly, anyway). Call it whatever seems appropriate—enlightenment, fulfillment, spiritual maturity, happiness, self-realization—it has to be earned, and to be earned it has to be lived, and that means bringing it into our daily lives and working on it. Instant gratifications are not the deepest gratifications, I suspect, though Lord knows they certainly have their charms. The emphasis is definitely on the practice, not the doctrine, and especially on practicing what you preach; there is a general recognition that there are many paths, and that they are a further manifestation of crucial natural diversity. I might also note for serious backsliders that the

play is as serious as the work, and there is a great willingness to celebrate; nobody is interested in a spirit whose holiness is constantly announced with sour piety and narrow self-righteousness.

*

Combining the three elements gives a loose idea of what I take to be bioregionalism: a decentralized, self-determined mode of social organization; a culture predicated upon biological integrities and acting in respectful accord; and a society which honors and abets the spiritual development of its members. Or so the theory goes. However, it's not mere theory, for there have been many cultures founded essentially upon those principles; for example, it has been the dominant cultural mode of inhabitation on this continent. The point is not to go back, but to take the best forward. Renewal, not some misty retreat into what was.

Theories, ideas, notions—they have their generative and reclamative values, and certainly a loveliness, but without the palpable intelligence of practice they remain hovering in the nether regions of nifty entertainments or degrade into more flamboyant fads and diversions like literary movements and hula-hoops. Practice is what puts the heart to work. If theory establishes the game, practice is the gamble, and the first rule of all gambling games has it like this: you can play bad and win; you can play good and lose; but if you play good over the long haul you're gonna come out alright.

Bioregional practice (or applied strategy) can take as many forms as the imagination and nerves, but for purpose of example I've hacked it into two broad categories, resistance and renewal. Resistance involves a struggle between the bioregional forces (who represent intelligence, excellence, and care) and the forces of heartlessness (who represent a greed so lifeless and forsaken it can't even pass as ignorance). In a way, I think it really is that simple, that there is, always, a choice about how we will live our lives, that there is a state of constant opportunity for both spiritual succor and carnal delight, and that the way we choose to live is the deepest expression of who we truly are. If we consistently choose against the richest possibilities of life, against kindness, against beauty, against love and sweet regard, then we aren't much. Our only claim to dignity is trying our best to do what we think is right, to put some heart in it, some soul, flower and root. We're going to fall on our asses a lot, founder on our pettiness and covetousness and sloth, but at least there is the effort, and that's surely better than being just another quivering piece of the national cultural jello. Or so it seems to me.

However, the primary focus of resistance is not the homogeneous American supraculture—that can be resisted for the most part simply by refusing to participate, while at the same time trying to live our lives the way we think we should (knowing we'll get no encouragement whatsoever from the colonial overstructure). Rather, the focus of resistance is against the continuing destruction of natural systems. We can survive the ruthless homogeneity of national culture because there are many holes we can slip through, but we cannot survive if the natural systems that sustain us are destroyed. That has to be stopped if we want to continue living on this planet. That's not "environmentalism"; it's ecology with a vengeance. Personally, I think we should develop a Sophoclean appreciation for the laws of nature, and submit. Only within the fractional time frame of fossil-fuel industrialization have we begun to seriously insult the environment and impudently violate the conditions of life. We've done a great deal of damage in a very short time, and only because of the amazing flexibility of natural systems have we gotten away with it so far. But I don't think we'll destroy the planet; she will destroy us first, which is perhaps only to say we'll destroy ourselves. The most crucial point of resistance is choosing not to.

> "The chances of bioregionalism succeeding, like the chances of survival itself, are beside the point. If one person, or a few, or a community of people, live more fulfilling lives from bioregional practice, then it's successful."

*

And then we must try to prevent others from doing it for us all, since by allowing monopoly-capital centralized government (which, like monotheism, is not so much putting all your eggs in one basket as dropping your one egg in a blender), we have given them the power to make such remote-control decisions. The way to prevent it is five-fold: by being a model for an alternative; by knowing more than they do; by being politically astute; by protecting what we value; and by any means necessary. (I think it's important to note that there is nearly complete agreement that nonviolence is the best means available, and that the use of violence is always a sad admission of desperation. Besides, they have all the money, guns, and lawyers. People advocating violent means are probably not very interested in living much longer.)

I think political smarts are best applied in the local community and county. Most crucial land use decisions, for instance, are made at the county level by boards of supervisors. The representative-to-constituent ratio is obviously much better in a county than in a country, and therefore informed and spirited constituents have a far greater influence on decisions and policies. Work to elect sympathetic representatives. Put some money where your heart is. Go to your share of the generally boring meetings and hearings. Challenge faulty information (thus the importance of knowing more than they do). Create alternatives. Stand your ground.

Buying land is also a strong political move; "ownership" is the best protection against gross environmental abuse, just as living on the land is the best defense against mass-media gelatin culture, assuming the quality of information influences the quality of thought. Owning land also affords increased political leverage within the present system. Besides, bioregionalism without a tangible land base would be like love without sex; the circuits of association wouldn't be complete. (Of course, it isn't necessary to own land to either appreciate it or resist its destruction, and I hope nobody infers that bioregionalism is for land aristocracy.)

*

The growth and strength of the "environmental movement" in the 1970s has encouraged awareness about the destruction of natural systems and the consequences of such callous disregard. This is all to the good, and we should continue to stay in their faces on critical issues. But it's going to be continual crisis ecology unless we come up with a persuasive economic alternative; otherwise, most people will go on choosing progress over maturity, for progress is deeply equated with payroll, and money, to most people, means life. It's that cold. It's also basically true, and many friends share my chagrin that it took us so long to grasp that truism. It now seems painfully obvious that the economic system must be transformed if we hope to protect natural systems from destruction in the name of Mammon. Economics seems to baffle everyone, especially me. I have no prescriptions to offer, except to note that it doesn't have to be *one* economic system, and that any economics should include a fair measure of value. What's needed is an economy that takes into true account the cost of biospheric destruction and at the same time feeds the family. People must be convinced that it's in their best economic interest to maintain healthy biological systems. The best place to meet this challenge is where you live—that is, personally and within the community.

It's probably also fairly plain that changing the economic system will involve changing our conception of what constitutes a fulfilled life and cracking the cultural mania for mindless consumption and its attendant waste. To realize what is alive within us, the who of who we are, we have to know what we truly need, and what is enough. As Marshall Sahlins has pointed out, affluence can be attained either through increasing production or reducing needs. Since increased production usually means ravaged natural systems, the best strategy seems the reduction of needs, and hopefully the consequent recognition that enough is plenty. A truly affluent society is one of material sufficiency and spiritual riches.

While we're keeping up this resistance in our daily lives—and I think it is in the quality of daily life rather than momentary thrills that the heart is proven—we can begin repairing the natural systems that have been damaged. Logged and mined watersheds need to be repaired. Streams have to be cleared. Trees planted. Check dams built to stop gully erosion. Long-term management strategies developed. Tough campaigns waged to secure funding for the work. There's a strong effort in this direction happening in Northern California now, much of it through worker co-ops and citizens' groups, with increasingly cooperative help from local and state agencies. This work has really just begun, and the field is wide open. So far it seems to satisfy the two feelings that prompted it: the sense that we have a responsibility to renew what we've wasted, and the need to practice "right livelihood," or work that provides a living while promoting the spirit.

Natural system renewal (or rehabilitation, or enhancement, or whatever other names it goes by) could well be our first environmental art. It requires a thorough knowledge of how natural systems work, delicate perceptions of specific sites, the development of appropriate techniques, and hard physical work of the kind that puts you to bed after dinner. What finer work than healing the Earth, where the rewards are both in the doing and the results? It deserves our participation and support. For the irrefutable fact of the matter is that if we want to explore the bioregional possibility, we've got to work, got to get dirty—either by sitting on our asses at environmental hearings or by busting them planting trees in the rain. Sniveling don't make it.

The chances of bioregionalism succeeding, like the chances of survival itself, are beside the point. If one person, or a few, or a community of people, live more fulfilling lives from bioregional practice, then it's successful. This country has a twisted idea of success: it is almost always a quantitative judgement—salary, wins, the number of rooms in the house, the number of people you command. Since bioregionalism by temperament is qualitative, the basis of judgment should be shifted accordingly. What they call a subculture, we call friends.

Most of the people I talk with feel we have a fighting chance to stop environmental destruction within 50 years and to turn the culture around within 800 to 1000 years. "Fighting chance" translates as long odds but good company, and bioregionalism is obviously directed at people whose hearts put a little gamble in their blood. Since we won't live to see the results of this hoped-for transformation, we might as well live to start it right, with the finest expressions of spirit and style we can muster, keeping in mind that there's only a functional difference between the flower and the root, that essentially they are part of the same abiding faith.

The Sun still rises every morning. Dig in.

(First published in **Coevolution Quarterly**, Winter 1981.)

MORE THAN JUST SAVING WHAT'S LEFT

Peter Berg

Anyone who has seen miles of elaborately constructed highway closed by a contamination crew in full protective gear attempting to clean up a chemical spill, or heard of an entire town being evacuated because of a similar calamity—and nearly everyone has by now—can sense that environmental disruptions aren't just "issues" anymore. They are widespread facts of life that are approaching plague proportions. A deep civilization crisis is underway, one that can cause social suicide. Our greatest threats no longer come from natural disasters but from the means we use to subdue nature.

We need a positive politics that views the Late Industrial crisis as a transition toward a society that is based *in* rather than *on top of* life. There needs to be a full pronouncement of values and thorough implementation of social, economic, technological, and cultural practices that affirm the natural basis of the human species in life-sustaining processes of the planetary biosphere.

Classic environmentalism has bred a peculiar negative political malaise among its adherents. Alerted to fresh horrors almost daily, they research the extent of each new life-threatening situation, rush to protest it, and campaign exhaustively to prevent a future occurrence. It's a valuable service, of course, but imagine a hospital that consists only of an emergency room. No maternity care, no pediatric clinic, no promising therapy: just mangled trauma cases. Many of them are lost or drag on in wilting protraction, and if a few are saved there are always more than can be handled jamming through the door. Rescuing the environment has become like running a battlefield aid station in a war against a killing machine that operates just beyond reach, and that shifts its ground after each seeming defeat. No one can doubt the moral basis of environmentalism, but the essentially defensive terms of its endless struggle mitigate against ever stopping the slaughter. Environmentalists have found themselves in the position of knowing how bad things are but are only capable of making a deal.

Why hasn't there been a more positive political approach to valuing the earth and reverencing life?

One reason is that shocked bewilderment at the massive failures of Late Industrial society is still mounting. Our optimistic attempts to carry out beneficial activities, and our deliberate hope for the future, seem always subject to instant miniaturization by the next Late Industrial avalanche. Can growing a garden, for instance, actually deal with the problem of increasingly destructive and poisonous agribusiness? What are the future consequences of engineering food sources? Suppose nuclear power is finally shut down, what do we do with wastes that have already accumulated? How about other poisons that have been released and could eventually cripple the genetic basis for life? Once considered to be extremist questions about remote possibilities, now they can be heard in classrooms, workers' meetings, supermarket waiting lines, and dinner conversations. Disillusionment and even panic will result unless they are seen as central issues in our lives.

Which leads to the main reason why people haven't been able to fully express their priorities for the fate of the human species and the planetary biosphere: the fact that political structures have become welded to the industrial direction of society. Everyone knows that clean water is necessary and that industrial processes inevitably pollute it, but there aren't effective political forums to establish local alternative ways to make a living.

Nutritious food is necessary but there is no direct political means to implement organic permaculture policies. Fossil fuel dependency is a losing proposition and nuclear power is a truly dead end, but the established political apparatus rejects strong renewable energy programs as being unrealistic.

It's time to develop the political means for directing society toward restoring and maintaining the natural systems that ultimately support all life. *Bioregions* are the natural locales in which everyone lives. *Reinhabitation* of bioregions, creating adaptive cultures that follow the unique characteristics of climate, watersheds, soils, land forms, and native plants and animals that define these places, is the appropriate direction for a transition from Late Industrial society. Environmentalism, at best, reaches its zenith in a standoff. It's time to shift from just saving what's left and begin to assert bioregional programs for reinhabitation.

The first step is to unmask Late Industrial wrappings from issues to show they are actually based on bioregional realities. "Jobs versus environment" is a typical disguise. Who really wants to work in an industry that will cause one's own death or distribute lethal consequences to others? When workers or managers defend these industries they aren't defining jobs as employment in something they necessarily want to do, they're talking about getting an income to pay their bills. All industries depend, however, on some natural characteristics of the places where they are located. It may be direct exploitation as in the case of mining, or indirect dependency as when a favorable climate or rich agricultural base permits a density of population that can be drawn into high technol-

Speaking For Douglas Fir

The bioregional movement is an educational exercise, first of all. Next, when you really get down to brass tacks, what it really means is that you have people who say: *I'm not going to move.* That's where it gets new. People say I'm going to stay here, and you could count on me being here 20 years from now. What that immediately does is make a politically-empowered community possible. Bioregionalism has this concrete base that it builds from: human beings that live in place together for the long run. In North America that's a new thing!

Human beings who are planning on living together in the same place will wish to include the non-human in their sense of community. This also is new, to say our community does not end at the human boundaries, we are in a community with certain trees, plants, birds, animals. The conversation is with the whole thing. That's community political life.

The next step might be that you have an issue, and you testify at a hearing. You say: I speak as a local, a local who is committed to being here the rest of my life, and who fully expects my children and my grandchildren to be living here. Consequently, my view of the issue is a long-range view, and I request that

you have a long-range view in mind. I'm not here to talk about a 20 year logging plan. I'm here to talk about a 500 year logging plan. Does your logging plan address 500 years? If not, you are not meeting your responsibility to local people.

Another person by this time takes the stand, from your same group, and says: I'm a member of this community who also intends to live here in the long run, and one of my friends, Douglas Fir, can't be here tonight. So I'm speaking for Douglas Fir. That point of view has come to me by spending time out in the hills, and walking with the trees, and sitting underneath the trees, and seeing how it seems with them. Then speak a sensitive and ecologically-sound long-range position from the standpoint of the tree side of the community. We've done this in Northern California, in particular a character who always calls himself "Ponderosa Pine." You can see how it goes from there. It's so simple. Such common sense. And so easily grasped by children.

— **Gary Snyder,** *from "Regenerate Culture!" an interview in* **The New Catalyst**, *No. 2, Jan./Feb. 1986.*

The Culture Of Cities

We must create in every region people who will be accustomed, from school onward, to humanist attitudes, cooperative methods, rational controls. These people will know in detail where they live and how they live: they will be united by a common feeling for their landscape, their literature and language, their local ways, and out of their own self-respect they will have a sympathetic understanding with other regions and different local peculiarities. They will be actively interested in the form and culture of their locality, which means their community and their own personalities. Such people will contribute to our land-planning, our industry planning, our community planning the authority of their own understanding, and the pressure of their own desires.

— **Lewis Mumford**, *from* **The Culture of Cities**, *1938.*

ogy or service industries. They all must eventually deal with the consequences of their operations on natural systems: minerals become harder to find so strip-mining craters begin to diminish Allegheny Mountains or High Plains farmland; Los Angeles becomes too smog- shrouded for its automobile-bound population to endure; the computer boom almost instantly overcrowds the natural confines of Silicon Valley. A political response to continuously denuding and fouling life-places is to insist on employment that *recreates* rather than destroys the natural wholeness that invited inhabitation in the first place.

Once issues are read back through to their roots in the characteristics of a bioregion, a reinhabitory political program can begin to take shape. For instance, agricultural and natural resources policies can obviously be linked to restoring and maintaining watersheds, soils, and native plants and animals. Energy sources should be those that are naturally available on a renewable basis in each life-place, and both distribution systems and uses for energy should be scaled in ways that don't displace natural systems. Community development in all its aspects from economic activities and housing to social services and transportation should be aimed toward bioregional self-reliance.

"No one can doubt the moral basis of environmentalism, but the essentially defensive terms of its endless struggle mitigate against ever stopping the slaughter. Environmentalists have found themselves in the position of knowing how bad things are but are only capable of making a deal. Why hasn't there been a more positive political approach to valuing the earth and reverencing life?"

Education and cultural activities should teach and celebrate the interdependence of human beings with other forms of life.

There are four different inhabitory zones within every bioregion and each of these warrants a distinct focus for reinhabitation.

CITIES need to undertake programs that reduce their drain on bioregion-wide resources while welcoming back a more natural presence. Green City platforms can, for example, promote neighborhood self-reliance through assisting block-size cooperatives to undertake a range of new activities: retrofitting houses for renewable energy; tilling community gardens: arranging city/country work and recreation exchanges. They could demand new employment in everything from operating small-scale recycling centers to producing goods for civic and neighborhood use from recycled materials. Most of the street space now occupied by parked cars could be vacated by operating neighborhood-based transportation systems to complement mass transit, and city soil could then be uncovered from asphalt to grow food or support wild corridors of native vegetation.

SUBURBS can adopt Green city proposals and also restore an agricultural presence on the land they occupy by encouraging food production where there are now lawns, and nourishing it with recycled household water and wastes.

RURAL AREAS are the working life-support foundations for most of a bioregion's population. They urgently require help to remove exploitation threats and to nurture sustainable practices. Country-based information systems that link into urban media should be developed to create greater awareness of an overall bioregional identity. Rural programs can also demand employment of local people as bioregional stewards to undertake restoration and maintenance projects, and as bioregional guides to educate vacationers and oversee their participation in those projects.

WILDERNESS is the enduring source of a bioregion's spirit and regenerative power. It must be maintained for its own sake and as a reservoir for reaffirming natural systems through reinhabitation. Access to wilderness should become a public right on the same level as learning to read and write with equipment provided freely and instruction carried out by those who can share their respect for wild places.

Constituencies for bioregional programs can be assembled around position statements of short-term and long-term goals that are appropriate to areas of inhabitation. Green City statements would, for example, oppose high-rise condominium apartment construction as a short-term goal and demand decentralized renewable energy housing in the long-term. Suburban groups would block further development of nearby farmland and also insist on water and waste recycling systems for the future. Rural groups would stand against present pesticide and herbicide spraying while proposing support for long-term permaculture and natural resources enhancement projects. Wilderness groups can immediately advocate intensified protection for wild places and future redirection of policies away from tourism and toward education.

Daniel O. Stolpe.

Naturally bordered locales provide the best organizational basis for these constituencies; creek watersheds, river valleys, plains, mountain ranges, or estuarial areas. An initial strategy can be to present a statement of positions on issues for endorsement by town councils and candidates for local, county, state, and even federal offices. Eventual recognition of naturally determined districts within larger bioregional political boundaries would continuously be sought as a long-range goal.

Everyone lives within some bioregion so everyone can gain from participation in the formation of a political platform that represents their life-place. What are the planks for your area? Find out and begin recovering autonomy to lead a reinhabitory life.

(First published in **Raise the Stakes** No.8., Fall 1983.)

BIOREGIONAL PERSPECTIVES

Gary Snyder

"The Region is the elsewhere of civilization." — *Max Cafard*

The little nations of the past lived within territories that conformed to some set of natural criteria. The culture areas of the major native groups of North America overlapped, as one would expect, almost exactly with broadly defined major bioregions as A.L. Kroeber noted in *Cultural and Natural Areas of North America* (1947). That older human experience of a fluid, indistinct, but genuine home region, was gradually replaced—across Eurasia—by the arbitrary and often violently imposed boundaries of emerging national states. These imposed borders sometimes cut across biotic areas and ethnic zones alike. Inhabitants lost ecological knowledge and community solidarity. In the old ways, the flora and fauna and landforms are also *part of the culture*. The world of culture and nature, which is actual, is almost a shadow world now, and the insubstantial world of political jurisdictions and rarefied economies is what passes for reality. We live in a backwards time. We can regain some small sense of that old membership by discovering the original lineaments of our land, and steering—at least in the home territory, and in mind—by those rather than the borders of arbitrary nations, states and counties.

Regions are "interpenetrating bodies in semi-simultaneous spaces" (Max Cafard, "The Surre(gion)alist Manifesto," *Mesechabe*, Autumn, 1989). Biota, watersheds, landforms, elevations, are just a few of the facets that regions are defined by. Culture areas, in the same way, have subsets such as dialects, religions, sorts of arrow-release, types of tools, myth-motifs, musical scales, art-styles. One sort of regional outline would be floristic. The Coastal Douglas fir, as the definitive tree of the Pacific northwest, is an example. (I knew it intimately as a boy growing up on a farm between Lake Washington and Puget Sound. The local people, the Snohomish, called it *Lukta tciyats*, "wide needles.") Its northern limit is around the Skeena River in British Columbia. It is found west of the crest through Washington, Oregon, and northern California. The southern coastal limit of Douglas fir is about the same as that of salmon, which do not run south of the Big Sur River. Inland it grows down the west slope of the Sierra as far south as the north fork of the San Joaquin River. That describes the boundary of a larger natural region that runs across three states and one international border.

The presence of this tree signifies a rainfall and a temperature range, and will indicate what your agriculture might be, how steep the pitch of the roof, what raincoats you'd need. You don't have to know such details to get by in the modern cities of Portland or Bellingham. But if you do know what is taught by plants and weather, you are more in on the gossip and can truly feel more at home. The sum of a field's forces becomes what we call very loosely the "spirit of the place." To know the spirit of a place is to realize that you are a part of a part and that the whole is made of parts, each of which is whole. You start with the part you are whole in.

As quixotic as these ideas may seem, they have a reservoir of strength and possibility behind them. The spring of 1984, a month after equinox, Gary Holthaus and I drove down from Anchorage to Haines, Alaska. We went around the upper edge of the basin of the Copper River, skirted some tributaries of the Yukon, and went over Haines summit. It was White and Black spruce taiga all the way, still frozen up. Dropping down from the pass to saltwater at Chilkat inlet we were immediately in forests of large Sitka spruce, skunk cabbage poking out in the swamps; it was spring. That's a bioregional border leap. I was honored the next day by an invitation to Raven House, to have coffee with Austin Hammond and a circle of other Tlingit elders, and to hear some long and deeply entwined discourses on the responsibilities of people to their places. As we looked out his front window to hanging glaciers on the peaks beyond the saltwater, Hammond spoke of empires and civilizations in metaphors of glaciers. He described how great alien forces—industrial civilization in this case—advance and retreat, and how settled people can wait it out.

Sometime in the mid-seventies at a conference of Native American leaders and activists in Bozeman, Montana, I heard a Crow elder say something similar. "You know I think if people stay somewhere long enough— even white people—the spirits will begin to speak to them. It's the power of the spirits coming up from the land. The spirits and the old powers aren't lost, they just need people to be around long enough and the spirits will begin to influence them."

Bioregional awareness teaches us in *specific* ways. It is not enough to just "love nature" or to want to "be in harmony with Gaia." Our relation to the natural world takes place in a *place*, and it must be grounded in information and experience. For example, "real people" have an easy familiarity with the local plants. This is so unexceptional a kind of knowledge that everyone in Europe, Asia, and Africa used to take it for granted. Many contemporary Americans don't even *know* that they don't "know the plants," which is indeed a measure of alienation. Knowing a bit about the flora, we could enjoy questions like: where do Alaska and Mexico meet? It would be somewhere on the north coast of California, where Canada Jay and Sitka Spruce lace together with manzanita and Blue oak.

But instead of "northern California" let's call it Shasta Bioregion. The present state of California (the old Alta California territory) falls into at least three natural divisions, and the northern third looks, as the Douglas fir example shows, well to

the north. The boundaries of this northern third would roughly run from the Klamath-Rogue River divide south to the San Francisco bay, and up the delta where the Sacramento and the San Joaquin Rivers join. The line would then go east to the Sierra Crest, and take that as a distinct border and follow it north to Susanville. The watershed divide then angles broadly northeastward along the edge of the Modoc Plateau to the Warner Range and Goose Lake.

East of the divide is the Great Basin, north of Shasta is the Cascadia/Columbia region, and then farther north is what we call Ish river country, which is the drainages of Puget Sound and the Straits of Georgia. Why should we do this kind of visualization? Again I will say: it prepares us to begin to be at home in this landscape. There are tens of millions of people in North America who were physically born here but who are not actually living here intellectually, imaginatively, or morally. Native Americans, to be sure, have a prior claim to the term native. But as they love this land they will welcome the conversion of the millions of immigrant psyches into fellow "native Americans." For the non-Native American to become at home on this continent, he or she must be *born again* in this hemisphere, on this continent, properly called Turtle Island.

That is to say, we must consciously fully accept and recognize that this is where we live, and grasp the fact that our descendants will be here for millenia to come. Then we must honor this land's great antiquity—its wildness—learn it—defend it—and work to hand it on to the children (of all beings) of the future with its biodiversity and health intact. Europe or Africa or Asia will then be seen as the place our ancestors came from, places we might want to know about and to visit, but not "home." Home, deeply, spiritually, must be here. Calling this place "America" is to name it after a stranger. "Turtle Island" is the name given to this continent by Native Americans based on creation mythology. The United States, Canada, Mexico, are passing political entities; they have their legitimacies to be sure, but they will lose their mandate if they continue to abuse the land. "The

> "*Bioregional awareness teaches us in specific ways. It is not enough to just "love nature" or to want to "be in harmony with Gaia." Our relation to the natural world takes place in a place, and it must be grounded in information and experience.*"

State is destroyed, but the mountains and rivers remain."

But this work is not just for the newcomers of the western hemisphere, Australia, Africa, or Siberia, a worldwide purification of mind is called for—the exercise of seeing the surface of the planet for what it is—by nature. With this kind of consciousness, people turn up at hearings and in front of trucks and bulldozers to defend the land or trees. Showing solidarity with a region! What an odd idea at first. Bioregionalism is the entry of place into the dialectic of history. Also we might say that there are "classes" that have so far been overlooked—the animals, rivers, rocks, and grasses—now entering history.

> "Showing solidarity with a region! What an odd idea at first. Bioregionalism is the entry of place into the dialectic of history. Also we might say that there are "classes" that have so far been overlooked—the animals, rivers, rocks, and grasses—now entering history."

These ideas provoke predictable and usually uninformed reactions. People fear the small society and the critique of the state. It is difficult to see, when one has been raised under it, that it is the state itself which is inherently greedy, de-stabilizing, entropic, disorderly, and illegitimate. Cities cite parochialism, regional strife, "unacceptable" expressions of cultural diversity, and so forth. Our philosophies, world religions, and histories are biased towards uniformity, universality, and centralization—in a word, the ideology of monotheism. Certainly under specific conditions neighboring groups have wrangled for centuries—interminable memories and hostilities cooking away like radioactive waste; it's still at work in the Middle East. The ongoing ethnic and political miseries of parts of Europe and the Middle East sometimes go back as far as the Roman Empire. This is not something that can be attributed to the combativeness of "human nature" per se. Prior to the expansion of early empires, the occasional strife of tribes and natural nations was almost familial. With the rise of the state the scale of the destructiveness and malevolence of warfare makes a huge leap.

In the times when people did not have much accumulated surplus, there was no big temptation to move in on other regions. I'll give an example from my own part of the world (I describe my location as: on the western slope of the northern Sierra Nevada, in the Yuba River watershed, north of the south Fork at the 3,000 foot elevation, in a community of Black oak, Incense cedar, Madrone, Douglas fir, and Ponderosa pine). The west slope of the Sierra Nevada has winter rain and snowfall, with a different set of plants from the dry east slope. In pre-white times, the Native people living across the range had little temptation to venture over, because their skills were specific to their own area, and they could go hungry in an unfamiliar biome. It takes a long education to know the edible plants, where to find them, and how to prepare them. So the Washo of the Sierra east side traded their pine nuts and obsidian for the acorns, yew bows, and abalone shells of the Miwuk and Maidu to the west. The two sides met and camped together for weeks in the summer Sierra meadows, their joint commons. (Dedicated raiding cultures, "barbarians," evolve as a response to nearby civilizations and their riches. Genghis Khan, at an audience in his yurt near lake Baikal, was reported to have said, "Heaven is exasperated with the decadence and luxury of China.")

There are numerous examples of relatively peaceful small-culture coexistence all over the world. There have always been multi-lingual persons peacefully trading and travelling across large areas. Differences were often eased by shared spiritual perspectives or ceremonial institutions, and the multitude of myths and tales that cross language barriers. What about the deep divisions caused by religion? It must be said that most religious exclusiveness is the odd specialty of the Judaeo-Christian/Islamic faith, which is a recent and (overall) minority development in the world. Asian religion, and the whole world of folk religion, animism and shamanism, appreciates or at least tolerates diversity. (It seems that the really serious cultural disputes are caused by different tastes in food. When I was chokersetting in Eastern Oregon one of my crew was a Wasco man whose wife was a Chehalis women from the west side. He told me that when they got in fights she would call him a "goddamn grasshopper eater" and he'd shout back "fisheater!")

People already sense, in some way, that they live in geographic regions comprising natural systems, of water, air and land. Now they are becoming aware of them, and seeing if we are overstressing these systems and rhythms. At the scale of the bioregion, people can understand the flow of natural systems, whereas at the global, or national, levels, the mind boggles. The systems are so varied, the climates so different. But the bioregion is something that people *do* understand.

So you have the region, and that's the right scale; and you have the sense of systems, that's the right philosophy. If you put the two of them together, you get ecological consciousness.

— **Kirkpatrick Sale**, *from an interview in* **The New Catalyst**, *Spring 1987.*

Cultural pluralism and multi-lingualism is the planetary norm. We seek the balance between cosmopolitan pluralism and deep local consciousness. We are asking how the whole human race can regain self-determination in place, after centuries of having been disenfranchised by hierarchy and/or centralized power. Do not confuse this exercise with "nationalism" which is exactly the opposite, the imposter, the puppet of the State, the grinning ghost of the lost community.

So this is one sort of start. The bioregional movement is not just a rural program, it is as much for the restoration of urban neighborhood life and the greening of the cities. All of us are fluently moving in multiple realms that include irrigation districts, solid-waste management jurisdictions, long distance area code zones and such. Planet Drum Foundation, based in the Bay Area, works with many other local groups for the regeneration of the city as a living place, with projects like the identification and restoration of urban creeks. There are groups worldwide working with third and fourth world people revisualizing territories and playfully finding appropriate names for their newly-realized old regions. Three continental bioregional congresses have been held on Turtle Island.

As sure as impermanence, the nations of the world will eventually be more sensitively defined, and the lineaments of the blue earth will begin to re-shape the politics. The requirements of sustainable economies, ecologically sensitive agriculture, strong and vivid community life, wild habitat—and the second law of thermodynamics—all lead this way. I also realize that right now this is a kind of theater as much as it is ecological politics. Not just street theater, but visionary mountain, field, and stream theater. As Jim Dodge says, "The chances of bioregionalism succeeding…are beside the point. If one person, or a few, or a community of people, live more fulfilling lives from bioregional practice, then it's successful." May it all speed the further deconstruction of the superpowers.

"Regional politics do not take place in Washington, Moscow, and other *seats of power*. Regional power does not *sit*; it flows everywhere. Through watersheds and bloodstreams. Through nervous systems and food chains. The regions are everywhere and nowhere. We are all illegals. We are natives and we are restless. We have no country; we live in the country. We are off the Inter-State. The Region is against the Regime—any Regime. Regions are anarchic." (Cafard)

(First published in **The Practice of The Wild**, San Francisco: North Point, 1990.)

REVALUING HOME: Feminism And Bioregionalism

Judith Plant

Several years ago, at a conference about regional development, in a workshop with native women, I asked Marie Smallface for some guidance: "What is the best thing for white people to do in the midst of the cultural and environmental havoc *created* by white people?"

She spoke directly and said, "Find a place and stay there." She went on to talk about how she thought it made more sense to be "of" the land you're struggling to save. Ultimately, she meant, staying home.

Bioregionalists express the same idea. Yet, at the same time home has been a very isolated place for women. To be different from this traditional situation, home, as such, needs understanding, valuing, and redefining. Here a partnership between bioregionalism and feminism can provide fertile ground for deep societal changes. For both perspectives value "all our relations"—with nature and with humankind,— and both value home.

Without feminism, it seems that the bioregional view is not going to bring about the shift in attitude that is required to live an ecologically harmonious life. We have to put our own house in order. Our relations with the earth reflect our relationships with each other.

Redefining and Revaluing Home

Bioregional action is based on local control and decentralization; nonviolence; sustainable lifestyles; and on a revaluing and redefining of home.

In considering the notion of home, bioregionalists turn towards ecology. The word itself comes from the Greek *oikos*, for home—an indication that home is much broader than simply the nuclear family. As it is in the natural world, where all life is connected and inter-related, teeming with diversity and complexities, so it is with human domestic life. Here is the scene of *human* ecology, or what Murray Bookchin refers to as "social ecology." Home becomes the locus of

liberation from a culture of violence, because it is here where people really have a measure of control over the creation of nonviolent values. It is where the consequences of political decisions are felt.

Feminism has everything to do with social relations and human ecology. The schism between the personal and the political has kept this valuable information from informing and directing political decisions. Feminists have given this a lot of thought; and not just abstractly, but thought based on experience. Since time-out-of-mind, women have had a history—or herstory—with home. Feminism has helped people understand how women have been isolated at home and, in turn, has articulated the value of women's work at home. This work has been done in the context of a society which has traditionally undervalued both home *and* women.

The Personal As Political

"All the issues are related. Now nobody can deal with all the issues—there isn't energy and time. But we can deal with *our* issues—the ones that affect us immediately—in a way that relates them to all the others.

And I think that we had better because otherwise we're bound to fail." — Joanna Russ, from *Reweaving the Web of Life*.

Dealing with *our* issues is the bioregional method. When bioregionalists talk about Forestry's cut-and-run mentality, they are speaking from their hearts, from their own experience. Clear-cutting the watershed which is the vital artery that supports the environment in which one lives stirs the emotions and the intellect together in

"Women of Europe," anonymous.

a powerful expression. To be an environmentalist takes on a deep, personal meaning.

It is because of this personal connection with political decisions and actions that the bioregional process helps people to see that what is valued personally is the same as what is valued politically. Seems common sense enough but, as many have experienced in political activism (in the alternative politics of the Left in the 60s, for instance), there has been a blind spot in seeing this relationship. So exploitative behavior in the market was viewed as unrelated to exploitative behavior interpersonally. The connection between personal values and political ones was missed. It was because of this blind spot, or inability to make this connection, that many women broke away from Left politics.

Is The Revaluing of Home a Double Bind for Women?

To avoid alienating women again, we have to

This is a whole new kind of home-grown politics. The bioregional movement is in some very profound way political. It is not largely concerned with the political institutions that now exist but with replacing those with new, organic and regionally-based ones. This is the sort of politics, I think, that is very much like what Students for a Deomocratic Society (SDS) was looking for. You look at the Port Huron statement in 1962—it has no ecological sense, really, because it wasn't until the late '60s and *Silent Spring*'s effects that this began to dawn on people. But nonetheless, the vision of a future America that the Port Huron statement embodies is not all that different in terms of participatory democracy, community empowerment, workplace deomocracy, etc., from what the bioregional movement is pointing toward. It's probably a kind of organic outgrowth of what happened in the '60s. We've grown up!

— **Kirkpatrick Sal***e, from an interview in* **The New Catalyst,** *Spring 1987.*

make sure that bioregionalism does not leave women in a double bind. As bioregionalists place new value on home, on the domestic, everyday life, those values and activities generally associated with women are now believed to be healthy activities that need to be maintained and developed.

At the same time, the historical and, indeed, present reality is that these life activities have been undervalued and have been a source of oppression for women.

> "Women are nurturers: we keep the systems we work in together (the family, service jobs in wage labor) by nurturing. The social relations of our nurturance work account on the one hand for our oppression (sacrificing our own interests for those of men and children) and, on the other hand, for our potential strength as bearers of a radical culture: we support an ethic of sharing, co-operation, and collective involvement that stands in clear opposition to an ethic based on individualism, competition, and private profit." — Ferguson and Folbre, *The Unhappy Marriage of Patriarchy and Capitalism.*

What remains valuable in mainstream society, and deep within our beings, has a dollar sign attached to it, and generally has nothing to do with home. In fact, home is more and more being sacrificed for economic ends. What is important goes on in the public sphere—politics and economics—and a person's worth is gauged in monetary terms. Within this ideology, domestic life has meant that some are subservient to others. Traditionally this has been women, as slaves, servants and wives. Children quickly learn that what goes on at home is unimportant compared to the values "out there."

Out of the Bind

Based on the strong, educated hunches of feminists, the only way out of this bind is to take the view that, culturally, society is in a transformational, transitional phase. We are attempting to move out of culturally-defined sex roles which value one over the other, toward a culture that places positive value on the active involvement of all people in domestic life. For it is here where culture is shaped.

> "Societies that do not elaborate the opposition of male and female and place positive value on the conjugal relationships and the involvement of both men and women in the home seem to be most

egalitarian in terms of sex roles. When a man is involved in domestic labor, in child care and cooking, he cannot establish an aura of authority and distance. And when public decisions are made in the household, women may have a legitimate public role." — Rosaldo, *Women, Culture, and Society: A Theoretical Overview.*

The polarization of women and men, as either/or, is the social organization from which we have emerged. There has been little, if any, tolerance for gradations or complexities. You are either one or the other. Part of this problem is thinking in pairs of opposites and, as with most dualities, one is thought to be preferred over the other.

In actual fact, human beings have the capacity for a wide range of behaviors. People now know that men are capable of gentleness and women can be assertive. Yet, still, mainstream society persists in valuing tendencies associated with maleness over those associated with femaleness.

The task remains to outsmart ourselves. Harmonizing all our relations, making the connections, is potentially the footing for a quantum leap in evolution. It's not simply a question of rights but of actually saving the species from itself.

It is no easy transition to a valuing of the domestic. For men, it is very difficult to find a place in a sphere of life they have been socialized to avoid and consider unimportant. Similarly for women who are so tempted to prove themselves according to patriarchal society's measuring stick.

Paying consistent attention to how we do things, to process, seems vital to the reconstruction of healthy relationships with the earth and with each other. Bioregionalism and ecology can guide us in our relations with nature, just as feminism can aid in an understanding of our human relationships. These two theories, coupled with inspiration from the natural world, could bring women and men together, with integrity and dignity, in bioregional community.

> "To put feminist values of equality, mutual aid, and respect for life in their place requires a society where people are engaged in face-to-face relations and where nature inspires us with the sanctity of life and the need to give back to others that which we receive from them." — Alexandra Devon, *Kick It Over.*

(First published in **The New Catalyst** No.2, Jan./Feb. 1986.)

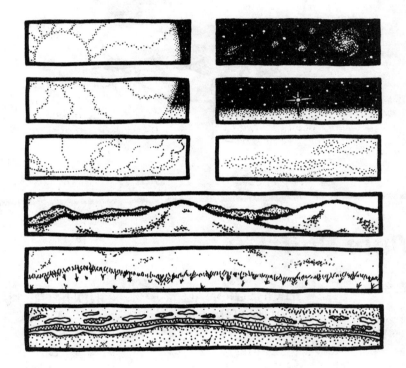

T'AI : PEACE

Drawing by Rob Messick.

Paradigm Shift

	BIOREGIONAL PARADIGM	INDUSTRIO-SCIENTIFIC PARADIGM
Scale	Region Community	State Nation/World
Economy	Conservation Stability Self-Sufficiency Cooperation	Exploitation Change/Progress World Economy Competition
Polity	Decentralization Complementarity Diversity	Centralization Hierarchy Uniformity
Society	Symbiosis Evolution Division	Polarization Growth/Violence Monoculture

— **Kirkpatrick Sale** *from* **Dwellers in the Land**, *San Francisco: Sierra Club Books, 1985.*

IN POCKETS OF RESISTANCE:
The Back-To-The-Land Movement Matures

Christopher Plant

Deep in the coastal rainforest, seven or eight hundred miles north of Vancouver, B.C., the tenderly cared-for log cabin with cedar shake roof still stands on a little bluff over-looking the Tseax River. Surrounded by breathtakingly beautiful snow- capped mountains, the care that has clearly gone into the place reflects the fact that, for someone, this has been a miniature paradise. Eagles wheel above the tall spruce and cottonwood trees, and the protected backwaters still provide a secret refuge for the moose, finding safety from hunters there through the long winter months. The tiny Pelton wheel, though, that provided generous, but by no means-trouble-free electric power from the creek, is now stopped. And the rustic, cedar-bough gate of the old goat-pen creaks on its wooden hinges as it swings carelessly in the occasional gust of wind.

This old homestead—typical of many in B.C.—is suffering right now. Built originally by English pioneers in the early years of the century, it was sold in 1968 by the one remaining white settler to a young, enthusiastic couple—part of a group of four or five—during the "new wave" of back-to-the- landers. The newcomers, fleeing America and the Vietnam draft, poured their best years of love and devotion into the place, and for a long time subsisted almost entirely on what they grew.

But, after ten years, and with two small children, the isolation—70 miles on a rough logging road to the nearest town—was too much. Their hopes of building a lasting community of friends did not materialize for one reason or another and, with bitter irony, paradise became a prison. The growing children deserved something better, and long-buried personal aspirations gnawed at their sense of identity. With the war long over, the couple took heart, braced themselves, and left—back to the east coast of the U.S. After three or more years, and two further attempts by people to make it there, their place was finally sold to an unknown buyer. Within weeks of the sale, the majestic 100 acres of rainforest was clear-cut, destined for the multinational market in 2 x 4s. A dream had ended.

*

Far away, where the coast mountains meet the interior plateau, and where the sun is hot and the air dry from having dropped its heavy load of rainfall, a narrow valley, tucked between the mountains, is vibrant with human hope and energy. Here, the 20 or so young families of *this* region's "new wave" have been luckier. True, a spirited attempt at living in a large commune withered on the vine. But the larger community has survived initial hardships and, importantly, the people have stayed in place, fired with the conscious intention of reinhabiting the land and forming a close-knit village-type of community to sustain themselves and future generations through time.

They meet and celebrate often, work together frequently, support one another whenever possible, and are active in a host of self- initiated organizations ranging from a food co-op to an ecological society and the Green Party of B.C. Hands planted firmly in the soil, they grow bountiful amounts of organic food and manage to support themselves one way or another by practicing either the skills they have learned here, like fine carpentry or vegetable- growing, or the trades they came with from the "old" world: as mechanics, electricians, nurses or publishers. Plans for the future, for the younger generation (none of whom attend regular school) to carry on when it is their time, include market gardening, an organic tree nursery for silviculture, and fish- farming. Inspired by the need to develop radically new ways of being in the world—a new culture of caring for one another and one's local place, and a new politics that empowers communities to make local decisions about local resources—*this* group has lost little of the idealism that fired the imaginations of those seeking to forge an alternative model for the future in the backwoods of B.C. *This* dream lives on...

> I n the Mattole Valley in California, and in the Ozarks, they have gone so far as to create alternative political institutions—congresses. Representatives from parts of the valley or plateau attend these congresses and they hammer out public policy positions that are quite different from those of the official state and country legislatures. The long-term hope is that people will say, well, the official legislators don't speak for us at all. Let's give our allegiance instead to these bioregionalist congresses which really *do* seem to be speaking to our issues. So the vision is exactly that we do it for ourselves. But we can't do it alone, and probably not even in a small neighbourhood or a small community. But if we get enough of those together then yes, we can do it by ourselves and make the present political forms obsolete and irrelevant.
>
> — **Kirkpatrick Sale,** *from an interview in* **The New Catalyst,** *Spring, 1987.*

*

You're equally likely to encounter either one of these scenarios today. For, in a world where wilderness is fast diminishing, western Canada is still very much a wild place, open to opportunities for building "new worlds" that simply don't exist in Europe, say, or most parts of North America, for that matter. But, as economic times have gotten tougher and mainstream politics more right-wing, the dominant trend has been away from the back-to-the-land dream, for it's harder now to make it on next to nothing.

Yet the movement matures, all the same, and with some reassuring threads of continuity. The warm Gulf Islands of the west coast, although more populated than before by people with money, remain a haven for artists of all kinds and a wonderland of home-grown architecture. In the Cariboo, a group once fired by Marx and Mao expand the number of their communally-run farms; slowly attract ever more adherents to their spartan way of life from the ranks of small town down-and-out street people; and maintain, unequivocally, that their aim is still, as ever, "to bring about an agrarian revolution in this country."

Others pass both ways: in and out of the dream. Tired of farming rocks up north, a friend quits "the good life" for the city, to become an environmental lawyer, highly valued by those who remain. Travelling the other way, an engineering student bids a safe but boring career farewell, finds a country niche and, eventually, becomes an expert on alternate energy systems. And, in the Kootenay mountain range, the Slocan Valley— once a hippie mecca, now much depopulated because of the economic depression there—has given birth to a new batch of foresters and ecologists. In their efforts to stop clear-cutting and to protect fragile watersheds, they wage a steady uphill battle to influence provincial forest policy.

With government and industry set to squeeze the last remaining resource dollar from these lands, it has been the struggles to preserve the last remaining wilderness in B.C. that has united current back-to-the-landers with their city contemporaries. Meares Island, South Moresby, the Stein River Valley—these and many other threatened areas have become household words, as the Megamachine pursues its deadly business. Opposition to this madness has sparked a renaissance within the broad alternative movement, fuelled by increasingly tangible threats to local ecosystems. Groups who left the rat-race to "get away from it all" find themselves, instead, "on the front lines," at the very frontier, quite prepared to sit in front of bulldozers, or spike trees, if necessary, to stop the desecration.

As a measure of this renaissance, countless single issue groups have formed, from north to south and east to west, struggling to save a watershed, prevent another dam, or stop a toxic waste dump from being built. More significant, perhaps, are the tentative steps toward uniting such diverse groups around a common view. Bioregionalism holds out this promise.

*

Rooted in the politics of place, the bioregional view expressly values natural, biological regions as well as the diverse cultures which they spawn. A decentralist, localist perspective, bioregionalism appeals strongly to all those who reject the tendency to ever-increased centralization, in both city and country. Whether it's restoring and greening city neighborhoods, or "reinhabiting" damaged rural lands and making them flourish once again, bioregionalism promotes the notion of sustainability of nature and culture over time. As such, it has attracted back-to-the-landers old and new, and provides common ground for the many other diverse strands of the alternatives movement: the feminist, green, cooperative and peace movements, for example.

Gatherings such as the Hat Creek Survival Gathering, now in its ninth year—originally begun to stop a coal-fired electricity-generating mega-project at Hat Creek, but continued long after the battle was won—are taking on the character of bioregional congresses. The hope is that, like their counterparts in the U.S., these congresses may eventually become the alternative decision-making bodies for different bioregions: models for an enlightened future where regions self-organize to live sustainably within their carrying capacities over the long term.

Reminiscent of the enthusiasm of by-gone years, tempered now with a streak of "older" realism, the bioregional movement dares still to call forth planet-healing ideals that were so much a part of the original back-to-the-land impulse. The wheel turns full circle. Now, however, the movement has experience on its side, a fact that is reflected in its much more clearly defined philosophy and direction, as well as in its consensus process and general tolerance of those who move in similar directions but on different paths.

*

As wave succeeds wave, the movement for a land-based alternative to modern industrial society in western Canada seems not to die, rather just to change its form from time to time. Although for some the dream of backwoods life has fizzled out, going "back-to-the-land" still *is* a viable alternative in British Columbia. Strengthened by the additional energy of bioregionalism, the movement continues to offer health and hope for a more ecological future as it matures. "Alive and well," said one poet a couple of years ago about the movement, "in pockets of resistance, still struggling we are…"

(First published **Kanada: Ein Express Reisehandbuch**, Ed. Maria Feltes and Thomas Feltes. Germany: Mundo Verlag, 1989.)

WHERE YOU AT? — A Bioregional Quiz

Compiled by: Leonard Charles, Jim Dodge, Lynn Milliman, Victoria Stockley.

What follows is a self-scoring test on basic environmental perception of place. Scoring is done on the honor system, so if you fudge, cheat, or elude, you also get an idea of where you're at. The quiz is culture-bound, favoring those people who live in the country over city dwellers, and scores can be adjusted accordingly. Most of the questions, however, are of such a basic nature that undue allowances are not necessary.

1. Trace the water you drink from precipitation to tap.

2. How many days till the moon is full? (Slack of two days allowed.)

3. What soil series are you standing on?

4. What was the total rainfall in your area last year (July- June)? (Slack: 1 inch for every 20 inches.)

5. When was the last time a fire burned your area?

6. What were the primary subsistence techniques of the culture that lived in your area before you?

7. Name five native edible plants in your region and their season(s) of availability.

8. From what direction do winter storms generally come in your region?

9. Where does your garbage go?

10. How long is the growing season where you live?

11. On what day of the year are the shadows the shortest where you live?

12. When do the deer rut in your region, and when are the young born?

13. Name five grasses in your area. Are any of them native?

14. Name five resident and five migratory birds in your area.

15. What is the land use history of where you live?

16. What primary ecological event/process influenced the land form where you live? (Bonus special: what's the evidence?)

17. What species have become extinct in your area?

18. What are the major plant associations in your region?

19. From where you're reading this, point north.

20. What spring wildflower is consistently among the first to bloom where you live?

Scoring:

0-3   You have your head up your ass.

    4-7   It's hard to be in two places at once when you're not anywhere at all.

    8-12   A fairly firm grasp of the obvious.

      13-16   You're paying attention.

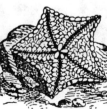

    17-19   You know where you're at.

    20   You not only know where you're at, you know where it's at.

"Salmon Circle," by Alison Lang.

Part Two

LIVING IN PLACE

Living-in-place means following the necessities and pleasures of life as they are uniquely presented by a particular site, and evolving ways to ensure long-term occupancy of that site. A society which practices living-in-place keeps a balance with its region of support through links between human lives, other living things, and the processes of the planet—seasons, weather, water cycles—as revealed by the place itself. It is the opposite of a society which **makes a living** through short-term destructive exploitation of land and life." — *Peter Berg and Raymond Dasmann*

This definitive statement by Peter Berg and Raymond Dasmann appeared in 1978 in the final chapter of the first bioregional anthology, *Reinhabiting A Separate Country: A Bioregional Anthology of Northern California*. Also introduced in this essay were such other basic terms, such as "reinhabitation," "bioregions," "watersheds" and "terrain of consciousness."

Earlier on, in 1974, the people at Planet Drum Foundation put out a "bioregional bundle" called *North Pacific Rim Alive*—"the first effort at thinking about a specific place," according to Peter Berg. From this collection, the wonderfully imaginative "Future Primitive" represented a breakthrough in perception, and therefore strategy, for post-industrial society: the need "to integrate our cultures with nature…at the level of the ecosystem which everywhere has a common structure and progression but everywhere varies specifically in composition and function according to time and place."

Living Here, written in 1977 by twelve different people of "the first self-conscious bioregional group in the country" is an excellent example of a bioregional presentation. It includes a map and a description of the watershed; a description of the original native plant and animal species, including the human cultures there; the story of how these were all almost destroyed by "those who came to live off the watershed, instead of directly in it;" and, finally, thoughts about reinhabitation and restoration.

All three of these publications were the fruit of the tremendously creative thinking going on at Planet Drum Foundation during the '70s. They gave a common vocabulary and orientation to the experience of many people who were already living "bioregionally" but not calling it that.

"Living-in-place" is not a new phenomenon but rather an age-old way of human adaptation which was successful for thousands of generations, until the rise of patriarchy and the present-day exploitative industrial civilization. Gwaganad's testimony of her ties to her place, and the spiritual connection between food, place and people, poignantly illustrate both past and present experience of native peoples whose home places are constantly under the threat of destruction. She speaks for us all, for we were all native to some place at some time in our ancestral past, and it is our natural right to become native to some place again.

In his esssay on the Hudson River Valley, Thomas Berry celebrates the integrating idea that each region is a single organic community of rivers, meadows, forests, wildlife, air and rain, soil and sunshine, including the humans and their dwelling places. This perspective overcomes the artificial split developed over the last few centuries between humans and nature, and between urban and rural areas. What affects one affects them all. "We are all in some manner needed by one another."

Home is the place where we live, with our human families, in our human communities, within our biotic communities. As Luanne Armstrong says, we are created by our home, our place, "shaped, each day, by living in it." In turn, we must learn to cooperate in its processes and yield to its limit, at the same time learning to love our place as part of ourselves.

DON'T MOVE!

Without further rhetoric or utopian scheming, I have a simple suggestion that if followed would begin to bring wilderness, farmers, people, and their economies back. That is: don't move. Stay still. Once you find a place that feels halfway right, and it seems time, settle down with a vow not to move any more. Then, taking a look at one place on earth, one circle of people, one realm of beings over time, conviviality and maintenance will improve. School boards and planning commissions will have better people on them, and larger and more widely concerned audiences will be attending. Small environmental issues will be attended to. More voters will turn out, because local issues at least make a difference, can be won—and national scale politics too might improve, with enough folks getting out there. People begin to really notice the plants, birds, stars, when they see themselves as members of a place. Not only do they begin to work the soil, they go out hiking, explore the back country or the beach, get on the Freddies' ass for mismanaging Peoples' land, and doing that as locals counts! Early settlers, old folks, are valued and respected, we make an effort to learn their stories and pass them on to our children, who will live here too. We look deeply back in time to the original inhabitants, and too far ahead to our own descendants, in the mind of knowing a context, with its own kind of tools, boots, songs. Mainstream thinkers have overlooked it: real people stay put. And when things are coasting along OK, they can also take off and travel, there's no delight like swapping stories downstream. Don't Move! I'd say this really works because here on our side of the Sierra, Yuba river country, we can begin to see some fruits of a mere fifteen years inhabitation, it looks good.

— **Gary Snyder**, *from* **Upriver Downriver** *No.10. 1987.*

REINHABITING CALIFORNIA

Peter Berg and Raymond F. Dasmann

A change is taking place in California. It cannot be easily quantified or evaluated since many who are involved do not want to be counted or publicized. But the direction is becoming clear. The change involves the spread of communities of people who are trying a new approach to living on and with the land. We call this phenomenon reinhabitation, a process that involves learning to live-in-place.

Living-in-place means following the necessities and pleasures of life as they are uniquely presented by a particular site, and evolving ways to ensure long-term occupancy of that site. A society which practices living-in-place keeps a balance with its region of support through links between human lives, other living things, and the processes of the planet—seasons, weather, water cycles—as revealed by the place itself. It is the opposite of a society which *makes a living* through short-term destructive exploitation of land and life. Living-in-place is an age-old way of existence, disrupted in some parts of the world a few millenia ago by the rise of exploitative civilization and more generally during the past two centuries by the spread of industrial civilization. It is not, however, to be thought of as antagonistic to civilization, in the more humane sense of that word, but may be the only way in which a truly civilized existence can be maintained.

In nearly every region of North America, including most of California, natural life-support systems have been severely weakened. The original wealth of biotic diversity has been largely spent and altered toward a narrow range of mostly non- native crops and stock. Chronic misuse has ruined huge areas of once-rich farm, forest, and range land. Wastes from absurdly dense industrial concentrations have left some places almost unlivable. But, regardless of the *endless frontier* delusion and invader mentality that came to dominate in North America, removing one species or native people after another to make-a- living for the invaders, we now know that human life depends ultimately on the continuation of other life. Living-in-place provides for such continuation. It has be-

come a necessity if people intend to stay in any region without further changing it in ever more dangerous directions.

Once all California was inhabited by people who used the land lightly and seldom did lasting harm to its life-sustaining capacity. Most of them have gone. But if the life-destructive path of technological society is to be diverted into life- sustaining directions, the land must be reinhabited. *Reinhabitation* means learning to live-in-place in an area that has been disrupted and injured through past exploitation. It involves becoming native to a place through becoming aware of the particular ecological relationships that operate within and around it. It means understanding activities and evolving social behavior that will enrich the life of that place, restore its life-supporting systems, and establish an ecologically and socially sustainable pattern of existence within it. Simply stated it involves becoming fully alive in and with a place. It involves applying for membership in a biotic community and ceasing to be its exploiter.

Useful information for reinhabitants can come from a wide range of sources. Studies of local native inhabitants, in particular the experiences of those who have lived there before, both those who tried to make a living and those who lived-in-place, can contribute. Reinhabitants can apply this information toward shaping their own life patterns and establishing relationships with the land and life around them. This will help determine the nature of the bioregion within which they are learning to live- in-place.

Reinhabitation involves developing a bioregional identity, something most North Americans have lost, or have never possessed. We define *bioregion* in a sense different from the biotic province of Raymond Dasmann (1973) or the biogeographical province of Miklos Udvardy (1975). The term refers both to geographical terrain and a terrain of consciousness—to a place and the ideas that have developed about how to live in that place. Within a bioregion the conditions that influence life are similar and these in turn have influenced human occupancy.

A bioregion can be determined initially by use of climatology, physiography, animal and plant geography, natural history and other descriptive natural sciences. The final boundaries of a bioregion are best described by the people who have lived within it, through human recognition of the realities of living-in- place. All life on the planet is interconnected in a few obvious ways, and in many more that remain barely explored. But there is a distinct resonance among living things and the factors which influence them that occurs specifically within each separate place on the planet. Discovering and describing that resonance is a way to describe a bioregion....

"We now know that human life depends ultimately on the continuation of other life."

Biologically, the California biotic province, which forms the heart of the bioregion, is not only unique but somewhat incredible—a west coast refuge for obscure species, full of endemic forms of plants and animals. It is a Mediterranean climatic region unlike any other in North America. It is a place of survival for once wide-spread species as well as a place where other distinct forms evolved. Anthropologically it is also unique, a refuge for a great variety of non-agricultural peoples on a continent where agriculture had become dominant.

During the century and a half that invader society has occupied northern California, a primary sense of location has been provided by surveyors dividing up the land. We know more about property lines than we do about the life that moves under, over, and through them. People are bombarded with information about the prices of things, but seldom learn their real biospheric cost. They are encouraged to measure the dimensions of things without ever learning their places in the continuity of bioregional life.

Within the bioregion is one major watershed, that of the Sacramento-San Joaquin River system which drains from all of the Sierra-Nevada, Cascade, and interior Coast Ranges and flows through the broad plain of the Central Valley. Coastally, smaller watersheds are significant, those of the Salinas, Russian, Eel, Mad, Klamath and Smith Rivers. The Klamath River is anomalous in that it drains from an area that belongs to a different bioregion. So too does the Pit River which joins the Sacramento. Otherwise the drainage systems help to define and tie together the life of the bioregion, and the characteristics of watersheds point out the necessities which those who would live-in-place must recognize.

Our real *period of discovery* has just begun. The bioregion is only barely recognized in terms of how life systems relate to each other within it. It is still an anxious mystery whether we will be able to continue living here. How many people can the bioregion carry without destroying it further? What kinds of activities should be encouraged? Which ones are too ruinous to continue? How can people find out about bioregional criteria in a way that they will feel these exist for their mutual benefit rather than as an imposed set of regulations?

Natural watersheds could receive prominent recognition as the frameworks within which communities are organized. The network of springs, creeks, and rivers flowing together in a specific area exerts a dominant influence on all non-human life there; it is the basic designer of local life. Floods and droughts in northern California remind us that watersheds affect human lives as well, but their full importance is more subtle and pervasive. Native communities were developed expressly around local water supplies and tribal boundaries were often set by the limits of watersheds. Pioneer settlements followed the same pattern, often displacing native groups with the intention of securing their water.

Defining the local watershed, restricting growth and development to fit the limits of water supplies, planning to maintain these and restore the free flowing condition of tributaries that are blocked or the purity of any which have been polluted, and exploring the relationships with the larger water systems connecting to it could become primary directions for reinhabitory communities. They could view themselves as centered on and responsible for the watershed.

People have been part of the bioregion's life for a long time. The greatest part of that time has been a positive rather than negative experience for other life sharing the place. In describing how as many as 500 separate tribal *republics* lived side by side in California for at least 15,000 years without serious hostility toward each other or disruption of life-systems around them, Jack Forbes (1971) points out a critical difference between invaders and inhabitants. "Native Californians...felt themselves to be something other than independent, autonomous individuals. They perceived themselves as being deeply bound together with other people (and with the surrounding non-human forms of life) in a complex interconnected web of life, that is to say, a true community.... All creatures and all things were...brothers and sisters. From this idea came the basic principle of non-exploitation, of respect and reverence for all creatures, a principle extremely hostile to the kind of economic development typical of modern society and destructive of human morals. (It was this principle, I suspect, which more than anything else preserved California in its *natural* state for 15,000 years, and it is the steady violation of this principle which, in a century and a half, has brought California to the verge of destruction."

Reinhabitants are as different from invaders as these were from the original inhabitants. They want to fit into the place, which requires preserving the place to fit into. Their most basic goals are to restore and maintain watersheds, topsoil, and native species, elements of obvious necessity for in-place existence because they determine the essential conditions of water, food, and stable diversity. Their aims might include developing contemporary bioregional cultures that celebrate the continuity of life where they live, and new region-to-region forms of participation with other cultures based on our mutuality as a species in the planetary biosphere. Shifting to a reinhabitory society, however, requires basic changes in present-day social directions, economics, and politics.

Economics

Northern California is biologically rich—perhaps the richest bioregion in North America. Its present-day economics are generally based on exploiting this richness for maximum short- term profits. The natural systems that create conditions of abundance in the region are both short-term and

long-term. There's good soil, but it took thousands of years to form. There are still some great forests left but they grew over centuries; and none have fully recovered that were logged in historic times.

Reinhabitory economics would seek sufficiency rather than profit. They might be more aptly termed *ecologics* since their object is to successfully maintain natural life-system continuities while enjoying them and using them to live. Most current forms of economic activity that rely on the bioregion's natural conditions could continue in a reinhabitory society, but they would be altered to account for the short and long-term variations in their cycles.

The Central Valley has become one of the planet's food centers. The current scale of agriculture there is huge; thousands of square miles under cultivation to produce multiple annual crops. Fossil-fuel-dependent heavy equipment appears at every stage of farming operations, and there is a steadily rising rate of artificial fertilizer use. Most of the land is owned or leased by absentee agribusiness corporations. It's a naturally productive place. Northern California has a temperate climate, a steady supply of water, and the topsoil is some of the richest in North America. But the current scale of agriculture is untenable over the long-term. Fossil fuel and chemical fertilizer can only become more expensive, and the soil is simultaneously being ruined and blown away.

There needs to be massive redistribution of land to create smaller farms. They would concentrate on growing a wider range of food species (including native food plants), increasing the nutritional value of crops, maintaining the soil, employing alternatives to fossil fuels, and developing small-scale marketing systems. More people would be involved, thereby creating jobs and lightening the population load on the cities.

Forests have to be allowed to rebuild themselves. Clearcutting ruins their capability to provide a long-term renewable resource. Watershed-based reforestation and stream restoration projects are necessary everywhere that logging has been done. Cut trees are currently being processed wastefully; tops, stumps, and branches are left behind, and whole logs are shipped away to be processed elsewhere and sold back in the region. Crafts that use every part of the tree should be employed to make maximum use of the materials while employing a greater number of regional people. Fisheries have to be carefully protected. They provide a long-

"Coyote Pointing," by Daniel O. Stolpe.

term life-support of rich protein, if used correctly, or a quickly emptied biological niche, if mishandled. Catching fish and maintaining the fisheries have to be seen as parts of the same concern.

Reinhabitory consciousness can multiply the opportunities for employment within the bioregion. New reinhabitory livelihoods based on exchanging information, cooperative planning, administering exchanges of labor and tools, intra- and inter- regional networking, and watershed media emphasizing bioregional rather than city-

consumer information could replace a few centralized positions with many decentralized ones. The goals of restoring and maintaining watersheds, topsoil and native species invite the creation of many jobs to simply un-do the bioregional damage that invader society has already done.

(First published in **Reinhabiting A Separate Country. A Bioregional Anthology of Northern California.** Ed. Peter Berg. San Francisco: Planet Drum Foundation, 1978.)

FUTURE PRIMITIVE

Jeremiah Gorsline and L. Freeman House

Future Primitive is spoken here as two voices. In reality, these voices represent the best cullings from readings in dozens of authors and scholars and from months of discussion with many people up and down the west coast of North America. It is an on-going collaboration which has hardly begun.

Humanity is an implicit and beneficial element of nature. Cultural history of the genus reveals a two million year span of successful adaptation during which people collected their food and materials from naturally productive geo-biotic regions and locales. A cultivation of the wild. The term *primitive* refers to this long and stable phase of human culture—so persistent it survives today on the most marginal lands. The replacement of this very successful adaptive culture with an exploitative/industrial culture occurred only very recently in the North Pacific Range. Human presence in the New World dates back at least twenty thousand years. From Mid- to Late-Wisconsin glaciation, populations began to grow and spread until encountering the continental margins. Through a process of bio- cultural evolution the journey over earth became a union with her body.

A simple shift in mode, in perception, in culture…the sheath of worldculture could drop away…revealing an endless and radiant landscape of the imagination. Human culture rising out of natural succession…its best aspiration harmonious interaction with the larger community, the ecosystem…a simple rearrangement of hierarchies…nothing to be afraid of, total security at both ends. Teaching history as an arm of biology for a generation would do it. Or do I have to lay down in front of that damned bulldozer again? I'm walking across the field toward Fishtown. The light is very clean and soft, an early spring day. The plants and trees are radiant from within and I am alert enough to see the radiance. Fishtown is built on pilings over the river, old gillnetters' shacks now occupied by artists and contemplatives. It lies about a mile from the paved road. Half the walk is over cultivated field, half through the woods, straight up over the hill and then the river. As I walk over the hill I'm paying attention to the trees and the ground. The river comes into view and suddenly I'm

stunned by the realization that I am not the same person who started the walk! I am transformed by a ceremony residing in the land itself. The place dictates the mandate for human activities there and that mandate can be perceived directly through a ceremony that lives in the woods like an almost tangible creature. I am transformed, transfixed; I am hung on the line to dry like a flapping raggedy flannel shirt.

We have been awakened to the richness and complexity of the primitive mind which merges sanctity, food, life and death—where culture is integrated with nature at the level of the *particular ecosystem* and employs for its cognition a body of metaphor drawn from and structured in relation to that ecosystem. We have found therein a mode of thinking parallel to modern science but operating at the entirely different level of sensible intuition; a tradition that prepared the ground for the neolithic revolution; a science of the *concrete*, where nature is the model for culture because the mind has been nourished and weaned on nature; a *logic* that *recognizes* soil fertility, the magic of animals, the continuum of mind between species. Successful culture is a semi- permeable membrane between man and nature. We are witnessing North America's post-industrial phase right now, during which human society strives to remain predominant over nature. No mere extrapolation from present to future seems possible. We are in transition from one condition of symbiotic balance—the primitive—to another which we will call the *future primitive*…a condition having the attributes of a mature ecosystem: stable, diverse, in symbiotic balance again.

Now I'm half crazed with it: I'm carrying a cockle shell in my palm as I walk and hitch around the countryside. It cuts into my hand just enough to keep me alert. I want to perceive those natural ceremonies and processions wherever I go. Maybe I'll go mad but I'm gaining a language. I can talk to almost anyone now and it's not stiff or wierd. Hitching to the dentist this morning along Chuckanut Drive, a narrow two-lane blacktop clinging to the cliffs running up the east side of Northern Puget Sound, fine vistas of the San Juan Islands, very little traffic this time of year. A cheerful middle-aged fisherman picks me up after a while. I pocket my cockle. He fishes on the Radio, dragging for hake which are sold to the fish-meal plant and ground up into pellets which are fed to hatchery salmon. I know another guy on the Radio and I tell him that I have to smell that fish-meal process, the damned plant's in La Conner, where I live. We feel friendly toward each other. He asks what do I do in La Conner, just foolin' away my unemployment, hah? I tell him what's in the North Pacific Rim, how it's strung together by salmon, fir, cedar, bear, the Japanese current, the weather; how 99% of human habitation there has been successful; how there's a real economy which everyone shares that has nothing to do with American or Russian or Japanese bucks. He digs it at once, doesn't even care about Japs ripping off "American" fish. He asks Are you religious? I say Well, ah, I think the planet's alive, yes I suppose I'm religious, but it's not out there, it's all over the place, it's in here. He says Yeah, well I'm not very religious either. But that economy, I can understand that, I've always thought I could get very close with a Japanese woman—now I could tell her, look, we're all in the same boat, whad'ya wanna do next? I give him his next line— yeah, eat another piece of this salmon. We laugh and drive on through Bellingham. He drops me right at the dentist's door and we part friends. I deliver to the dentist a copy of a poster we have managed to produce for the Drum concerning the rate of trade between the Japanese and the Ainu in 1792. White Rice. He's very happy to get it. Says Wow, the Hudson Bay Company was doing the same thing at the same time on this side with white flour!

The science of ecology provides us with a logic of integration: individuals join to form species/populations; populations join to form community/ecosystems; ecosystems join to form the biosphere. If we wish to integrate our cultures with nature we do so at the *level of the ecosystem* which everywhere has a common structure and progression but everywhere varies specifically in composition and function according to time and place. Compare this with the post-industrial ideal of *stewardship* whereby a single species assumes management of the biosphere in order to turn to its advantage all biological and physical processes. A single species dead-end.

Technology on the North Pacific Rim is boat technology. You can't walk around the Rim without a bulldozer in front of you to clear the trees. Bigfoot is a 22 year old ex-logger, tractor driver, peaviner, a friend of mine. Maybe a month ago he decided that the only reasonable way to live around here was to get into a boat that would row and sail, which would open up for him a 500-mile radius in which he could forage and cultivate the wild. Live that way, forget about logging hernias. He found a 26-foot Columbia River bowpicker hull which was sinking, raised it, put a foredeck and new gunwhales on it, intends to step a mast soon. It's a big boat with a lot of beam, but so well-shaped that one person can row it standing up with 14 foot sweeps. Last week he and Peter and I took it out. We rowed it up the channel a couple of miles against the current and then through the fish hole in the jetty, a tricky business. It was one of those typical days on the Rim—water above, water below, the definition of the horizon obscured into a dozen tones of pearl gray. A person in a boat on such a day floats in the center of a dimensionless cosmos; up, down, here, there, all obscured. A person in a boat is in the center of It. We worked our way along the jetty until we saw a cedar log big enough to cut shake bolts out of it. Drift-wood. We took a chainsaw, bucked it up, loaded it in the boat. Then found a big alder, perfectly seasoned, bucked it up for firewood and loaded it. As the tide goes out the fish hole dries up, so we hurried back out into the channel so as not to be stranded on the wrong side of the jetty. We rowed back on the channel, trying out various rowing styles; facing backwards, facing forwards, two men rowing together, etc. We got back before noon, not tired, but laughing, with more than half a cord of mixed shake-bolts and fire wood. Anxiety about survival has always been beside the point. The air was moist and tasty that morning and we felt good for the rest of the day.

A narrow climatic zone adjacent to the temperate North Pacific. Sea level to coast-mountain divide. Within this range there is a progression manifest in its life process. With the retreat of glaciers came the first communities—the lichens, mosses and grasses—forming a living cover over raw glacial till; reducing soil erosion and evaporation; building up organic matter. Next, willow and cottonwood seedlings, prostrate on the nitrogen-impoverished soil. Then, the alders: hosts to nitrogen-fixing bacteria. Nitrogen compounds leak from roots to soil. Leaves form a nitrogen-rich detritus. Organic matter accumulates. Community succession continues. As the alder thicket matures, hemlock and red cedar surge upward and shade out the alder. The new stands thicken. More organic matter is added to the soil. Conditions continue to change. Succession slows as energy is increasingly relegated from production to maintenance and protection. Growth slows. Life cycles, elaborate webs of association working toward symbiotic balance, more complex food chains, nutrient conservation and stability. In two hundred years the alder's gone. Incorporated into the forest soil.

This past month we ate nettles, many oysters, dandelion greens, salmon, cat-tail shoots, smelt, lambs' quarters, clams, mussels, and a lot of stuff from the grocery store. Less dependence on the grocery store than last year. The last of last summer's frozen strawberries for breakfast this morning. Five pound Dolly Varden trout in the channel, but I haven't learned to catch them yet. Garden still half an inch under water but the leeks and garlic holding tough. Milk from local cow-farmers. It's very early spring.

Rain forest. Hemlock-wapiti-deer-red cedar-sitka spruce biome. Duff and organic soil is deep. Wapiti browse, deer browse. Trails through the forest. Beds where they sleep. The challenge is to fit ourselves to this range in a way appropriate to the strategy and particulars of its regional succession, so that our cultures are once again a ceremony of interaction between species and ecosystem, matching the regional diversity. Events related to landmarks; a mythology of place; a landscape of events. The locale is one context containing the indigenous culture, appropriate to its time and place, ritualizing connections between species and habitat. Continuous with biology. A community of beings joined by rim and basin, air and watershed, food chains— ceremonies. Inhabiting river basin, estuary, mountainside and island, we proceed as part of the ceremony of this evolution. There is no independent existence.

Whispers from Suwa-no-se Island, in the Japanese Archipelago, poetry in the Micronesian Senate, Tlingit newspapers 300 miles in the back country. Neighbors and allies. My feet are here and my head's everywhere. Various locales are speaking through various people, communes, peoples. Wallace Stevens said, "There are men of a valley/Who are that valley...the soul...is composed of external world." Geobiotically, there is no sense in centralized national governments. Biologically, the industrial state is a travesty. Economics has been misunderstood for two thousand years. Growth economics and bio-engineering are thrusting us into an encapsulated toilet of a future. There will be corresponding committees, regional caucuses, continental congresses to deal with these considerations. We will strive for indigeneity and regional self-sufficiency. We will be informed by earthworms and plankton. We will study that authority which resides in place and act out our lives accordingly. There is no separate existence.

(First published in **Raise The Stakes** "North Pacific Rim Alive," Bundle #3, 1974.)

Drawing by Martha Tree.

LIVING HERE

The Frisco Bay Mussel Group

We who live around the San Francisco Bay-Sacramento River Estuary, all species ranging this watershed on the North Pacific Rim, feel a common resonance behind the quick beats of our separate lives; long-pulse rhythms of the region pronouncing itself through Winter-wet & Summer-dry, Something-flowering- anytime, Cool Fog, Tremor and Slide.

Borne-Native in the San Francisco Bay Region

The region proclaims itself clearly. It declares the space for holding our own distinct celebrations: Whale Migration & Salmon Run, Acorn Fall, Blackberry & Manzanita Fruit, Fawn Drop, Red Tide; processions and feasts which invite many other species, upon which many other species depend. The bay-river watershed carries these outpourings easily. They are borne, native, by the place. Their occurrence and the full life of the region are inseparable.

Human beings have lived here a long time. For thousands of years, the region held their celebrations easily. They ate enormous quantities of shellfish, acorns, salmon, berries, deer, buckeyes, grass seeds, and duck eggs. They cut countless tule reeds for mats, boats and baskets, burned over thousands of acres of dead grass, made trails everywhere, cleared land and packed down soil with villages. They netted fish from boats, strung fish traps across creeks and rivers, and dug up tidelands looking for clams and oysters. The region probably never held a species that had a greater effect upon it, but for thousands of years human beings were part of its continuous life. They lived directly in it, native.

The Shell Mound Cultures and the Ancient Kuksu Cult

Over four hundred shell mounds have been found in and around the Bay Area, and many of these mounds date back into the third, even the fourth millenium before the present. The mounds were for the most part composed of oyster, clam and mussel shells, but animal and fish remains also provide us with a pretty good idea of both the wildlife of the Bay Area during these early days, as well as the hunting and fishing practices of the first inhabitants. Deer, Elk, Sea Otter, Beaver, Squirrel, Rabbit, Gopher, Raccoon, Wild Cat, Wolf, Bear, Dog, Seal, Sea Lion, Whale, Porpoise, Canvasback Duck, Goose, Cormorant, Turtle, Skates, Thornbacks and other fish were all found within the mounds. They also contained the remains of some of the first settlers, and occasionally male bodies were found accompanied by pipes and weapons, and female bodies were found with mortar, pestle and awls. The large number of these mounds, as well as the range of artifacts, gives us some idea of the size and sophistication of this early culture. Along with a number of fishing and hunting tools and utensils, highly polished bone awls, graceful "charm stones," delicately worked stone pipes, bone whistles, stone labrets, and certain shell beads and pendants were also found in the debris.

The appearance of this Shell Mound Culture in the Bay Area during the fourth millenium before the present can perhaps best be understood in terms of the larger movements of people going on throughout the entire Pacific Basin and upon the Pacific Rim during this period of history, a period when sedentary fishing peoples began to experiment with fish poisons and food resources (the mound itself being an excellent open air "lab") thus leading to the invention of the cultivated crop and agriculture.

The largest shell mound in the Bay Area was found at Emeryville, and it was quite well known as the site of the Emeryville Shell Mound Park at the turn of the century. The mound was destroyed, and the main plant of the Sherwin-Williams Paint Company—"We cover the Earth"—was built on its spot in 1923. This mound was quite large—200 feet long, over 25 feet high, and over 50 feet wide—and visitors would note how during certain seasons, it was constructed to take full advantage of the sun setting directly between the narrows of the Golden Gate straits. The area is characterized today (coincidentally?) by a series of anonymous, brilliant wooden sculptures that have been raised on the land-fill areas adjoining the old park, and the reinhabitation of many of the abandoned industrial warehouses of Emeryville by artists, crafts people, and small press publishers in and around Shell Mound Road.

Although the Costanoan Indians may or may not have been the people who constructed these mounds, by the time of Spanish colonization the Costanoan people had occupied all the old mound areas of the East Bay and the San Francisco peninsula south to Monterey, while the Coastal Miwok peoples occupied Marin to the north. Clearly, by the time of European contact, the Sacramento River had become the key to the Indian geography of the Bay Area, and to follow the river inland was to come in contact with an increasingly populous and sophisticated Indian culture. Of the many fascinating Indian cultures occupying the inland foothills and the Valley, the Pomo peoples—per-

haps the most respected basket weavers in the New World—deserve special mention. The Pomo peoples in and around Clear Lake, which can be seen as the "capital district"for north central California Indian culture, seem to have had the greatest impact on the area's Indian cultures as a whole. In contrast to the Pomo way of life which has been richly documented, precious little is known about the Costanoan peoples who lived on the Bay. We do know that at the time of contact at least as many as 21,000 Costanoan Indians were living in this area, with another 4,000 Coastal Miwok Indians living in Marin. The Indian population for the Sacramento River Watershed area, moreover, was well over 140,000 people. By 1910, after less than two hundred years of disease and mistreatment introduced by the invaders, the Costanoan and Coastal Miwok cultures had been completely wiped out, and only 2,800 natives were still living in the greater Sacramento Watershed area—and most of them were living as far away from the center of colonial activity and civilization as they could. Visions of Gold, both Yankee & Conquistador, seem to have been the central agen-

AT HOME IN L.A.

Here in Echo Park in the original Spanish pueblo, I can see in the distance, dimmed by sunlit haze, evidence of the peculiar twisting and turning of the earth, in the upended, jumbled paleolithic land form of the east west Santa Monica mountains. The grid city of imported wood, steel, stucco, asphalt, concrete squares, oblongs, towers, circles, woven roots and grasses called Los Angeles transformed desert, from rock, from sand. Presiding tender mountain ridges within which water, streams and ancient habitat hide, once ocean bottom, now weathered rocks and pillow lava replicating waves on earth. Called mountains, the Santa Monica's home to the Gaabrieleno, to the Shoshone and Cumash, an airshed to the region. They are threatened along with the Verdugos and Santa Susanas by massive bulldozing; stiffened with concrete they are to be cut up and made into flatland for speculation and for growth.

From my room with a view I cannot see the stars, nor any native vegetation; the oaks are gone, the native grasses, the sycamores. The L.A. river, to my north, over the basalt rock of Echo Park, is channeled in vertical walls. Following floods in 1916, a decision was made to contain potential damage to structures by sending water to the sea. Shortsighted greed lost the opportunity to replenish the now degraded artesian waters and aquifers which sustain wetlands and marshlands. Since then, the streets, the freeways along with sewer pipes and drain pipes collect the rain which, no longer sinking downward, rushes to the beautiful Santa Monica Bay. Once the passageway to whale and dolphin, to seals and swordfish, the sea is thick with a layer of pesticides and toxic chemicals. House and industry, built in the flood plain, are protected. In turn, these inhabitants drink, flush, wash and dump offal and toxics into water, imported from far away in Colorado and Northern

cy of destruction.

The few reports of the Costanoan culture that survive are uniformly unflattering, and tell us more about the mind of the invader than they do about the facts of native culture. There is a bittersweet irony to these reports, a black humor that sounds at times as if the script had been written by Lenny Bruce. Consider this description of Jose Espinosa y Tello on the Costanoans of Monterey. "Men and women go naked feeding in the fields like brute beasts, or gathering seeds for the winter and engaging also in hunting and fishing. Although some of these natives have now been *reduced to obedience* [italics added] and form part of the Mission of San Carlos, they still preserve their former disposition and customs. Among other habits which they retain it has been noticed that in their leisure moments they will lie on the ground face downwards for whole hours with the greatest content." Clearly the Costanoans were the subject of vicious and unfair reporting, as were, of course, most of the Indians of North America. The anthropologist Kroeber, who accepts most of these reports at face value, tells us the Costanoans were a "dark, dirty, squalid and apathetic" people. "I have never seen one laugh." He reports one invader, Choris, as saying, "I have never seen one look you in the face." Nonetheless, reading between the lines, certain details do emerge, and these details suggest a very different portrait of these people. "Costanoan, from the Spanish, meaning a coastal people…Coyote, Eagle, Hummingbird sitting on a mountain top. When the ocean receded and the land appeared, it was Coyote who went down and created these coastal people…. They held the Sun, and the Redwood Tree, as Sacred…Sophisticated tule huts, sophisticated tule rafts…. A line survives from one of their dances: We dance on the brink of the World."

Very little is known about the Costanoan religion. We are told only that at the Mission San Jose the natives continued to hold their ancient winter solstice dance much to the chagrin of the officials. The existence of this dance among the Costanoans suggests that they were influenced by the famous Kuksu Cult, a widespread system of religious belief that served to unite many of the cultures of the Sacramento Watershed area. The

---

California, making green grass lawns and thick green vegetation lining freeways, making highrise bright hard green.

This is my home, a way station for the collection of mortgage interest, payments to the Department of Water and Power, Southern California Gas Company, Pacific Bell and taxes of all kinds. Only the air is free, and is often unbreathable. My home, in the absence of a social polity, is my temporary sanctuary; it is the one space which does not psychologically belong to the other. And from it, from this node in a network of grassroots workers, we challenge the underlying assumptions of growth in the basin. For this, we need a new language and new organizing, which uses old forms in new ways. Developing a community of spirit, we are sometimes able to halt the massive growth machine from obliterating our neighborhoods and our places of work. For instance, we've saved eighty thousand acres of native chapparall, coastal sage and rare riparian habitat in the Santa Monicas. It is all under attack.

Over my ridge is Elysian Park. Planted as an English landscape in the 19th century when much of the surrounding land was still desert, the real estate brokers were readying the hills for sale. For thirty years a Citizens' Committee has stopped one hundred and thirty incursions into the park. This year they want to cover the Elysian Park Reservoir and expand the Los Angeles Police Academy into the park, where homeless live in trees and pee on park rangers. This rock outcrop, once covered with canyon live oak woodland, was decimated by grazing sheep, rock quarries and dumping, now dry brown eucalyptus woodland, an import from Australia. They cut the water away in 1950 when they tore up Chavez Ravine for the Pasadena Freeway, and never gave it back. So there are periodic fires. The Committee has forced them to replace the picnic areas and grass in some areas. Once the backyard of the Spanish Roman city plaited along the diagonal sunline of the mediterranean, the area is like a hole in the L.A. landscape where time has stopped.

—Sue Nelson, *from* **Land and the People 1989**, *a prose-poem delivered at the 1989 U.S. Green Gathering , Eugene, Oregon.*

Kuksu Cult involved dance rituals and festivals, although it was primarily male-oriented (in counter-distinction to the ancient, female- oriented ghost religion and secret societies), the degree of sexual exclusivity varied from tribe to tribe, clan to clan. The secret Kuksu initiation ceremony conveyed moral, ethical and sacred teachings, and served to inform the initiates as to their place within the circle of all beings.

The Kuksu was always depicted as a terrifying figure, half man and half bird. Consider this description by Jaime de Angulo of the arrival of the Kuksu during the Winter Solstice Festivals among the Pomo. "Finally, just as the last rays of the sun were setting on the western shore of the lake, an extraordinary series of screams and yells started up again—but this time it was coming from the hills. With great excitement the people began to point towards the West. Off in the distance you could vaguely make out the outline of an old, dead tree. An owl was sitting on the top branch of the tree, and a man...or a bird...was hanging upside down, arms and legs spread stiff and still, from one of the bottom branches. He had feathers, lots of feathers growing out of the top of his head at various angles. Suddenly a fire shot up from the ground underneath him, and he was surrounded by smoke. When the smoke cleared, the man...or bird...whatever it was...had disappeared. "That was the Kuksu," Old Man Turtle said, "The Kuksu has returned."

It is not known when the Kuksu Cult first entered into this area, but the point of origin is thought to have been from the Southwest. Indeed the iconography of the Kuksu Cult, fire, owl, feathers, dead tree—has much in common with similar cults throughout the large Uto-Aztecan cultural area, and the Kuksu himself seems at least in some distant sense related to the great Aztec cult figure, Quetzalcoatl.

The appearance of the Kuksu always followed the ceremony held for the ghosts of the people who had died during the previous year. After the ghosts had been given their sendoff, on the last day of the festival, just at sunset, the Kuksu would arrive, his head ablaze with feathers of many cultures, a blaze equal to the rays of the setting sun, signifying (seemingly) that a new season, and a new Sun, had begun its cycle. The arrival of the Kuksu—with his strange high pitched whistle; his head, torso, and limbs all moving to the inaudible sound of three distinct and seemingly unrelated rhythms; and his bird's headdress an incredible shock of multi-colored feathers sticking out at various and seemingly random angles—the arrival of the Kuksu was the most important and powerful moment of the year.

The Kuksu Cult, therefore, certainly began as a Sun Cult of some order, but a Sun Cult that penetrated into an area where the Old Pleistocene Religion of the Dead and Ghost Cults were widely practiced. Indeed the Kuksu Cult in this area is often considered to be a Moon Cult too, as the native Indians held the Moon to be the night-time Sun. Hence the Kuksu Cult derived additional power, and was to an extent transformed by its close association with the older religion, and it came to have a central synthesizing impact on all the early Indian cultures of this area.

A few hundred years ago some new people moved in and began to impose a non-native way of life over the entire watershed. Instead of living directly in it, they began living off of it, on top of it. Dams, canals and pipelines were built to shift "surplus" water away from life-systems in rivers, creeks, lakes, and marshes which had always required it. Oysters and clams were stripped from the bayshore in a few years and their beds filled in with garbage and crushed hillsides to create waterfront real estate. Within a short time, redwood and fir forests became houses and San Francisco Bay turned into a huge toilet for sewage and factory wastes. Generations born here called themselves "native" but kept pushing the watershed's life to exhaustion. Nearly all habitats for native species were destroyed. Attempts by many species to maintain themselves were stopped through outright slaughter or intolerable despoilation. Some of the largest are lost to the region now; tule elk, grizzly bear and condor.

It was extremely profitable for a few of the new people to live here this way. Anything could be seen as unused surplus by a non-native eye and it was easy to find markets elsewhere for much of it. But profits began slipping as native life-forms vanished. The place withered quickly and became increasingly less liveable for all of the people in it.

Watershed

San Francisco Bay is the lower end of a vast watershed, beginning at the highest ridges of the Sierra Nevada and the inner Coast Range, continuing through the Central Valley, ending at Golden Gate. Watershed is the peak experience; selecting among bodies of water, watershed divides rainfall/runoff by direction, this rainwater to the Russian River, this to the Bay and Delta, this to the Pacific Ocean.

Watershed often divides plants, animal lives, far-off views— which watershed are you in now? Once divided, water flows in and out of steep mountain canyons, through flat valleys, into marshy, muddy bays and estuaries, always downhill, getting increasingly salty past the Sacramento-San Joaquin River confluence near Antioch, until it becomes one with the ocean in the Bay.

Watershed is a whole, defines what is upriver/downriver, what the space is we roam in, in our own bodies of water. Watershed is the universe of our water body experience. When you follow a watershed, it teaches, leads you on in. When you cut a watershed with roads, dams and ditches, it bleeds, erodes, floods. Watershed defines place, wind, food, pathways, ceremonies and chants. Enter into that flowing moment of watershed living, in this place, celebrate the return of salmon and herring, dream of waters merging, enlarge the watershed with your own self, until you are in it totally, until you are it.

Watershed is a living organism: rivers and streams and underground flows are veins and arteries; marshes are the pollution-removing kidneys; water to drink; water is the cosmic sense organ of the earth, the dimpled skin between above and below; water rhythms show us moon, season, shape and sense of land.

Flowing, tumbling water wears away hard granite, soft sandstone, creates the watershed form with what remains, brings forth nutriment for ocean creatures, creates beautiful beaches, the sound of the river turning is a low moan, waterfalls roar, water over rock.

Watershed landscape was history: we build where it's flat, avoid floods, water the crops, hunt animals at the dark waterhole. The mud flats around the Bay come from 19th-century Sierra Nevada hydraulic-mining clay sediments. Flood control dams and channelized streams come from reactions to the 1955 Northern California floods. Disturbances of the river spread upstream as well as downstream; too much silt means no salmon spawning, no clarity for fishing, flooding at the raised river mouth.

Water falls by gravity, rises by levity.

We climb the watershed, to the ridge top, to glimpse what lies beyond, what we can see, well grounded along the ridge, but intrigued, curious as all mammals are, to see, to see what lies beyond our sight, beyond sense perception?

Down inside the watershed, a few peaks draw our attention: Mt. Hamilton in the south Bay; wind-clean San Bruno Mountain to the west, the wooded sides of Mount Tamalpais in the central and north Bay, the spread-out devil of Mt. Diablo uplifted from the sea to the east, the volcanic lava cap of Mount St. Helena, the highest, sliding in and out of view as we travel the lower Russian River watershed. From inside our Pleistocene-drowned Bay valley, we need climb only a short way to rise up high enough to see for fifty miles; Ohlone and Miwok Indians watched each other's fires across the Bay at night, kept an eye on fishing and shellmound rubbish heaps during the day, eyes up on circling hawks.

Water and plants, land and animals are at home, a living whole, an ecosystem in a biotic region. When the water system is cut or altered, all else is affected. When plants are destroyed, land covered for urbanity, water changes, becomes sluggish, then ravages towns in floods, dries up creeks in summer, goes underground when overused.

So much of the healthy plant and animal life in our watershed region has been damaged or destroyed, we will need generations to restore it, to return the original healthy native/wild ecosystem to make our peace with this water body.

All around the Bay, there are tens of thousands of acres of diked-off tidelands which could be res-

Metaphor For A City

The proper metaphor for a city, after all, is not the "machine for living" that was dreamed of by techno-freak architects like LeCorbusier thirty years ago. The proper model is a living eco-system with appropriate niches for a great variety of beings. A city's diversity, one of its main delights, should be biological as well as social. It needs the magical and mysterious vitality of nature as well as society.

— **Ernest Callenbach,** *from* **Raise the Stakes**,

tored to pickleweed/cordgrass salt marsh, the planet's intense biologically productive habitat, where the edge of the sea transfers food from land to water creatures.

Damming all creeks for flood control has been our constant practice, this great fear and unwillingness to live with watershed events. Now these creeks, watercourses through the land, wider, deeper, drier than before, need rehabilitation, to make them able-bodied again, released from bonds of concrete and riprap. To restore all creeks, to make them flow full of power, working for us and all wild life, is also our work, is right action.

Look around your town. Find the creek, follow it down, figure out—what to do? Do it, right, now.

When forests are transformed into housing developments, there is an illusion of prosperity which masks the hollowness felt by people who live in them. Landscapes full of buildings become depressing. Jobs that require annihilating living things or manufacturing monotonous garbage breed self-contempt. Constant exposure to other people or television without an opening into the naturally-evolved graces of the planet is oppressive and demeaning. There is a feeling that one's life is being used. Used up.

Non-native culture, live-in colonialism, becomes its own worst threat. Rejection of living within the boundaries of natural life-systems requires mammoth amounts of labor and energy to build, rebuild, and keep up artificial ones. By reducing the diversity of life in the region, non-native culture constantly narrows opportunities for social and personal self-preservation. There's a steady movement through extinction of native life towards self-extinction.

Species: Familiar and Ghost

The uniqueness of each place comes in part from ecology and climate, but even more from the biota, the animals and plants that live there, shaping the landscape, its character, and one another as they evolve together. Each species which forms a strand of a living community has its own history and has entered the regional fabric at some point in geologic time, bringing the mysterious information of its own previous being.

This subtle and deeply resonant wisdom of place deserves respect and reverence, for those who thoughtlessly destroy information so long in the gathering are guilty of a crime against consciousness. The shrines where uniqueness and subtlety are concentrated should not heedlessly be plowed or paved over. The dappled carpets of *Stipa* bunchgrass, constellation with shooting stars and *Fritillaria*, the solitary digger bees and dancing *Hydropsyche* are not replaceable by crude expanses of opportunistic weeds, wild oats and thistle, houseflies and Argentine ants.

Two hundred years ago, San Francisco Bay and the land rimming it was a natural paradise. Nutrients, washed down from the mountain slopes all around the great Central Valley, were carried to and accumulated in the Bay, which abounded with fish and oysters, harbor seals, sea otters and dolphins. Indian villages were more numerous along its shores than anywhere else in California. The rich alluvial deposits of the tidal flats were crowned with vast marshes, a magnet for awesome hordes of migratory ducks and geese and also the great food producer for the Bay's water creatures, while landward grew lush meadows of bunch grass, where thousands of tule elk grazed.

In the sand dunes now overlain by the sod of Golden Gate Park, grizzly bears dug out ground squirrels among the yellow lupines and dune tansies. The tule elk and grizzlies are long gone now and the dune tansy is making a last precarious stand on a few small scraps of land soon to be built upon near the ocean beach. Two small but lovely species of butterflies, which once hovered over the flowering vales of San Francisco and nowhere else, have winked out forever, one in the last century, one in this. The beautiful San Francisco garter snake, which lived in little fault ponds along the San Andreas, has been seldom seen since developers destroyed most of its habitat in the early 1900s. A marvelous web of native plants and insects, some found nowhere else, still survives on the ridge and upper slopes of San Bruno Mountain, but development plans are closing in fast.

The sea otters have been hunted from the Bay, and most of the dolphins and harbor seals are gone. Some of the Bay's invertebrates, native shrimps and mussels, are being crowded out by competing species brought inadvertently from distant seas on the hulls of ships.

In Lake Merced, an estuary which gradually became fresh thousands of years ago, there are fresh-water opossum shrimp and fresh-water tentacled sea worms. Both have so far been able to survive the vagaries of managing the lake for trout fishing.

Golden eagles nested commonly along the

eastbay hills and hunted jackrabbits on the flatlands below. A few remain, reminders of the time when they and the great California condors wheeled high in the skies over San Francisco Bay.

The natural communities which persist are precious fragmented holograms of the once great San Francisco ecosystem. We should protect it and as much as possible restore it, for these living roots which penetrate far into the past not only maintain the biological integrity of our home region, but nourish our spirit and sense of place as well.

Winter-wet and Summer-dry, Something-flower-ing-anytime, Cool Fog, Tremor and Slide will remain. The region's unique resonance will continue to sound behind whatever celebrations are carried by it, and proclaim itself more clearly than any declarations made about it. Reinhabitants of the place, people who want to maintain a full life for themselves and for the watershed, are shaping human celebrations which respond to that resonance. Celebrations which depend on but can be shared by other species. Lives which can be part of the region proclaiming itself.

(San Francisco, 1977.)

MISH MEDITATION

We are the Mish of Ish River Country
We are a new tribe of dwellers in this land.
We are a rainbow tribe—
original people, new people,
people with roots going back a few generations,
red people, white people, black people,
yellow people, brown people.
We come together to protect and restore this place,
to rebuild community,
and to sow the seeds of a new culture—
a culture of this place, in this place.
We come together in community
not only with the many-colored people,
but also with the flying people, the swimming people,
the four-legged people, the plant people,
and the past and future people.
Because we know that
as we shape our common destiny,
we must consider all our relations.
We are a diverse people.
We are a rainbow tribe, a new tribe.
We are the Mish of Ish River Country.

— Lance Scott

SPEAKING IN THE HAIDA WAY

Gwaganad

*T*he human connection with the land is often eloquently stated by the native people. Here, Gwaganad of Haada Gwaii (the Queen Charlotte Islands), shares her experience of what it is to live with nature. Her statement was made before the Honorable Mr. Justice Harry McKay (here called Kilsli) in British Columbia's Supreme Court on November 6, 1985, in the matter of the application by Frank Beban Logging and Western Forest Products Ltd. for an injunction to prohibit Haida picketing of logging roads on Lyell Island, South Moresby.

"Kilsli, Kilsligana, Kiljadgana, Taaxwilaas. Your Honor, chiefs, ladies held in high esteem, friends. I thank you for this opportunity to speak today. I was aware that I could get a lawyer, but I feel you lose if you go through another person.

"My first language is Haida. My second language is English. Therefore I can express myself better in English. I feel through another person, a lawyer, they also speak another language, and I would have lost what I hope to help Kilsli understand and feel.

"Since the beginning of time—I have been told this through our oral stories—since the beginning of time the Haidas have been on the Queen Charlotte Islands.

"That was our place, given to us.

"We were put on the islands as caretakers of this land.

"Approximately 200 years ago foreigners came to that land. The Haida are very hospitable people. The people came. They were welcomed. We shared. They told us that perhaps there is a better way to live, a different religion, education in schools. The Haida tried this way. The potlatches were outlawed. In many schools my father attended in Kokalitza, the Haida language was not allowed to be spoken. He was punished if he used his language. To this day, Watson Price, my father, understands every word of the Haida language, but he doesn't speak it.

"So the people came. We tried their way. Their language. Their education. Their way of worship. It is clear to me that they are not managing our lands well. If this continues, there will be nothing left for my children and my grandchildren to come.

I feel that the people governing us should give us a chance to manage the land the way we know how it should be.

"It seems that the other cultures don't see trees. They see money. It's take and take and take from the earth. That's not the way it is in my mind.

"On Lyell Island—I want to address Lyell Island and South Moresby, the injunction being served on us. I want to say why that concerns me. To me it is a home of our ancestors. As Lily stated, our ancestors are still there. It is my childhood. Every spring come March my father and mother would take me down to Burnaby Narrows. We stayed there till June. It's wonderful memories I had. I am thankful to my parents for bringing me up the traditional way. There was concern on the Indian agent's part that I missed too much school. But how can you tell them that I was at school?

"Because of that upbringing, because I was brought down to Lyell Island area, Burnaby Narrows and living off the land— that's why I feel the way I do about my culture and the land.

"In those early years the first lesson in my life that I remember is respect. I was taught to respect the land. I was taught to respect the food that comes from the land. I was taught that everything had a meaning. Every insect had a meaning and none of those things were to be held lightly. The food was never to be taken for granted. In gathering the food—the nearest I can translate—I can say to gather food is a spiritual experience for me.

"We are a nation of people at risk today. They say that to make a culture the language is important. I am proud to say I speak my language, but not too many more people in my age do. So you can say in a sense, if this keeps up, the language is going fast. In the past the culture was in very much jeopardy when the potlatching was outlawed. We almost lost ourselves as a people. That culture has been revived in the past few years. There is pride in being a Haida, pride in being a Native. The only thing we can hold on to to maintain that pride and dignity as a people is the land. It's from the land we get our food, it's from the land we get our strength. From the sea we get our energy. If this land such as Lyell Island is logged off as they want to log it off…and they will go on logging. We have watched this for many years. I have read records that our forefathers fought in 1913. It's been an ongoing fight. But no-one is really hearing us. They said they wouldn't log Lyell Island at first and now I hear they are going to go ahead. So today I am here because pretty soon all we are going to be fighting for is stumps. When Frank Beban and his crew are through and there are stumps left on Lyell Island, they got a place to go. We, the Haida people, will be on the Island. I don't want my children and my future grandchildren to inherit stumps. They say, *Don't be concerned, we're planting trees again. Wait for the second growth. It will be just like before.* I travel all around the Island a lot with my family. I see lots of things. This summer I got to see second growth and it pained me a great deal, because I kept hearing there is second growth coming. I saw twenty-year-old second growth around Salt Lagoon. They were planted so close that the trees couldn't grow big. They were small and there was no light getting into them. They couldn't grow. You could see and you could feel that they could not grow. Therefore, I don't feel too hopeful when I hear second growth.

"I want to touch now on another very important area in my life as a food gatherer. It is my job, my purpose, to insure that I gather certain food for my husband and my children, and I want to share one part. It's called *gkow*. That's herring roe on kelp. In the spring the herring come and they spawn on kelp. For many years now I have been harvesting that and putting it away for the winter. But so far I haven't heard what—why is food gathering spiritual?

"It's a spiritual thing that happens. It doesn't just happen every year. You can't take that for granted. We can't take that for granted because everything in the environment has to be perfect. The climate has to be perfect, the water temperature, the kelp have to be ready and the herring have to want to spawn.

"But I want to share what goes on in my spiritual self, in my body, come February. And I feel it's an important point. That's what makes me as a Haida different from you, Kilsli. My body feels that it's time to spawn. It gets ready in February. I get a longing to be on the sea. I constantly watch the ocean surrounding the island where the herring spawn. My body is kind of on edge in anticipation.

"Finally the day comes when it spawns. The water gets all milky around it. I know I am supposed to speak for myself, but I share this experience with all the friends, the lady friends, that we pick together this wonderful feeling on the day that it happens, the excitement, the relief that the herring did indeed come this year. And you don't quite feel complete until you are right out on the ocean with your hands in the water harvesting the kelp, the roe on kelp, and then your body feels

"The Earth"

This is us, the Earth. We realize it sooner or later, but there is no getting around it. If we do not learn to live in harmony with the food chains, with the ecosystems, then gradually they will come out of balance, and then they will die. It is all a circle/cycle and we are in it; we can not escape.

The Earth, clothed in sweet greenness, Mother of all life, we are here.

— **Baden Powell**, *from* **Reinhabiting a Separate Country: A Bioregional Anthology of Northern California**. *San Francisco: Planet Drum Foundation, 1978.*

right. That cycle is complete.

"And it's not quite perfect until you eat your first batch of herring roe on kelp. I don't know how to say it well, but your body almost rejoices in that first feed. It feels right. If you listen to your body it tells you a lot of things. If you put something wrong in it, your body feels it. If you put something right in it, your body feels it. Your spiritual self feels it. In order to make me complete I need the right food from the land. I also need to prepare it myself. I have to harvest it myself. The same thing goes for fish, the fish that we gather for the winter. But I wanted to elaborate on the harvesting of kelp to give you an idea of how it feels as Haida to harvest food.

"So I want to stress that it's the land that helps us maintain our culture. It is an important, important part of our culture. Without that land, I fear very much for the future of the Haida nation. Like I said before, I don't want my children to inherit

stumps. I want my children and my grandchildren to grow up with pride and dignity as a member of the Haida nation. I fear that if we take that land, we may lose the dignity and the pride of being a Haida. Without that there is no—there is no way that I can see that we could carry on with pride and dignity. I feel very strongly—that's why I came down to express my concern for my children and grandchildren.

"So today, if that injunction goes through and the logging continues—and there is a saying up there, they say, *Log it to the beach.* Then what? What will be left and who will be left? We can't go anywhere else but the Island.

"I study a lot about our brothers on the mainland, the North American Plains Indians in their history. They moved a lot because they were forced to. Some moved north, south, east, west, back up against the mountains and back again.

"We as Haida people can't move anymore west.

Home

Whenever I think I might be in danger of becoming learned and even wise, I go home. When I am lost, homesick, depressed, tired, burned out, elated, having mystic visions, wanting to share my joy, I go home. I have been doing it for years now. Most of the time I've lived there. Occasionally, I work in other places, other cultures, knowing that the time will come when it will call me, and, as inexorably as a kite heading for the earth, I will go there. When I am living there, going home means going outside, to the lake, the mountains, my favourite hill where I watch the ospreys play wind games. When I am away, it means driving every spare weekend to catch a few days there.

None of this is metaphorical. Home is where I was born, where I grew up, where I have lived most of my life. Wherever else I live, what I continue to refer to as home is *this* place; not just an owned place, but a wholly lived-in place. I have tried, a few times, and rather naively, to explain the depth of this tie to other people. They look at me puzzled; one friend said, "it's your bottom line, like religion."

Well, sort of. But all my explanations end up sounding like the sentimental brand of nature-loving mush that I try to avoid. Yet there should be a place for it—a description for what has been and still is the most central, deepest and longest relationship of my life....

And I lived, explored, grew there. Sliding down gravel slopes on the neighbor's half-wild horses; swimming out into the lake, all four of us, my brothers and sister, leaving the tame town kids behind on the beach; running over the driftwood in the half- frozen bay in the spring, daring each other, daring myself, to climb rocks and cliffs I was only half sure I could manage; becoming surefooted without noticing it, and sure of myself, picking up knowledge along the way, of animals, and plants, and fire, and wood, and hay and fruit and gardening. Taking chances. All of us—my brothers, my sister and I—inveterate risk-takers, in different ways: one a tree-faller; one a horse- trainer; one, for lack of a better label, a raging ecofeminist peacenik; one a social worker and new father at 43.

We never asked permission. We took hor-

We can go over into the ocean is all. So when the logging is gone, is done, if it goes through and there are stumps left, the loggers will have gone and we will be there as we have been since the beginning of time. Left with very little to work with as a people.

"Again I want to thank you, Kilsli, for this opportunity to speak and share my culture. Thank you very much."

(First published in **Ruebsaat's Magazine**, No. 20, and later appeared in **The New Catalyst**, No. 6, Winter 1986/87 and **Healing The Wounds: The Promise of Ecofeminism**, Ed. Judith Plant. Philadelphia and Santa Cruz: New Society Publishers, 1989.)

rendous and what probably looked like terrifying chances, but always with the feeling that we would be okay. We drove tractors at six and got rifles at ten; I got my first horse at nine, a half-broken three year-old mare. We had a perfectly ordinary, if somewhat isolated, country upbringing. Except for high school which was, for all of us, hideous. But that's another story....

As for my "relationship" with that place—I don't know what else to call it, though it sounds pretentious—I have stood on the mountain and said, "I love you," as I would say to an utterly beloved person, and not felt foolish. This "relationship" has, in some way, determined all of my major life decisions. When I could have stayed in university, I came home instead. And whenever I came back, battered, bruised and exhausted—from a marriage, from school, from surviving in a world I didn't understand—it healed me, whether it took six months or six years, and let me go again.

I know it intimately, this place, as I could know a lover's body, each curve and bump, each joining and parting, each scar and nick and mole. Some parts I know better than others: the farm, the center, the place which is *absolutely* home.

It occurred to me the other night as I looked out the windows of my rented house in a borrowed city, that it is harder to see a place when you don't have a relationship with it. It's like looking at a crowd of strangers among whom may be eventual friends. But such faces are only revealed over time.

I am created by my home, not as a mother might have created me, but as a teacher, a grandmother, an elder. I was shaped, each day, by living in it, by standing still in it, by learning it. It has made me a connoisseur of color, light, texture, taste, feel, all of it coming in, as real as making love, only this—this has never palled, never bored me, never lessened.

I have sat patiently through conversations in which "the land" gets mentioned in hushed and reverent tones, trying not to say anything. When I live there, my reverence is close and unable to be spoken. It's what I live within: like air, invisible, but necessary. As I wrote in a poem once: "When I leave, it allows me, when I return, it ignores me as water ignores rain."

— **Luanne Armstrong**, *extracted from "Home,"* **The New Catalyst** *No.15, Fall 1989.*

THE HUDSON RIVER VALLEY:
A Bioregional Story

Thomas Berry

The world of life, of spontaneity, the world of dawn and sunset and starlight, the world of soil and sunshine, of meadow and woodland, of hickory and oak and maple and hemlock and pineland forests, of wildlife dwelling around us, of the river and its well-being—all of this some of us are discovering for the first time as the integral community in which we live.

Here we experience the reality and the values that evoke in us our deepest moments of reflection, our revelatory experience of the ultimate mystery of things. Here, in this intimate presence of the valley in all its vitality, we receive those larger intuitions that lead us to dance and sing, intuitions that activate our imaginative powers in their most creative functions. This, too, is what inspires our weddings, our home life, and our joy in our children. Even our deepest human sensitivities emerge from our region, our place, our specific habitat, for the earth does not give itself to us in a global sameness. It gives itself to us in arctic and tropical regions, in seashore and desert, in prairie-lands and woodlands, in mountains and valleys. Out of each a unique shaping of life takes place, a community, an integral community of all the geological as well as the biological and the human components. Each region is a single community so intimately related that any benefit or any injury is immediately experienced throughout the entire community.

So it is also with ourselves. We who live here in the Hudson River Valley constitute a single organic community with the river and the lowlands and the surrounding hills, with the sunlight and the rain, with the grasses and the trees and all the living creatures about us. We are all in some manner needed by one another. We may disdain the insects and the lowly plankton in the river, we may resent the heat of summer or the ice of winter, we may try to impose our mechanistic patterns on the biological rhythms of the region, but as soon as any one of these natural functions is disturbed in its proper expression, we are in trouble, and there is no further support to which we can appeal.

The natural world has produced its present variety, its abundance, and the creative interactions of all its components through billions of experiments. To shatter all this in the belief that we can gain by thwarting nature in its basic spontaneities is a brash and foolish thing, as is amply demonstrated by many of our past activities. If we do not alter our attitude and our activities, our children and grandchildren will live not only amid the ruins of the industrial world, but also amid the ruins of the natural world itself. That this will not happen, that the valley will be healed where it is damaged, preserved in its present integrity and renewed in its creative possibilities, is the hope that is before us.

Just now we are, as it were, returning to the valley, finding our place once again after a long period of alienation. At such a moment in our own history, as well as in the history of the region, we need first of all an extreme sensitivity to the needs of all the various components of the valley community—the needs of the river, the soil, the air; the needs of the various living forms that inhabit the valley; and the special needs of the human community dwelling here in the valley. We need to know how these relate to one another. Prior to our coming from abroad, all of these components of the region had worked out a mutually enhancing relationship. The valley was flourishing.

When we arrived we brought with us an attitude that the region was here for our exploitation. Even though we broke our treaties with the Indian tribes, we did recognize their rights and made treaties with them. It never entered our minds that we should also have made treaties with the river and with the land and with the region as a whole. In this we failed to do what even God did after the flood: "I set my rainbow in the cloud and it shall be a sign of the convenant between me and the earth. When I bring clouds over the earth and the rainbow is seen in the clouds, I will remember my covenant which is between me and you and every living creature of all flesh; and the waters shall never again become a flood to destroy all flesh."

Such a treaty, or some such spiritual bond, between ourselves and the natural world, is needed, a bonding based on the principle of mutual enhancement. The river and its valley are neither our enemy to be conquered, nor our servant to be controlled, nor our lover to be seduced. The river is a pervasive presence beyond all these. It is the ultimate psychic as well as the physical context out of which we emerge into being and by which we are nourished, guided, healed, and fulfilled. As the gulls soaring above the river in its estuary region, as the blossoms along its banks, the fish within its waters, so, too, the river is a celebration of existence, of life lived in intimate association with the sky, the winds from every direction, the sunlight. The river is the bindin presence throughout the valley community. We do not live primarily in Poughkeepsie or Peekskill, Newburgh or Yonkers.

We live primarily along the river or in the valley. We are river people and valley people. That fact determines more than anything else the way we live, the foods we eat, the clothes we wear, how we travel. It also provides the content and context for celebrating life in its most sublime meaning.

We celebrate the valley not in some generalized planetary context, but in the specific setting that we have indicated. It is a celebration of our place, but our place as story, for we need only look about us to appreciate the grandeur of these surroundings. The grandeur of the valley is expressed most fully in its story.

The story, as we have seen, is a poignant one, a story with its glory, but not without its tragedy. Now the story begins to express the greatest change from a sense of the valley as subservient to human exploitation to a sense of the valley as an integral natural community which is itself the basic reality and the basic value, and of the human as having its true glory as a functioning member, rather than as a conquering invader, of this community. Our role is to be the instrument whereby the valley celebrates itself. The valley is both the object and the subject of the celebration. It is our high privilege to articulate this celebration in the stories we tell and in the songs we sing.

(First published in **The Dream of the Earth**. San Francisco: Sierra Club Books, 1988.)

The River That Runs Both Ways

Reinhabit The Hudson Estuary

THE SALMON CIRCLE

Fraser Lang and Alison Lang

Chorus ROCK

       F#-
And the salmon circle from the sea to the sea, up the rivers of life
D   E   F#-
endlessly, and they always return to the place they began, for a million years they
D   E   F#-
swam and swam and swam

Verse (1,2,4)

        F#-   G#-
Round the rocks in the pool, in the river below, they are
F#-   B7   F#-
turning and turning Oh so slow, and they've been there forever in that
G#-   F#-   B7
sacred dance, round and round they go, it's a water romance And the (to Chorus)

Verse 3

F#-   G#-   F#-   B7
Red backs, moving in the stream; Hump backs dancing in a dream;
F#-   G#-   F#-   B7
Nose to tail, they circle round and round, Go back to the spawning ground
(to Chorus)

(2)
To the long slow rhythm of a four-year cycle,
to the pounding beat of the oceans that are like a
drum that sounds clear across the globe,
and it's calling its children,
it's calling its children home.

(4)
By the taste of the waters they return to the source
lay down their eggs feel the life force
resting safe in the gravel pass the winter through,
these great fish are dying
but in the spring life renews.

THE SALMON DANCE

Women and men alternate in a circle, and begin moving in a counterclockwise direction making the salmon motion. Put your hands in front of you, palms together, forming the salmon's nose. Then make swimming, bobbing, swaying movements as you go around the circle. Feel the scales growing on your skin.

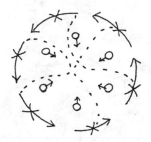

After the first chorus make two circles, the women on the inside, the men on the outside.

With the first verse, begin circling, the outside circle counterclockwise, the inside circle clockwise.

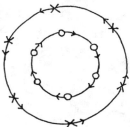

After the chorus, the men's circle stops and the women find alternate positions in the outside circle. They begin a weave with the men continuing counterclockwise and the women clockwise.

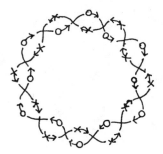

Women leave the weave circle and form a stationary spawning circle in the middle. The men's circle continues to spin and the men make dashes through the women's circle.

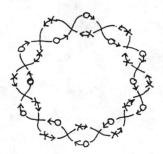

At the end of the chorus, the men's circle stops and the women rejoin it, and they begin the weave, the same as the second verse.

At the end of the final chorus, "And they swam and swam and swam...," the circle stops and everybody joins hands and comes into the center with their hands raised above their heads. This is repeated a second time ending in a circle, raising their hands above their heads, then bending forward in the salmon's final death.

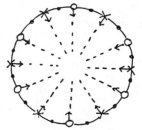

— **Alison Lang, from North American Bioregional Congress III Proceedings, 1989.**

Design by Rob Messick.

Part Three

NATURE, CULTURE AND COMMUNITY

"Our understanding must grow to encompass a union of nature and culture in which the sacredness of all life is honored. As long as we saw all other life as outside and apart from ourselves, we treated it carelessly. Embracing the interconnectedness of all life, we can again weave together the rift between sacred and secular, and the totality will be seen as sacred."
— *Nancy Jack Todd and John Todd*

The web of life on earth is a vast interdependency, maintaining a balance of tensions within which all species find some part to play. Yet, within historic times, humans have got out of joint with the whole. Cultures everywhere have been broken up by the on-rush of commercial empires. This is the global problem that humanity faces. The demand is to build new cultures, new communities—to extend the adaptive, caring practices of community even beyond our own people, embracing other species and surrounding ecosystems.

Certain leaps of consciousness will be required for the new life- ways to emerge. The effort of understanding is greatly supported by the recent work of Lynn Margulis and other workers in the natural sciences. The contemporary view of nature is profoundly social, providing fact and metaphor that inspire cooperative action. Cooperation, community building, is the strategy of nature.

Speaking of the new, positive approach to evolution, Nancy Jack Todd and John Todd, in *Bioshelters, Ocean Arks, City Farming*, lay out a history of the transition from a mechanical to an organic perspective, beginning in 17th century Europe. Humans are viewed as participants in creation rather than mere observers, or controllers. From the same book, the Todds outline a basic paradigm of "design" in nature, to help orient activities within a biological framework.

"Totem Salmon" illustrates the relations between human cultures and a grand scale ecosystem, the North Pacific Rim. "Totem Salmon" is noteworthy as one of the first bioregional sketches in the early days of the Planet Drum Foundation before the term "bioregion" came into use. Here is a classic "all-species" essay.

Through culture and community, humans find their place in nature. "How Humans Adapt" and "Culture is the Missing Link" briefly state the case.

No Foreign Land brings us to the topic of community. As a result of alienation, civilized people often lack any image of being "at home" in community. Wilf Pelletier takes us there, giving us an inside view of everyday experience in his own native village. The promise of community is that we shall get to be ourselves.

Judith Plant's "Searching for Common Ground" and Helen Forsey's "Community: Meeting our Deepest Needs" continue the discussion of how best to care for each other and our places. The necessary connections between ecofeminism and bioregionalism are clarified. Concerns of domestic life are brought forward and valued. Marnie Muller's "Bioregionalism/Western Culture/Women"—once again an early formulation, preceding the term ecofeminism—draws the several themes together with an overview of patriarchal history and a commitment in the present to regenerate our homeplaces.

The summary essay, "Earth Diet, Earth Culture," is a model of bioregional description, comparing the ways in which successive societies, primitive and modern, have adapted to place in the San Francisco River watershed, New Mexico. A focus on diet highlights crucial differences in cultural adaptation.

Nature, culture, community...chant these words and be reminded of primary connections, worlds within worlds.

Networking Nature

Fossil evidence of primeval microbial life, the decoding of DNA, and discoveries about the composition of our own cells have exploded established ideas about the origins of life and the dynamics of evolution on earth.

First, they have shown the folly of considering people as special, apart and supreme. The microscope has gradually exposed the vastness of the microcosm and is now giving us a startling view of our true place in nature. It now appears that microbes— also called micro-organisms, germs, bugs, protozoans, and bacteria, depending on the context—are not only the building blocks of life, but occupy and are indispensable to every known living structure on the earth today. From the paramecium to the human race, all life forms are meticulously organized, sophisticated aggregates of evolving microbial life. Far from leaving micro-organisms behind on an evolutionary "ladder," we are both surrounded by them and composed of them. Having survived in an unbroken line from the beginnings of life, all organisms today are equally evolved.

This realization sharply shows up the conceit and presumption of attempting to measure evolution by a linear progression from the simple—so-called lower—to the more complex (with humans as the absolute "highest" forms at the top of the hierarchy). As we shall see, the simplest and most ancient organisms are not only the forebears and the present substrate of the earth's biota, but they are ready to expand and alter themselves and the rest of life, should we "higher" organisms be so foolish as to annihilate ourselves.

Next, the view of evolution as chronic bloody competition among individuals and species, a popular distortion of Darwin's notion of "survival of the fittest," dissolves before a new view of continual cooperation, strong interaction, and mutual dependence among life forms. Life did not take over the globe by combat, but by networking.

—**Lynn Margulis and Dorian Sagan,** *from* **Micro- cosmos: Four Billion Years of Microbial Evolution**, *New York: Summit Books, 1986.*

DESIGN SHOULD FOLLOW, NOT OPPOSE, THE LAWS OF LIFE

Nancy Jack Todd
and John Todd

The cell is the basic unit and building block of life. As such it is an entity complete unto itself. This is most easily pictured by bringing to mind the kind of one-celled creature frequently perused in introductory biology courses, the most popular usually being the amoeba. Like all other simple and primitive organisms, it is self-contained. It carries out, at the microscopic level, all the basic attributes of life, including food gathering, feeding, excretion, respiration, purification, and reproduction. The same is as true of a cell in our own kidneys, a butterfly's wing, or a sumac leaf, as it is in the independently inclined amoeba.

ii. The cell participates directly in the fundamental functioning of the whole organism. There is a high degree of interaction and cooperation between cells. At the dawn of life on Earth, evolution was triggered when different kinds of organisms invaded or enfolded each other to produce composite organisms ranging from fungi and lichens to the higher plants and animals. Over eons of time the cooperation and interdependence between formerly unrelated organisms has grown ever more complex. Basic to biological functioning has been the bringing together of normally distinct organisms, the combined activities of which create new organisms. Concomitantly, many of the ancient, less complex precursors of present life forms, like bacteria, spirochetes, and blue green algae, still persist as independent entities. As such they continue to play a basic and major ecological role in the overall metabolism of the planet.

iii. The fact that organisms are at once complete, independent and autonomous, yet interdependent with other life forms, is a paradox to basic life. However whole and complete its structure, no organism is an island unto itself. Nature depends upon connections through different levels of biological organization. The connections are always immediate and near by. There is an unbroken continuum from cell to organism to the large ecosystem and beyond to the bioregion and on again ultimately to the whole planet. Further, although, through differentiation, related cells become organisms that range from insects to trees, ancient biological patterns are not abandoned but maintained through vast reaches of time. In this way nature is extremely conservative— and this characteristic is a unity that permeates all of life.

iv. The ecosystem is the next level of organization and is analogous to an organism, the differences being that the boundaries are less distinct, the length between the components longer, and the couplings looser. An ecosystem is an interacting system of living organisms and their non-living environment. In a sense, the environment is the home within which organisms live. A pond is one of the simplest ecosystems to visualize because it is contained in a bowl of land and its boundaries are easily discerned. An ecosystem can also be defined in terms of contained relationships—the ecosystem of the food chain or the relationships of the essential gases which are controlled by organisms are examples. When a pond is exposed to sunlight, the algae give off the oxygen essential to the survival of the animals. The bacteria and animals produce carbon dioxide which the algae and other plants need in order to live. Populations of smaller fish are kept in check by predators. Predators in turn are regulated by even larger predators like herons as well as by their own reproductive biology in that they produce fewer offspring. To make an anthropomorphic evaluation of such an arrangement as dog-eat-dog would miss the deeper meaning of nature. Just as all of us must live to eat, all life forms consume others yet also have a function beyond their own particular existence. In the end, all life is eaten or decays, that new life may be born and the larger life continue. Whereas organisms are outwardly defined by a particular structure or surface or architecture, such as bark or skin or scales, topographically ecosystems are defined by the diminishing or outer limits of the relationships. While the definition of boundary in a pond is contained by the banks, more often

one ecosystem, like a field, will blend into others like that of a wood or a neighboring lawn. An ecosystem is not just an assembly of creatures but, because of the integrity of its structures and the mixed relationships, it is a definable entity, a meta-organism. Just as relationships in animals are expressed through a central nervous system, an ecosystem like a pond expresses relationships as a gestalt—as the sum of its parts acting in dynamic concert.

v. Nature is not static. The natural world lives in flux and understands change. In a wooded area an abandoned lawn left to itself reverts to a meadow and then, within brief decades, to a woods. During this period—technically termed ecological succession—structural changes take place. The landscape becomes more diverse, stable and often less vulnerable to perturbations. In contrast, more

From A Mechanical To An Ecological Worldview

For some time now there have been tremors threatening to undermine the edifice of Descartes and Newton and the acceptance of the strictly causal nature of physical phenomena. Early in this century the general relativity theory of Albert Einstein abolished the concept of absolute space and time, and with it the mechanistic world view. Since that time the cosmology on which we have built our political, economic and social structures has no longer fit the theories being involved on the frontiers of scientific theory and advanced thought. In spite of the daily evidence of our senses and the quantity of information pouring in from the media, books, and scientific journals—deserts expanding, forests dwindling, species vanishing at the rate of one a day, widespread social unrest— we continue to act as though none of this has anything to do with us and our behavior. Reports are published on limits to growth, on the finite carrying capacity of the Earth, on repression and injustice, yet economic and political strategies, both capitalist and communist, continue to be based on assumptions of indefinite exploitation and continued

growth. This reflects our world view which was built on now outdated concepts but is no longer cohesive with emerging scientific thought. Gradually, however, as general loss of faith and confidence are becoming evident, this paradigm is fading and another is emerging. As the concept of a mechanistic universe and a schizophrenic attitude to nature are relinquished, we find ourselves on the verge of a cosmology potentially far more cohesive intellectually, more sound intuitively, and more peaceful spiritually.

It begins to become increasingly apparent then that with the slow dissolving of the mechanistic world view, we are evolving a new or renewed awareness of the universe— one that is internally consistent. No longer must we gloss over the discrepancies between the spiritual and the material, the sacred and the secular. The scientific paradigm points to acceptance of the cosmic dance of Shiva and the dance of quanta—and all of us participate, creatures of light-energy, star matter, all are dancers. The ancients watched the sky and saw with their hearts. Eastern mystics see with the inner eye, and humanly derived systems, most of our towns and cities for example, indicate a frame of mind that could be called early successional. Structural relationships are defined and fixed at the outset and the pattern is hard to change as conditions change. We tend to build, destroy, rebuild, destroy and rebuild again. Too often we lock ourselves into inflexible designs which inhibit maturation in a given society or community.

vi. The bioregion, beyond the ecosystem, is the next over-riding structural unit, forming a cluster of ecosystems arranged topographically and climatically to produce a distinct region. A bioregion is easy to recognize but hard to define. It can be framed by a great river valley, by mountain ranges or a coast. Usually it is categorized by distinctive vegetation and climate. Yet even a bioregion is not an island unto itself, for it blends outward to join with others to comprise a biographical province. The hardwood forested land east of the Great Plains extending southward from southern Canada almost to the Gulf of Mexico is one such great province. Such provinces in turn interconnect and blend to form the Earth's

---

now physicists have looked at the universe with telescope and microscope and all seem to have come to a commonality of understanding. The physicist John Wheeler maintained that the most important aspect of the quantum principle is that it destroyed the concept of the world as "sitting out there." The act of observation in itself makes the observer a participator. Making a measurement, even of an electron, changes the state of the electron to that degree so the universe will never again be quite the same. He concluded, "In some strange sense the universe is a participatory universe."

The idea is an overwhelming one. Just as we are beginning to reassume some responsibility for our actions in the context of the Earth, a question of a larger context and consequence arises. Yet no matter how far-reaching our ultimate accountability, it seems common sense that it is here, with the Earth and each other, that the healing must begin. And if because we have discarded their myths we can no longer look to the ancient gods for instructions as to how to proceed, science re-embedded in the cosmology of a participatory universe and a sense of the sacred may yet prove to be an appropriate guide....

The chance to participate in a process so much larger than ourselves holds out to us, the heirs of the age of science and technology, the possibility of a new set of instructions—or perhaps the eternal instructions—in a language, that of science, which we understand and accept. The Native American spokesman, Chief Black Elk, once declared that "All life is holy and good to tell," but we chose not to listen. Yet we cannot ignore the rest of life indefinitely. Our understanding must grow to encompass a union of nature and culture in which the sacredness of all life is honored. As long as we saw all other life as outside and apart from ourselves, we treated it carelessly. Embracing the interconnectedness of all life, we can again weave together the rift between sacred and secular, and the totality will be seen as sacred. Perhaps, now, with a synthesis of knowledge of fields as disparate as quantum physics, astronomy, ecology, religion, holography, anthropology, and the contemplation of sacred art, architecture, and geometry, certain harmonies are beginning to be heard, or heard again, and our sense of the world, rather than being cacaphonous and diffuse with the claims of economists and environmentalists, communists and capitalists, the secular and the sacred, begins to make more sense, and ring true. Perhaps a cosmology that is at once beyond memory and still just out of reach of present knowledge, yet somehow alive within us, is unfolding. The stars are still there to remind us that we are both trivial and non-trivial. One way of reaching out toward what we want to bring into being is a careful reassessment of how we are to live; where under the shining sky, in what relation to the sun and the solar winds, and how we are to best care for the living, celestial matter that is the small portion of the Earth on which we find ourselves.

— Nancy Jack Todd and John Todd, from Bioshelters, Ocean Arks, City Farming: Ecology as the Basis of Design. San Francisco: Sierra Club Books, 1984.

canopy—until eventually we come around to Gaia.

(First published in **Bioshelters, Ocean Arks, City Farming: Ecology as the Basis of Design**. San Francisco: Sierra Club Books, 1984.)

Culture Is The Missing Link

We are children of the green globe

We say we are children of the green globe, living things upon the planet. The fact inspires us with a sort of pride. The theory of evolution is our genesis story. It places our feet on the ground. The perspectives of biology comprise our metaphysics. Our philosophy thrives on the prospect that all things move, change, flow in Cosmos. Change flows through us and all around us, and *we* are changing too. This is the cosmic situation in which all animals carry out their habits of adaptation, including ourselves.

We are animals

For pre-historic folks, probably the issue never came up, whether they were to regard themselves as animals or not. And in civilized times the question only really surfaced in the last century. Since Darwin, the answer has been yes, we are animals. We are one species among millions on earth. We are planetary beings, of the order of primate.

We are social animals

We were together even in the trees. Later, out on the savannas we moved in bands, gathering and hunting. We hung out around the campfire, at peace with one another, in harmony with our environment. Bodies close, we sat gazing into the fire, safe in our togetherness. We talked of the life that was common to us, told stories recounting the ways of a people, passing on wholeness.

We are cultural animals

Wholeness or organization is a feature of all living forms. In an anthropological view, culture was the whole form of the human being. It spanned the generations. It was the self-governing, adaptive unit. It was an organized set of customs, an integrated way of life in which the aims of the group and the selves of the group became one. Despite its shortcomings, it was the original appropriate society.

We lost our cultures

Civilization destroyed original cultures and their ecologies. So what's to be done? We can't go back. We must go ahead. We have to invent the human groups which can adapt to these present circumstances.

We will build new cultures

We need to recreate the conditions of organization that produce whole humans; get behind the process, and do it consciously. Our method is social. We get together with others who are searching for an alternative to industrial civilization, and who perceive the power of society to reorganize itself. We agree to undertake a conscious experiment: try out living together in one place, a quiet place, where thought can go on, care can go on (with or without a culture, the self needs a home).

Sharing a global perspective, and using the method of inquiry, we try to create a new culture that is adaptive to this particular time and place on the planet. We offer the hope that others could do this too. Small society provides the means to restore ourselves to each other and to Nature.

— **Van Andruss and Eleanor Wright**, *first published in* **The Catalist**, *April-May, 1984.*

TOTEM SALMON

L. Freeman House

"An Indian gave me a piece of fresh salmon roasted, which I ate with relish. This was the first salmon I had seen and it convinced me we were in the waters of the Pacific Ocean."
— from the journal of Meriweather Lewis at the headwaters of the Lehmi River, August 3, 1805.

Salmon is a totem animal of the North Pacific Range. Only salmon, as a species, informs us humans, as a species, of the vastness and unity of the North Pacific Ocean and its rim. The buried memories of our ancient human migrations, the weak abstractions of our geographies, our struggles toward a science of biology do nothing to inform us of the power and benevolence of our place. Totemism is a method of perceiving power, goodness, and mutuality in *locale* through the recognition of and respect for the vitality, spirit and interdependence of other species. In the case of the North Pacific Rim, no other species informs us so well as the salmon, whose migrations define the boundaries of the range which supports us all.

For time without increment, salmon have fed and informed bear, porpoise, eagle, killer whale. For the past twenty to thirty thousand years, salmon have fed and shaped the spirit of Yurok, Chinook, Salish, Kwakiutl, Haida, Tsimshian, Aleut, Yukagir, Koryak, Chuckchi & Ainu—to name a few of those old time peoples who ordered their daily lives and the flow of generations according to the delicate timing and thrust of the salmon population.

Asian and North American salmon range and feed together in great thousand mile gyres, in schools numbering in the millions, all around the North Pacific, then divide into families and split off from this great species celebration to breed and spawn in specific homes in the great rivers and innumerable streams of the North Pacific Rim. The great rivers, the Klamath, the Columbia, the Fraser, the Skeena, the Stikine, the Yukon, the Anadyr, the Amur, are spawning homes for the ubiquitous salmon and drainage routes for vast portions of the planetary watershed.

*

The central North American plains, until a century ago, were served and informed by their own totem population, the buffalo. (Imagine for a mo-

ment what this range might be like today, had the buffalo there been respected and protected.) The buffalo were destroyed through the need for expansion by industrial capital, and by that ultimate expression of heedless anthropomorphism, the American political concept of Manifest Destiny. First the enormous herds were divided by the new transcontinental railroads, then they were shot down one by one by an adventurous and enormously inefficient fur trade. Within a generation, the species that had informed humans how to live indigenously was gone. From that time on, peoples of that range have wandered a course of random environmental destruction, little informed by the power of the earth, and generation by generation have become less alive because of their loneliness.

Now international industrial capital has set its sight on the North Pacific, the penultimate theater for unlimited industrial expansion. A whole new technology is tooling up for the purpose of mining the ocean floors of minerals which have been exhausted terrestrially. The Japanese, in the course of their wild adulation of growth economy, having exhausted their terrestrial *and* marine resources, now have huge factory ships fishing the mid-Pacific salmon migrations, taking immature fish and decimating that population immeasurably.

It is the nature of industrial capital that it has no interest in preserving indigenous populations, since capital is mobile and can move on once a "resource" has been exhausted. Indigenous populations cannot flee this rapacity because of their biological marriage to habitat. What is not generally recognized is that the *human* species is also an indigenous population. We, too, are inextricably married to place. We can only be kept constantly informed of our situation as a species through regard and recognition of brethren species. The life of the wild salmon population is of essence to the life of the human population.

The Names of Salmon

The English "salmon" derives from the Latin "salire", to leap. The word for salmon in the Chinook Jargon, a put-together language made up of elements of native dialects in Northwestern North America and of elements of English and French, is derived from the English, "sammon." The Pacific salmon, *Onchorynchus*, is to be distinguished from the Atlantic salmon, *Salmo*. The names of subspecies are generally derived from native Siberian names for the fish. There are seven varieties of salmon which range and feed in the North Pacific. At the northern extreme of their range they frequent and feed in the Bering Sea, but at the southern extreme are rarely found south of forty-one degrees. These are their names:

Onchorynchus chavica: called King, Chinook, Tyee, Spring, Quinnat
(Northern Hokkaido to the Sacramento River);

O.kisutch: called Coho, Silver
(Monterey Bay to the Kamchatka Peninsula);

O.nerka: called Sockeye, Red, Blueback, Nerka
(Fraser River to the Kurile Islands);

O.gorbucha: called Pink, Humpbacked, Humpie
(Columbia River to Korea);

O.keta: called Chum, Dog, Keta
(Puget Sound to Korea);

O.masu: called Cherry, Masu
(Amur River to the Pusan River of Korea);

Salmo gairdneri: called Steelhead Trout
(Monterey Bay to the Stikine in Alaska).

Salmon Mind

Salmon eggs are deposited in more or less evenly graded gravel with enough cold water running over them to maintain an even temperature but not enough to disturb the eggs. The eggs are a brilliant translucent orange-red, about the size of buckshot. Sockeyes will spawn in lakes rather than streams. A single female will deposit up to several thousand eggs in a single "redd" or nest.

After a gestation period of 50 days to three months, the "alevins" hatch out with yolk sacs still attached. The babies nestle in the gravel for several weeks until the yolk sac is gone and they have gained an inch in size. At this point, they emerge from the gravel as "fry", quick and light-shy. It is at this stage of development that life is most perilous, the small fish being vulnerable to hungry larger salmon, other fish, water birds and snakes.

The fry feed at dawn and dusk and into the night on plantonic crustacea and nymphs, growing fastest in the summer when insects are most available. Many salmon remain in lakes and streams for a year, though pinks, dogs, and kings begin their journey to the sea in the first year, as fry.

The migration to salt water is an epic event involving millions of smolt (as the little salmon are called at this stage). On the Yukon River, this journey can be as long as 1800 miles, on the Amur 700-800. The fish travel in schools, at night to avoid predators, following the guidance of a single larger smolt who seems to make decisions for the school at obstructions, rapids, etc. Out of two million eggs, perhaps 200,000 fish have survived to make the migration.

On the way downstream, the smolt can be killed by 1) natural predators; 2) irrigation ditches which confuse and trap the fish; 3) undissolved human sewage; (4) turbine intakes at dams which act as meat grinders; 5) nitrogen rich water on the downstream side of dams; 6) wastes from pulp mills; 7) wastes from chemical plants; and 8) warm or oxygen-depleted water created by industrial flow-through or sedimentation.

Now the smolt will spend three to five months in estuaries and bays, gradually acclimatizing to salt water. They begin by feeding on zooplankton. As they grow larger and develop stronger teeth, they will eat crustaceans such as shrimp (which some biologists believe colors their flesh), euphasids, amphipods, copepods, pteropids and squid.

It is at this point in the consideration of salmon that biologists begin to slide off into weary human-centered metaphors for the talents and strengths of the fish. We are talking about the great ocean migrations of the salmon, wherein they range and feed for thousands of miles in the North Pacific, grow to maturity, and navigate unerringly back to the stream of their birth on a time schedule which can be predicted to within a few days.

In general, North American salmon make this circular journey in a counter-clockwise direction while Asian salmon move clockwise. Often the great schools' paths will mingle, sharing the search for food that has brought them halfway across the Pacific. Pinks make the circuit once and race home to spawn after two years; kings may take as much as four or five years. The enormous schools travel at a general rate of ten miles per day until the spawning urge takes them and they increase their speed to thirty miles per day. The fish are nearly always found in the top ten metres of water during the migrations.

No one really understands the mechanisms that guide the fish through the trackless ocean and back to a specific spot at a specific time. Evidence would seem to indicate that the circuits are printed on the genes of the individual fish. It is probable that neither a consciousness common to a school nor memorized information guides them. There is, however, plenty of room for speculation. This evidence is in as of 1968:

• The migration is in a circular motion, rather than to and fro, eliminating the possibility of the fish backtracking on themselves.

• Salmon find their ways to the spawning grounds as individuals, not in schools.

• Arrival of the fish at the spawning grounds is less variable than the seasonal changes in the weather, making the use of temperature gradients as guidance cues unlikely.

• The nearly constant overcast in the far North Pacific makes celestial navigation unlikely (but not impossible).

• Migration routes tend to be across open water even in areas where it would be easy to follow the

coast, so that the use of physical landmarks is eliminated.

• The fish swim actively downstream in and across the currents of the Pacific. The currents have subtle differences in salinity, but in order to use these differences as cues, the salmon would have to group up to near the edges of the streams, which they do not do.

• Seawater is an electrical conductor moving through the planet's magnetic field, thus the ocean currents generate small amounts of electrical potential. Some fish are able to detect such small amounts of voltage and there is reasonable speculation on the part of William Royce et al that salmon may have similar receptors and use the electricity as a navigational cue.

Salmon *always* find their way back to the stream or lake where they were born and spawn there again, generation after generation. As they approach fresh water, they have reached the peak of their physical and instinctual genius. Fat and shining and leaping, schools will swarm restlessly at the mouths of rivers and streams, waiting for optimal conditions of run-off. They feed voraciously now, generally on herring, for they will not feed again once they enter fresh water. This is the time to take salmon for meat. The flavor and texture of the flesh is at its very best and, eaten fresh, the strength of the fish will stay with the eater.

It is likely that the salmon use their keen sense of smell to identify their home estuary and to choose the right forks as they push upstream. Biologists have run experiments on the fish at this stage of their journey, plugging the salmon's nostrils. Without a sense of smell the spawning run tends to move in a random manner and the fish get lost.

The trip upstream is an enormous effort. Even in the absence of human improvements on the rivers, cataracts, rapids and waterfalls must be

> The symbioitic process goes on unceasingly. We organisms of the macrocosm continue to interact with and depend upon the microcosm, as well as upon each other. Certain families of plants (such as the pea family, including peas, beans, and relatives such as clover and vetch) cannot live in nitrogen-poor soil without the nitrogen that comes from such plants. Neither cows nor termites can diigest the cellulose of grass and wood without communities of microbes in their guts. Fully ten percent of our own dry body weight consists of bacteria, some of which, although they are not a congenital part of our bodies, we can't live without. No mere quirk of nature, such co-existence is the stuff of evolution itself.
>
> — **Lynn Margulis and Dorian Sagan, Micro-cosmos: Four Billion Years of Microbial Evolution**, *New York: Summit Books, 1986.*

overcome. In spite of obstacles, the fish travel between 30 and 90 miles a day until they have reached the spawning ground. The salmon now undergo striking physiological changes. Humpbacks will grow the hump for which they are named. Dogs grow long, sharp teeth and the upper mandible grows out and extends down over the lower. The body of the sockeye will turn fresh-blood red, its head an olive green. In general, the fish turn dark and bruised; the organism begins to consume itself. Drawing its last strength from ocean-gained fat, the flesh turns soft.

Now the salmon perform the breathtaking dance for which their entire lives have been in preparation. As they reach their spawning home, the fish pair off, male and female. A sort of courtship ensues, the male swimming back and forth over the female as she prepares the nest, rubbing and nudging her, then darting out to drive off other males. The female builds the nest with her tail, scooping out silt and smaller stones to a depth of several inches and in an area twice the length of the fish. Finally all that is left in the nest are larger stones. The crevasses and fissures between the stones will provide shelter for the eggs. The nest completed, the female assumes a rigid position over the center of it and the male approaches, curving his body up against hers. The eggs and clouds of milt are deposited simultaneously. The sperm, which stays alive in the water for seconds only, must enter the egg through a single tiny pore or micropyle, which itself closes over in a matter of minutes. In situations where the current is extremely fast, two males will sometimes serve a single female to ensure fertilization. The nest is covered and the process is repeated, for a day or a week, until the eggs are all deposited.

A single female will deposit from 2000 to 5000 eggs, but only a small percentage of these are destined to hatch. The rest are eaten by fish or birds, attacked by fungi, or washed downstream.

Now the fish, already decomposing, begin to die, and within days all have finished their migration. Their bodies are thrown up on the banks of streams and rivers, providing feast for bear and eagle.

Immortal Salmon: Native Relationships

Peoples who inhabited the North Pacific Range so successfully up until a few hundred years ago learned to eat fish from bears and eagles; learned to catch fish by wit and invention—bone hooks and seaweed lines, elegant weirs of hemlock root, spears and dipnets. The salmon were accorded the respect demanded by another people. When two peoples are bonded together by geography or find themselves at different levels on the same food chain, such respect is pragmatic rather than rhetorical. Fishiness is not alien, only different. Lines of communication between species are kept open and fresh by means of ritual, hunger tempered by respect on the occasion of each new spawning run.

All around the North Pacific Rim, with notably few tribal exceptions, a First Salmon Ceremony was practiced on the occasion of the year's first run up the rivers. The difference between these ceremonies is noted in Erna Gunther's monograph, *First Salmon Ceremonies in the Pacific Northwest.* More interesting are their similarities. Throughout the Rim there existed the notion that conscious spirit resides in all plants and animals. The salmon is always perceived as a person living a life similar to that of the people who catch it. Therefore, before it is safe to eat any plant or animal it is necessary to assure the creature that *there is no desire to offend.* Thus the ceremonies.

Further, the spirits of plants and animals were considered immortal. Do not the creatures and plants return each year? Tribal people assume a certain amount of responsibility in the continuity of this immortality and use the ceremonies as methods of assuring that proper respect for the runs, proper methods of fishing them, and proper methods of disposal of bones and viscera are practiced from generation to generation. The ceremonies have the practical effect of assuring the continuity of both species, salmon and human.

Yurok First Salmon

The old man ate from a separate pile of acorns and drank no water for a long time before first salmon.

A short time before first salmon the old man called his helper over from Rekwei to Welkwau.

On the sixth day before first salmon the old man said to his helper, "This is the last day you may eat freely. Beginning with tomorrow, you will not eat until evening, so eat freely today."

Then they built a path from the village to the sandspit, removing every pebble and leaf. They asked the people not to use the path.

On the night before, the old man prayed all night over his fire of angelica root. He prayed all night.

In the morning they came out of the sweat house, put on new deerskin blankets and tied back their long hair with otterskin, and walked down to the river on the clean path.

The men were lined up at the river fishing. "Continue to fish for eel, but not for sturgeon," the old man said. They sat down to wait for salmon.

In the afternoon, the first salmon came. "Stop running!" the old man shouted. The fish stopped, "Now run again!" The fish ran on. They did that together five times.

The old man shook his harpoon twice and spoke to the salmon. "You will stop running. As you pass every fishing place you will leave your scales, to the head of the river, ending there. Now run on." The fish listened and went on.

Soon the next salmon came up the river. The old man made four feints and speared the fish on the fifth. Across the river at Rekwei, a great wailing and crying went up, as if one of the people had died.

He hit the fish on the head with a rock and laid his otterskin tie across the salmon's belly. "I am glad I caught you. You will bring many salmon into the river. Rich people and poor people will be happy. And you will bring it about on the land that everything will grow that is good to eat."

As they took the salmon back to the village, all the people called out the names of all kinds of food they liked from the sea and everything else they wanted, dentalia shells and woodpecker scalps. The noise rose to the sky.

The fish was taken to the living house, cut into four pieces and cooked over a low fire of angelica root by the old man's niece. The old man and his helper took a few mouthsful. Then they went to the sweat house where they stayed the rest of the day and all the next night but did not sleep.

The women took the first salmon, what remained of its meat, its head, its guts, its tail and back, took it back to the river and threw it in. The crows and seagulls did not fight over the guts that year and plenty of salmon came up the river. (Working from A.L. Kroeber, *Indians of California*.)

Salmon Energetics

In 1972 and 1973 I fished Puget Sound and Southeastern Alaska aboard purse-seiners. In the spring of 1973, I became familiar with Michael Perlman's energetics analysis of agriculture in the United States; I wrote him at Chico State College

in California and he sent me a copy. The energetics approach to the study of the growing and gathering of food measures the energy which goes into the work and compares that figure with the energy potential in the food retrieved, all figures translated into calories. Perlman found that one-crop agribusiness expended five calories for every one retrieved, whereas an organic gardener working a small plot might expend as little as one calorie for every 16 retrieved.

These figures impressed me, as did the intelligence of the approach. There can be no doubt that some such criterion must inform human technology on the planet, given that the solar bath which is the source of all translatable energy in the biosphere is constant and finite. I decided to do a similar study to determine the efficiency of purse-seining as a method of securing protein, following Perlman's model.

During the summer of 1973, fishing out of Hoonah and Ketchikan, Alaska, I kept careful records of fuel consumed, calories expended by the men on board, fish caught in pounds, etc. I was pleased with myself. I saw myself as a rigorous lay scientist, Goethe studying botany. This mood of self-congratulation helped lift the depression caused by the generally repressed experience of random mechanical killing. (Purse-seiners carry no locker to stow the death in.)

To measure value in salmon is like trying to weigh spirit. For the moment, however, we will consider the value of salmon to lie in its high concentration of protein as a food source. I will use calories as a common denominator through which to consider the value of fuel consumed, man-hours expended, and protein retrieved. I used the following figures, culled either from Perlman or from Georg Borgstrom's *Fish as Food, Vol. II*.

• The "average" man consumes 3000 calories per day. These men were working harder and longer than any average and ate more to make up for it. I know because I was cooking for them. I've allowed them 4000 calories per day.

• One BTU=.252 calories

• One gallon of diesel fuel produces 167,375 BTUs or 42,178.5 calories.

• One pound of salmon provides 440.4 protein calories.

In the course of the season, 2466 gallons of fuel were consumed and 133 man-days expended in order to retreive 95,604 pounds of salmon. Our boat made an average catch for the fleet that year.

MAGICal Reflections: All Species Representation at the North American Bioregional Congress

The practice of keeping faith with another species, or with several other species, is a discipline. It is, we might say, a practice that requires practice. Individual persons wishing to act in this capacity should be intimately aware of the biology and ecology of their *familiars*. And they should know, too, the traditional myths and stories regarding these species that are told by indigenous people—such stories and songs often carry a keen awareness of the emotional character, the traits and the habits of other species, an awareness (honed over the generations of contact) far more nuanced and intimate than is commonly attainable by the civilized and literate intellect. Yet neither of these sources, the scientific or the storied, can take the place of direct, personal contact with other species on their own terms. Scientific evidence from ecology and ethology, like the insights embedded in totemic myths, provide us—at best—with "clues" for entering into a living rapport with other beings. Yet a genuine reciprocity and empathy with other shapes of intelligence is not easily come by, nor quickly achieved—this we all know.

Finally, the practice of maintaining such a rapport while being attentive to the voices and visions of human decision-makers is difficult indeed. It requires listening with one ear to the human speakers while lending the other to the wind whispering in the trees, to the churning voices of the river, to the beating of one's own heart. In this way we begin to bring the human community into resonance with the larger community of beings. We stand poised on the boundary betwen human culture and the wilderness, keeping the flow open—ensuring that the boundary functions more like a membrane and less like a barrier. This is a unique ritual—a kind of meditation for our time.

Once again, it is a practice that requires practice. It can be practiced following a deer-trail in the mountains, or while lying on the ground in one's backyard staring sideways into the deep forest of grass. It can be practiced at town meetings, and at regional congresses. Those of us who acted as species-intermediaries at NABC III suggest that any other folks interested in this work begin preparing themselves as soon as possible.

— **David Abram**, *from the MAGIC (Mischief, Animism, Geomancy, and Interspecies Communication) Committee report in the* **Proceedings of the Third North American Bioregional Congress** *(NABC III), 1989.*

Thus 104,544,181 calories were spent in order to retreive 38,662,257.6 protein calories, a loss at the rate of approximately 2.7 to 1.

Long before the figures were added up, I realized that they were inadequate to any true picture of the situation. If these figures represent a warp in the practice of energetics values, "true" figures would demonstrate a complete break with natural conservation. For while the figures on the "credit" side remain constant, the figures on the "debit" side only whisper of the actual costs. There are no figures (nor are there likely to be very soon) on the costs in terms of energy of taking fuel out of the ground, of refining it, of transporting it to Alaska (or Siberia or Hokkaido). Neither are there figures on the costs of tooling up to produce diesel engines, nor on the bio-mass of trees cut to build the boats, nor the production of metals for the new steel boats, nor their maintenance. Then one must consider the cost of building and maintaining a proliferation of competitive canneries, the costs of canning, the costs of shipping the canned and frozen product to the richer sections of the world market.

The nature of fuel and material shortages becomes more understandable when approached with these criteria. The commercial salmon fishery and indeed most industrial technology has reached the last stages of self-cannibalization.

So this small study can only be used practically as a comparative index for the study of efficiency in various modes of taking salmon. It is immediately apparent that numbers of people (labor-intensive) are more efficient in this frame of reference than numbers of fuel-gobbling engines (energy-intensive). Trollers with their smaller engines are more efficient than seiners; reef-netters and fish-traps which use engines minimally are more efficient than trollers, etc. The further we pursue these sorts of studies, the more we will become aware that the essential attractiveness of salmon as food lies in the fact that the fish returns to the eater. It is not necessary to pursue them in expensive machines at all: every adult fish returns to the river of its origin.

Craig and Hacker in *The History and Development of the Fisheries of the Columbia River* estimate that before the arrival of white people in the Columbia River Basin, the 50,000 or so people who lived there caught up to 18 million pounds of salmon per year without damaging the stock. Certainly this was the peak of efficiency in the history of the salmon fisheries in the North Pacific. In 1970, a thoroughly industrialized fleet took only 12 and one half million pounds from the Columbia River.

Fish Without Spirit: Canneries and Hatcheries

The history of the fishing industry on this coast is the history of the cannery. Methods for safely vacuum packing quantities of salmon were perfected on the Sacramento River of California in the 1870s. The gold had petered out and people were looking around at the other amazing sources of wealth the Pacific drainage offered them. Within 20 years, scores of canneries were built: at the mouth of the Columbia, on Puget Sound, and in Southeastern Alaska. The canning remained laborious, depending basically on the handwork of imported Chinese labor, until 1903 when the "iron chink," a mechanical fish dresser, was introduced. This machine increased the production capacity of the canneries tenfold and from that point, the race was on.

Early in the history of the fisheries, the canneries began to capitalize the process of fishing, acquiring outright the large and expensive purse-seiners and financing fishermen who were buying the smaller gill-netters. Thus the canning industry tends to control the fishermen. Skippers of cannery owned or financed boats must sell to the cannery at can-

nery prices or lose their boats. A fisherman who does not produce enough fish is also likely to lose his boat and so a fierce competitive rapaciousness is set up among the people who actually do the fishing.

It is characteristic of people who fish for a living that they want to continue to do what they are doing. One hears more well-informed conservation talk in fishermen's taverns than at any board meeting of the Sierra Club. The allegiance of the canneries on the other hand, is to market and capital. Once a resource is diminished to the point where it is no longer profitable to market it, capital can pull out and move on to another market.

Much is made of the freedom and independence of the fisherman. This myth is so pervasive that many bought fishermen believe it themselves, for people who are attracted to fishing are freedom loving people. But unless a person has accumulated enough money to own his own boat and gear, he has little to say about how he fishes, where he fishes, what he fishes for or to whom he sells it. Nor are his first-hand observations of the health of fish populations heeded. The canneries call the shots.

*

The reliance of a fishery on hatcheries is noisy evidence that natural provision is breaking or has broken down. Every national fishery on the North Pacific Rim is now heavily reliant on hatcheries with the exception of Alaska, where the myth of "inexhaustible natural resources" was dominant up until five or ten years ago. Now Alaska is busily building hatcheries against the time when forty years of creek robbing will catch up with them.

Almost a century ago the Japanese state seems to have decided that nature had provided rivers for industrial sewers. Since 60% of Japanese protein comes from fish products, some provision had to be made for the salmon. In 1889 the first Japanese hatchery was built at the headwaters of the Ishikari River on the island of Hokkaido. Today the Japanese fishery relies entirely on artificial propagation with 50 hatcheries on Hokkaido and 82 on Honshu. Over half the escapement is caught, killed and stripped of their eggs for the hatcheries. Little or no provision is made for the rest of the spawning population: the condition of the spawning grounds is generally ignored. Some few streams are maintained as "salmon culture rivers," i.e. the pollution is kept to a reasonable level, but the people are denied access to them. (There is no sportfishing for salmon in all of Japan, but some subsistence fishermen thrive as poachers on these few streams.)

In the United States, hatchery culture was moribund until the late 1950s due to misunderstanding of the salmon's diet. At that time, the "Oregon moist pellet" was developed as hatchery food and the potential of the hatcheries to deliver a large and healthy artifically propagated salmon population was greatly enhanced. Since that time, the King salmon run on the Sacramento River, once dead, has been revived. Fish and Game Departments in Washington and Oregon report that up to half the salmon catch is of hatchery origin.

Hatcheries put food on our tables at the expense of dependence on a self-perpetuating technology requiring ever more capital investment. Curious cultural attitudes grow out of dependence on artificially spawned salmon. One is led to believe that the hatchery fish are the property of the state, private herds with national identities. States act as if the *spectacle of wildlife* must be maintained at any cost, providing tax supported hatchery fish for sporters who drag their big boats behind big trucks for hundreds and thousands of miles, take a few salmon, leave many beer cans, and drag the boats back again. Meanwhile the miracle of self-regulating natural provision which the salmon have provided for many thousands of years is ignored.

Who Are The Salmon People?

It must be remembered that the Pacific salmon is *not* a particularly important source of world protein. The 1970 salmon catch for the entire North Pacific was 385,000 tons. Compare that figure with the top five fish protein catches for the same year:

Peruvian anchoveta - 10 million tons
Atlantic herring - 3.8 million tons
Atlantic cod - 3.1 million tons
Alaska walleye pollock - 1.7 million tons
South African pilchard - 1.1 million tons.

But locally, on the North Pacific Rim, the salmon has always been an extremely important source of protein as well as a monitor of the health of the region. The health of the wild species is infinitely more important than its appearance in the show-cases of New York delicatessens, on the tables of posh restaurants in London and Moscow, and on the shelves of endless suburban supermarkets in North America and Europe.

Some of the greatest of the commerical fisheries have failed. Kodiak and Bristol Bay are closed this year. Southeastern Alaska and the Columbia River wobble on the lip of failure. Only the Fraser River keeps Puget Sound alive. Japanese and Russian fleets fish the mid-Pacific taking young fish. The role of industry as provisioners of luxury food at the expense of the wild salmon and human populations is no longer tolerable.

The care of and access to wild populations of salmon needs to be undertaken by associations of people who live and subsist on or near the spawning grounds Such associations would replace Fish and Game Departments, not as law enforcement agencies, but as educational units, self-regulating and decentralized fishing fleets, and providers of ritual and ceremony which would celebrate the interdependence of species.

…Collectively operated canneries, smokehouses and freezer units assure the preservation of the fish for inexpensive local consumption. Trade councils decide on the value of the fish for trade with inland regions…

…People of the maritime regions, realizing salmon as creature and food move to protect the spawning grounds against dam builders, lumber interests, chemical plants. Slowly, slowly, the salmon population increases…

…Fisher-biologists alternatively work fishboats or traps and tend to the excellence of the spawning grounds…

…Fishboat embassies to keep Rim-wide communications open. Fish crews on the Skagit from Sapporo, from the Yukon. Fish crews on the Amur from the Fraser. Men, women, children…

It will be a great day each year when the fish return. Nothing else will be important on that day.

— La Conner, Washington. 1974.

(First published in **North Pacific Rim Alive,** Bundle No.3. San Francisco: Planet Drum Foundation, 1974.)

HOW HUMANS ADAPT

Kelly Booth

What is the adaptive unit for human beings? Is it the individual? This doesn't seem likely considering that humans are social animals and rely on social cooperation for their survival and well-being. Could it possibly be the state and its bureaucracies? It is doubtful that the government is capable of functioning like an adaptive organism. Could it be our modern mass society, so subject to consumer fads and fashions? Does this seem to provide the foundation for an adaptive social unit?

Unlike other organisms, humans do not have adaptive behavior fixed in their genes. They must learn it. But there is more to human adaptation than can be learned in the lifetime of one individual. Our hominid ancestors overcame this problem by having learned patterns registered in the customs of the group. There came to be stable groups with stable customs passed on from one generation to another.

The group became the unit of adaptation. The individual can only adapt by being a member of an adaptive community. If the individual is to act adaptively, the group as a whole would have to be like an adaptive "social organism."

What would this "social organism" look like? What kind of society would it be that could act in an organized and adaptive way?

It is difficult to see how we can approach such large questions, but there are two sources that may provide us with some clues. One source is biology and our observations of the natural world. What are the features of organisms that enable them to adapt to their environments? The second source is anthropology. Some forms of tribal organization have lasted for at least 40,000 years, and a few features may be as old as one, two, even three million years. Clearly, these forms were sustainable.

Organisms live in place. They are very finely adapted to their particular habitats and vary from one place to another according to their circumstances. They are highly integrated. Every function supports every other function in a remarkable harmony. There is no conflict or competition between organs. Such integration occurs only at a certain scale. A cell, organ or organism can only be so large and still be integrated. To partly overcome this limitation, larger organisms are differentiated into many levels of organization. A mammal is not just a mass of undifferentiated protoplasm. It is made up of cells, tissues and organs.

Tribal societies show these same features of place, integration and scale. Each culture, as a whole, was adapted to a particular place. The individual member finds its place in the culture while the culture as a whole finds its place in the natural environment.

Many tribes had a high degree of integration and mutual aid. Customs and roles cohered into a mutually supportive whole. There were few institutionalized conflicts of interest, no hierarchies or classes. Integration was limited to certain scales. Tribes could only be so big and still maintain the kinds of communication necessary for a common identity. They were comprised of smaller organized groups, such as bands, in which more intimate face to face interaction went on. These smaller groups were also limited in size.

The parallels between tribal societies and organisms are not coincidental. Integration, scale and sensitivity to a particular place are essential features of all adaptation. It seems highly unlikely that a human tribe would have been able to adapt if there were competition between its parts, no limits on scale, or no sensitivity to the uniqueness of its particular surroundings.

Integration, scale and a sensitivity to place are emphatically not found in mass society. The mass does not adapt to a particular place. Instead, it tries to standardize all places. Its relations to its natural

Mutual Aid: A Factor Of Evolution

Happily enough, competition is not the rule either in the animal world or in mankind. It is limited among animals to exceptional periods, and natural selection finds better fields for its activity. Better conditions are created by the *elimination of competition* by means of mutual aid and mutual support. In the great struggle for life—for the greatest possible fullness and intensity of life with the least waste of energy—natural selection continually seeks out the ways precisely for avoiding competition as much as possible. The ants combine in nests and nations; they pile up their stores, they rear their cattle—and thus avoid competition; and natural selection picks out of the ants' family the species which know best how to avoid competition, with its unavoidably deleterious consequences. Most of our birds slowly move southwards as the winter comes, or gather in numberless societies and undertake long journeys—and thus avoid competition. Many rodents fall asleep when the time comes that competition should set in; while other rodents store food for the winter, and gather in large villages for obtaining the necessary protection when at work. The reindeer, when the lichens are dry in the interior of the continent, migrate towards the sea. Buffaloes cross an immense continent in order to find plenty of food. And the beavers, when they grow numerous on a river, divide into two parties, and go, the old ones down the river, and the young ones up the river—and avoid competition. And when animals can neither fall asleep, nor migrate, nor lay in stores, nor themselves grow their food like the ants, they do what the titmouse does, and what Wallace has so charmingly described; they resort to new kinds of food—and thus, again, avoid competition.

"Don't compete!—competition is always injurious to the species, and you have plenty of resources to avoid it!" That is the *tendency* of nature, not always realized in full, but always present. That is the watchword which comes to us from the bush, the forest, the river, the ocean. "Therefore combine— practice mutual aid! That is the surest means for giving to each and to all the greatest safety, the best guarantee of existence and progress, bodily, intellectual, and moral."

— **Petr Kropotkin**, *from* **Mutual Aid: A Factor of Evolution**. *Boston: Porter Sargent Publishers.*

environment are coarse, crude and insensitive. Mass society is not integrated. There is exploitation, hierarchy and fragmentation. We find highly mobile individuals (or nuclear families) within an almost undifferentiated and unbounded mass extending to cover the globe. There is no sense of scale, or intermediate levels of organization.

In short, mass society does not have features essential for adaptation. It cannot be the unit of adaptation for human beings.

The unit that we are looking for is precisely the one that has been destroyed and devoured by modern industrial society. It is the small scale, integrated, self-governing community, having its own identity and its own customs which are adapted to its particular place.

(First published in **The Catalist**, April-May, 1984.)

HOME IS HERE

Wilfred Pelletier and Ted Poole

I had no money, no credit. There was no work on the reserve I could make money at. Once again, I was just another damn Indian. I had fallen back into survival, Indian style. What that means is that you work—sometimes you work like hell—but you're not an employee and you don't get paid money. You get paid in a different way—satisfactions, I suppose you'd call them—the good feeling of your body coming together with hard work, the good feeling of your life coming together because all the non-essentials have fallen away and the whole thing is just simple, very simple and primary. There's a direct line between your head and your hands and your belly. Money, the middleman of survival, has been eliminated. Everything you do is directly related to survival: the wood you cut, the water you draw, the garden you plant, the berries you pick, the fish you catch—and that's your life. And that was our life, but not all of it. There was another element in our survival: the people.

Every day somebody would drop in—some woman would drop in and say, "Well, we had this soup last night. If you want it, it's left over. There's enough there for three or four people, but I can't heat it up now because there's eight of us." And there were three of us, so we'd have soup. Or somebody'd drop in with potatoes, or after they'd made bread: "I want you to try my bread." And every day they came. It had nothing to do with them wanting us to try their bread. They were feeding us. And it wasn't just kindness or thoughtfulness, not charity. It was a way of life, or survival. They sustained us because, with Indians, if the community doesn't survive, no one survives.

*

I've come home dozens of times, hundreds of times, and no one has ever asked me where I came from or what I'm doing now or where I'm living now or how much money I make or what sort of job I have or any of these questions which are so common in white society. What that means is that the people in that community don't place any importance on these things. They like me and love me as I like and love them, and when I come home they are happy to see me and they don't see anyone except Wilf, who was once a little boy and who's now older and bigger and a man, but who is still Wilf, really unchanged. I haven't become any-

thing, I'm not somebody; I'm just who I always was—Wilf. I don't have to account for myself, I don't have to impress anyone, I don't have to explain myself, I don't have to do anything. I'm allowed just to be, and that is the greatest freedom I know. That is what I mean when I say I've come home. And that is life, total life. And that is the world. There isn't anything outside of that.

Yeah, that's all there is except that one other thing, and that one other thing—I don't know what it is. It can be called "the job," or I guess it could be given lots of names. Anyway, there are hundreds of Indian people like me who go home, but only for a few days, a weekend or whatever, and then they go back to that job. They're a toolmaker or a student or a factory worker or something; they leave and go back to that job. Even though the reserve is all there is. And I don't know…oh, I can talk about economic necessity, the need to survive and so on, and there aren't any jobs on the reserve so you have to go outside to find a job. All that. But I know that doesn't explain it. You're damned if you do and damned if you don't. Everyone has to decide for himself what poverty is, what survival is—to be rich in relationships and poor in possessions, or the other way around. For Indians, it seems to be a choice between staying home and having very little (which is really everything) and going away in order to achieve relative affluence (which is nothing). I do know that the whole thing I'm talking about of going home, that's what religion is all about. Those people want to go home, all the people in the world. And I wonder…I don't think there are very many who get home any more through organized religion because the people who are trying to lead the way don't know where they're going. What I mean by going home is finding your own people—not just your blood relations, your *whole* family, wherever they may be anywhere in the world. And I guess that means recognition: knowing the members of your family at a glance and having them know you. People who accept you without question. Because if your medium of exchange is not love, you can't survive.

*

…So I was lost before I was thirty years old, wandering around in a fog of half-truths and falsehoods. I knew that, but I didn't know what to do about it—where to go or how to get out of it. Then one day I came smack bang into reality. I suppose it sounds silly, but what happened was that I saw a dandelion. Here I was, a middle-aged man surrounded with dandelions all my life. Then I saw one. But there was nothing that stood between me and that dandelion, that's what I mean: no classifications, no categories, no words, not even the word "dandelion." Nothing. And that dandelion was not just a thing, one of a million yellow things that were bright and pretty and very common. That dandelion was a being, a living being that accepted and included me totally. I felt like I was standing in the center of the sun with those cool yellow petals going out from my feet and away into the distance forever.

I said I saw a dandelion for the first time. But it really wasn't the first time. I learned that too because there was a flash of remembrance in that experience—no when or where, just a flash— but enough so I knew that when I was a very young child I lived in that reality all the time. Those remembrances of reality began to happen to me more and more often and they were all about just simple things, really very little simple things, and none of them ever lasted very long. But they were what I lived for.

I suppose lots of people have experiences which actualize their identity, their totality. Experiences of oneness with the earth. I remember hearing a man singing in the middle of the night. Everyone was asleep, and way off somewhere he was singing. Indian singing—chanting. He had no drum, just the voice. And the voice seemed to go down into the earth, and shake the earth and come up into me. And that experience was an experience of oneness. I've had that experience, too, hearing a wolf howling, and like the Indian singing, the song of the wolf has no words. And the feeling it gives me also has no words.

*

Then I took a look around. I saw city halls, courthouses, houses of parliament, churches, schools, and universities by the hundreds and thousands. I saw systems—systems for managing the land, the air, and the water; systems for managing human behavior; systems for managing religion; systems for managing learning; systems for managing food, shelter, clothing; systems for managing love and procreation: a vast complex of carefully engineered systems. I saw millions of people working, not for themselves, but for someone else. I saw millions of people doing, not what they themselves want to do, but what someone else wants them to do. I saw the depressing evidence of a people who have externalized and institutionalized—in fact, have tried to standardize—the very nature of humanity. I saw a whole people who've lost the way of life and in its place have built a mechanical monster which does most of their hard work, carries their water, delivers their food, raises their kids, makes their decisions, says their prayers, transports them, "informs" them, entertains them, and controls the people it serves, absolutely. I also saw that the monster, unable to manage itself, was running wild, totally out of control, ripping the land to pieces, spreading poisons, filling the air with filth, dumping garbage and shit in the rivers and lakes and oceans. I saw all that, and I saw the people, millions of them, crowded together in cities, living side by side in towns, villages, rural areas. But I didn't see a single community.

Still, I knew of some. There were a few *bona fide* communities left in America, all of them Indian or Eskimo. A community is invisible from the outside—just a collection of people. But from the inside it is a living organism that manages itself. Not engineered, not planned; just growing there—a sort of happening that flourishes or shrivels depending on the climate around it. A community has no institutions, no agencies, no forms of extraneous government, because *there are no departments of activity.* There's only a way of life, and all the activities are just naturally in that flow, all the things that people find it necessary to do in order to survive. In the communities I was thinking of, the people know nothing of Justice or Religion or Education or Equality or Culture or any of those big institutional concepts. Their language has no words of that sort in it. But the people themselves are just and learned and religious and equal. Those people don't even know they are a community. The word itself has no meaning for them.

Another thing they have no awareness of and certainly no word for, but which I have observed lots of times, is something I have come to call community consciousness. I'm not sure I can describe it except to say it's common ground, a kind of corporate consciousness that is shared by everybody in that community and used by everyone. Maybe the best word for it is "trust"—a kind of trust that people outside that community can hardly imagine and which the people inside that community cannot name. I think it must be closely related to the kind of consciousness you see in a flock of sandpipers. Fifty or sixty individual birds are all packed together into one dense flock and they're going to beat hell, turning this way and that, diving and climbing, cutting around in tight circles, and that flock stays right together, stays the same shape all the time. And not one bird runs into another. Each bird acts, flies, moves like every other bird. The flock behaves as one, one single organism. You can see the same thing in a school of fish and in some swarms of insects, too.

Optimum Scale

If I begin this discussion of the bioregional paradigm with the concept of scale it is because I believe it to be, at bottom, the single critical and decisive dominant of all human constructs, be they buildings, systems, or societies. No work of human ingenuity, however perfect otherwise, can possibly be successful if it is too small or, more to the usual point, too big, just as a door fails if it is too small to get through, a doorknob if it is too large to grasp; just as an economy fails if it is too small to provide shelter as well as food, a government if it is too large to let all its citizens know about and regularly influence its actions.

At the right scale human potential is unleashed, human comprehension magnified, human accomplishment multiplied. I would argue that the optimum scale is the bioregional, not so small as to be powerless and impoverished, not so large as to be ponderous and impervious, a scale at which, at last, human potential can match ecological reality.

— **Kirkpatrick Sale**, *from* **Dwellers in the Land**. *San Francisco: Sierra Club Books, 1985.*

Now, I don't know how they do that, those creatures, except that *they* don't do it; *it* does it. And I think this same thing, this same sensitivity or alertness or whatever, is present in tribal communities. For one thing, work is shared and produce is shared. People survive together as a group, not as individuals. They aren't into competition. But they aren't into cooperation either—never heard of either of those words. What they do just happens, just flows along. And they're not into organization either; no need for it, because that community is *organic*. Wherever people feel the need to organize it's because the normal condition of their society is dis-organized (not together). But I don't think the Western European way of organizing brings things together anyway, in the sense of human relations. From what I've seen, it usually does just the opposite. It gets things done, but it alienates people.

Let's say the council hall in an Indian community needs a new roof—maybe that would be a good example. Well, everybody knows that. It's been leaking here and there for quite a while and it's getting worse. And people have been talking about it, saying, "I guess the old hall needs a new roof." So all of a sudden one morning here's a guy up on the roof, tearing off the old shingles, and down on the ground there's several bundles of new, hand-split shakes—probably not enough to do the whole job, but enough to make a good start. Then after a while another guy comes along and sees the first guy on the roof. So he comes over and he doesn't say, "What are you doing up here?" because that's obvious, but he may say, "How's she look? Pretty rotten, I guess." Something like that. Then he takes off, and pretty soon he's back with a hammer or shingle hatchet and maybe some shingle nails or a couple of rolls of tarpaper. By afternoon there's a whole crew working on that roof, a pile of materials building up down there on the ground, kids taking the old shingles away— taking them home for kindling—dogs barking, women bringing cold lemonade and sandwiches. The whole community is involved and there's a lot of fun and laughter. Maybe next day another guy arrives with more bundles of shakes. In two or three days that whole job is finished, and they all end up having a big party in the "new" council hall.

All that because one guy decided to put a new roof on the hall. Now who was that guy? Was he a single isolated individual? Or was he the whole community? How can you tell? No meeting was called, no committees formed, no funds raised. There were no arguments about whether the roof should be covered with aluminum or duroid or tin or shakes and which was the cheapest and which would last the longest and all that. There was no foreman and no-one was hired and nobody questioned that guy's right to rip off the old roof. But there must have been some kind of "organization" going on in all that, because the job got done. It got done a lot quicker than if you hired professionals. And it wasn't work; it was fun.

(From **No Foreign Land: The Biography of a North American Indian.** Toronto: Random House of Canada Limited, 1973.)

Illustration by David LaChapelle.

Black Values

We need to recognize, I think, that Green values or bioregional values are not something wholly new or limited to native peoples. I know in the black community in my own family history, my roots are in the rural South, and the values that the people that I grew up with in my earliest years were bioregional. Ours was a politics, an economics, a lifestyle of place, and a real respect for the whole community, the community of beings—that was the most fundamental experience I had as a child. I experienced everything as connected, everything was related and you were to respect that and live out of that, and also to be humbled by the limits of what you knew. To recognize your own limitations and therefore to act more cautiously or to be responsible about how you lived in the place that you called home. So I think there's a whole tradition in our collective history that we're a part of, that we're growing out of. I think that's true too for rural culture in general. It's a part of Western culture, part of white people's own history that they need to also understand and reclaim.

— **Jeffrey Lewis**, *interview by Paul Cienfuegos and Ellen Rainwalker, from* **NABC III Proceedings**, *1989.*

SEARCHING FOR COMMON GROUND: Ecofeminism And Bioregionalism

Judith Plant

It is no accident that the concept of ecofeminism has emerged from the many tendencies within the movement for social change. Women and nature have had a long association throughout history and it is only now that the deepest meanings of this association are being understood. Just as ecologists have paid critical attention to the attitudes, social structures and rationalizations that have allowed the rape of the earth, so have feminists dug deeply to understand why society has rendered them second class citizens, at best.

Both schools of thought are now converging with similar analyses. The difference is that ecologists are scientists, basing their views of the interconnectedness of all things on the intellect, whereas feminists cannot help but come from the school of experience and have sought intellectual frameworks in order to try to make sense of their experience of subjugation. The coming together of the two gives us hope for an understanding of the world that has the potential to be rooted in "thinking feelingly."

Ecology and Women

Ecology is the study of the interdependence and interconnectedness of all living systems. As ecologists look at the consequences of changes in the environment, they are compelled to be critical of society. Because the natural world has been thought of as a *resource*, it has been exploited without regard for the life that it supports. Social ecology seeks ways to harmonize human and non-human nature, exploring how humans can meet their requirements for life and still live in harmony with their environments.

Ecology teaches us that life is in a constant state of change, as species seek ways to fit in particular environments which are, in turn, being shaped by the diversity of life within and around them. Adaptation is a *process*. Ecology helps develop an aware-ness of the need to incorporate these organic facts into our most general views of the world—those views that shape the way humans will *be* in the world.

Within human society, the idea of hierarchy has been used to justify social domination, and has been projected on to nature, thereby establishing an attitude of controlling the natural world. The convergence of feminism with ecology is occurring because of an increasing awareness that there are, in fact, no hierarchies in nature. A belief in the virtues of diversity and non-hierarchical organization is shared by both views.

Women have long been associated with nature: metaphorically, as in "Mother Earth," as well as with the naming of hurricanes and other natural disasters! Our language says it all: a "virgin" forest is one awaiting exploitation, as yet untouched by man [sic]. In society, too, women have been associated with the physical side of life. Our role has been "closer to nature," our "natural" work centered around human physical requirements: eating, sex, cleaning, the care of children and sick people. We have taken care of day-to-day life so that men have been able to go "out in the world," to create and enact methods of exploiting nature, including other human beings.

Historically, women have had no real power in the outside world, no place in decision-making and intellectual life. Today, however, ecology speaks for the earth, for the "other" in human/environmental relationships; and feminism speaks for the "other" in female/male relations. And ecofeminism, by speaking for *both* the original others, seeks to understand the interconnected roots of all domination, as well as ways to resist and change. The ecofeminist's task is one of developing the ability to take the place of the other when considering the consequences of possible actions, and ensuring that we do not forget that we are all part of one another.

Ecofeminism: Its Values and Dimensions

Why does patriarchal society want to forget its biological connections with nature? And why does it seek to gain control over life in the form of women, other peoples, or nature? And what, on earth, can we do about dismantling this process of domination? What kind of society could live in harmony with its environment? These questions form the basis of the ecofeminist perspective.

Before the world was mechanized and industrialized, the metaphor that explained self, society and the cosmos was the image of organism. This is not surprising, since most people were connected with the earth in their daily lives, living a subsistence existence. The earth was seen as female. And with two faces: one, the passive, nurturing mother; the other, wild and uncontrollable.

These images served as cultural constraints. The earth was seen to be alive, sensitive; it was considered unethical to do violence toward her. Who could conceive of killing a mother, or digging into her body for gold, or of mutilating her? But, as society began to shift from a subsistence economy to a market economy; as European cities grew and forested areas shrank; and as the people moved away from the immediate, daily organic relationships which had once been their basis for survival, peoples' cultural values—and thus their stories— had to change. The image of earth as passive and gentle receded. The "wrath and fury" of nature, as woman, was the quality that now justified the new idea of "power over nature." With the new technology, man [sic] would be able to subdue her.

The organic metaphor that once explained everything was replaced by mechanical images. By the mid-seventeenth century, society had rationalized the separation of itself from nature. With nature "dead" in this view, exploitation was purely a mechanical function and it proceeded apace. The

new images were of controlling and dominating: having power over nature. Where the nurturing image had once been a cultural restraint, the new image of mastery allowed the clearing of forests and the damming and poisoning of rivers. And human culture which, in organic terms, should reflect the wide diversity in nature, has now been reduced to mono-culture, a simplification solely for the benefit of marketing.

Since the subjugation of women and nature is a social construction, not a biologically determined fact, our position of inferiority can be changed. At the same time as we're creating the female as an independent individual, we can be healing the mind/body split.

Life struggles in nature—such as the fight to protect B.C.'s Stein River Valley and the many less-publicized ones—become feminist issues within the ecofeminist perspective. Once we understand the historical connections between women and nature and their subsequent oppression, we cannot help but take a stand on the war against nature. By participating in these environmental standoffs against those who are assuming the right to control the natural world, we are helping to create an awareness of domination at all levels.

Ecofeminism gives women and men common ground. While women may have been associated with nature, they have been socialized to think in the same dualities as men have and we feel just as alienated as do our brothers. The social system isn't good for either of us! Yet, we *are* the social system. We need some common ground from which to be critically self-conscious, to enable us to recognize and affect the deep structure of our relations, with each other and with our environment.

In addition to participating in forms of resistance, such as non- violent civil disobedience in support of environmental issues, we can also encourage, support and develop—within our communities— a cultural life which celebrates the many differences in nature, and encourages thought on the consequences of our actions, in all our relations.

Bioregionalism, with its emphasis on distinct regional cultures and identities strongly attached to their natural environments, may well be the kind of framework within which the philosophy of ecofeminism could realize its full potential as part of a practical social movement.

Bioregionalism: An Integrating Idea

Bioregionalism means learning to become native to place, fitting ourselves to a particular place, not fitting a place to our pre-determined tastes. It is living within the limits and the gifts provided by a place, creating a way of life that can be passed on to future generations. As Peter Berg and Raymond Dasmann have so eloquently stated, it "involves becoming native to a place through becoming aware of the particular ecological relationships that operate within and around it. It means understanding activities and evolving social behavior that will enrich the life of that place, restore its life-supporting systems, and establish an ecologically and socially sustainable pattern of existence within it. Simply stated, it involves becoming fully alive in and with a place. It involves applying for membership in a biotic community and ceasing to be its exploiter."

Understanding the limitations of political change—revolution— bioregionalists are taking a broader view, considering change in evolutionary terms. Rather than winning or losing, or taking sides, as being the ultimate objective, *process* has come to be seen as key to our survival. *How* we go about making decisions and how we act them out are as important as *what* we are trying to decide or do.

In evolutionary terms, a species' adaptation must be sustainable if the species is to survive. How can humans meet their requirements and live healthy lives? What would an ecologically sustainable human culture be like? It is in dealing with these questions that the bioregional movement and the philosophy of ecofeminism are very much interconnected.

Human adaptation has to do with culture. What has happened with the rise of civilization, and most recently with the notion of mass culture, is that what could be called bioregionally adapted human groups, *no longer can exist*. It's difficult to imagine how society could be structured other than through centralized institutions that service

> Competition in which the strong wins has been given a good deal more press than cooperation. But certain specifically weak organisms have survived in the long run by being part of collectives, while the so-called strong ones, never learning the trick of cooperation, have been dumped on to the scrap heap of evolutionary extinction.
>
> — **Lynn Margulis and Dorian Sagan,** *from* **Microcosmos: Four Billion Years of Microbial Evolutioin,** *New York: Summit Books, 1986.*

the many. In our culture almost every city exists beyond its carrying capacity; diverse regions are being exhausted and ecologically devastated.

Becoming native to a place—learning to live in it on a sustainable basis over time—is not just a matter of appropriate technology, home-grown food, or even "reinhabiting" the city. It has very much to do with a shift in morality, in the attitudes and behaviors of human beings. With the help of feminism, women especially have learned an intimate lesson about the way power works. We have painfully seen that it is the same attitude which allows violence toward us that justifies the rape of the earth. Literally, the images are the same. We also know that we are just as capable, generally speaking, of enacting the same kind of behavior.

The ideas of bioregionalism are being practiced all over the world—just rarely referred to as such. The name gives us common ground, however, like ecofeminism. But bioregionalism gives us something to practice and together they could be seen to offer a praxis—that is, a way of living what we're thinking. Here we can begin to develop an effective method of sharing with our male friends the lessons we have learned about power, as well as our hopes and aspirations for an egalitarian society—a society which would be based on the full participation and involvement of women and men in the process of adaptation and thus in the maintenance of healthy ecosystems.

Homing in on a New Image

One of the key ideas of bioregionalism is the decentralization of power: moving further and further toward self-governing forms of social organization. The further we move in this direction, the closer we get to what has traditionally been thought of as "woman's sphere"—that is, home and its close surroundings. Ideally, the bioregional view values home above all else, because it is here where new values and behaviors are actually created. Here, alternatives can root and flourish and become deeply embedded in our way of being.

This is not the same notion of home as the bungalow in the suburbs of western industrialized society! Rather, it is the place where we can learn the values of caring for and nurturing each other and our environments, and of paying attention to immediate human needs and feelings. It is a much broader term, reflecting the reality of human cultural requirements and our need to be sustainably adaptive within our non-human environments. The word ecology, in its very name, points us in this direction: *oikos*, the Greek root of "eco" means home.

The catch is that, in practice, home, with all its attendant roles, will not be anything different from what it has been throughout recent history *without* the enlightened perspective offered by feminism. Women's values, centered around life-giving, must be revalued, elevated from their once subordinate role. What women know from experience needs recognition and respect. We have had generations of experience in conciliation, dealing with interpersonal conflicts in daily domestic life. We know how to feel for others because we have practiced it.

At the same time, our work—tending to human physical requirements—has been undervalued. What has been considered material and physical has been thought to be "less than" the intellectual, the "outside" (of home) world. Women have been very much affected by this devaluation and this is reflected in our images of ourselves and our attitudes toward our work. Men, too, have been alienated from childcare and all the rest of daily domestic life which has a very nurturing effect on all who participate. Our society has devalued the source of its human-ness.

Home is the theater of our human ecology, and it is where we can effectively "think feelingly." Bioregionalism, essentially, is attempting to rebuild human and natural community. We know that it is non-adaptive to repeat the social organization which left women and children alone, at home, and men out in the world doing the "important" work. The *real work* is at home. It is not simply a question of fairness or equality, it is because, as a species, we have to actually work things out—just as it is in the so-called natural world—with all our relations. As part of this process, women and nature, indeed *humans* and nature, need a new image, as we mend our relations with each other and with the earth. Such an image will surely reflect what we are learning through the study of ecology, what we are coming to understand through feminism, and what we are experiencing by participating in the bioregional project.

(First published in **The New Catalyst**, No.10, Winter 1987/1988.)

COMMUNITY: Meeting Our Deepest Needs

Helen Forsey

When we look at human needs across cultures and over time, a recurring theme is the need for roots in the Earth, for a reliable, sustained relatedness to a particular area or locality. The multiple visions of people seeking and creating balanced, egalitarian, harmonious communities all have in common that element of sturdy rootedness. Bioregionalists call it "living in place"; most people would call it home. But the concept of "home" has been viciously distorted—coopted by capitalism to refer to an exchangeable piece of real estate; corrupted by patriarchy to mean a man's castle, where women and children are neither free nor safe. In this context, "homelessness" takes on for us a new and broader meaning, referring not only to the harsh realities faced by those who actually lack shelter, but also to a pervasive phenomenon of modern alienation even in the midst of creature comforts. It is time we reclaimed the concept of "home," and made it synonymous with the kind of community that ecofeminism strives to create.

Human beings have always created ways of living together; we are social animals after all. But, under patriarchy, those ways have been oppressive and harmful to people and to the Earth. More and more of us are realizing now—with the hope that it is not too late—that we must turn that phenomenon around.

So, in our various spots on this planet, groups of us cluster together again, more or less intentionally, in homesteads, neighborhoods and networks, to forge new ways of living and working together, new models of community that will comprise this essential turn-around. And we ask: How can we make the most of these efforts to create a new reality out of our best visions? What pitfalls do we need to watch out for and avoid, so as not to fall back into the old oppressive patterns? How can we build, from our small scattering of communities, a network of growing strength that can truly help to bring about the enormous cumulative changes that the world so desperately needs?

A fundamental part of the answer is that we need to be ready and able to draw on both our experience and our understanding, and allow the theory and the practice to nourish and deepen each other. Unless we can become aware of the meaning of our experience and reinterpret those meanings in our actions, we risk losing the valuable lessons we can learn from the experience....

As we build community, we need to learn to listen to each other and to ourselves, to be aware of our experience and to hear our own inner voices. Reflecting on those times in our lives where we have experienced wholeness, empowerment, joy, we can see those experiences as signposts for our deepest needs, indications of how those needs can be filled. This process is part of what the feminist poet and nonviolent activist, Barbara Deming, calls "remembering who we are." Whether the "relevance" of what is going on is immediately obvious or not, we need to allow our awareness and our understandings to surface. If something feels right, or wrong, there is probably a reason, whatever the experts or the bosses or the politicians may try to tell us. We need to begin to trust both our intuition and our common sense—as the feminist movement has long been encouraging women to do—and be willing to spend the time and energy, individually and collectively, to fit these together and build from what we learn.

Our experience and understandings as feminists and as ecologists are, of course, absolutely vital to this process. So much of our search is for an alternative to the alienation that permeates modern industrial society, where our inter-relationships with other humans, animals, plants and the Earth itself are distorted through power hierarchies and prescribed roles, electronic technology, plastic packaging and layers of concrete and asphalt. The basic causes of that alienation lie in patriarchal attitudes and structures, distance from nature and lack of knowledge and respect for its cycles and systems. If we fail to recognize this causality, we are apt to find ourselves recreating those same alienating structures in our attempts to build community, and any hope for the evolution of a true alternative will be doomed.

In fact, as we attempt to practice community, we find that this effort by itself does not automatically change our old behavior patterns and our accustomed ways of relating to each other and to the Earth. And to go on relating in the old ways threatens to destroy the community and the integrity of the alternative we sought. This contradiction has spelled the end of countless experiments in collectivity, with people coming to the tragic—and mistaken—conclusion that such alteratives run counter to human nature. I believe that it is not human nature itself which is at fault, but rather the stifled and distorted attitudes and behavior that *un*natural and oppressive societies have cultivated.

Thus, in order to make possible the necessary fundamental changes in all our relations, we need to continually develop our understanding and analysis of what must be changed and why, as well as our determination and ability to live and interact differently in our daily lives. Without such understanding, the old destructive patterns will tend to dominate our actions, preventing any real change; whereas theory alone, without practice, is sterile.

Alternative communities can, of course, take a multiplicity of forms, and this potential for endless variety is one of the most hopeful aspects of the communal movement. Communities can be neigh-

borhoods or villages, small homesteads or more geographically dispersed webs of commonality and interaction. We are not talking here about the patriarchy's repeated attempts to define "community" in its own oppressive terms, but rather about the many kinds of social experiments which are consistent with ecofeminist principles. To explore the characteristics that such communities tend to have in common would form the subject matter for an entire book, but I want to touch on a few of the elements that my experience tells me are essential for building sustainable alternatives.

First, community living is life-affirming and nonviolent. Community people come together out of love for each other and for the Earth, commitment to certain basic values, and a hope, however tenuous, for a better future. This commitment often involves anger, struggle, and pain, but that in no way cancels out the love or the continuing possibility of joy. Community does not represent a withdrawal from the struggle; instead, it is an affirmation that better ways do exist, and an expression of our determination to live those better ways in the here and now.

> **B**ioregionalism as a political and cultural movement can only emerge when the people of an area understand their history and the effects of the land on that history. Without understanding the land and the cultural adaptation to it, political action, even if it arises from the grassroots, is likely to make problems worse. The politics of place must be firmly rooted in the consciousness of place...
>
> — **Gary Coates and Julie Coates,** *from* **Co-Evolution Quarterly,** *Winter 1981.*

Communities value autonomy and self-reliance based on equality. Community people have a common urge to make their own decisions, control their own destinies, both as a group and as individuals. This implies responsibility, ")knowing what it takes to live," as one community woman put it, an ability to cope, and a willingness to share those capabilities. It also requires both an internal and an external balance—equality and respect within the group regardless of sex, race, class, age or other differences, and freedom from intervention from the outside. Once again, everything is connected. If inequalities and exploitation exist within the community, those attitudes and modes of behavior will threaten not only the cohesiveness of the group, but also its relations with its homeplace and the creatures that co- inhabit that place. And if control of decisions or resources is imposed from outside, the balance and cycles of the community's life are likely to be disrupted or destroyed. Without implying isolation, there needs to be a degree of autonomy which will permit the community to grow and flourish in the context of its own ecofeminist values.

Community demands openness, clarity, emotional connectedness and the ability and willingness to communicate about the things that matter. The inevitable problems faced by people living together cannot be resolved without honest and sensitive communication which builds trust and understanding. This is nowhere more true than in a group of people committed to new and better ways of relating. People in community must be willing to be vigilant and self-critical, as well as patient and generous, in addressing the group's internal dynamics; ready both to challenge and to affirm, keeping constantly in mind the principles of respect, equality, cooperation and caring that they have committed themselves to.

The issue of tolerance is a thorny one. How much are we willing to tolerate actions and attitudes that go against our cherished values? How do we handle such contradictions when they arise? Is it élitist or unrealistic to demand that everyone in the community be committed to ecofeminist ideals and practice? How accessible are these ideas to a wider public, and might our insistence on them prevent the growth of the very movement we wish to see spread?

How we answer these questions, and how, in practice, our communities deal with these situations, is indicative in each case of our own related-ness and respect for ourselves, other beings, and the Earth. Surely there are many answers, and none of them are simple. Community is not a simple solution to the world's problems. We know by now that simple solutions don't exist in any case; they are another of the patriarchy's lies. What community may be, however, is humanity's next evolutionary step, giving more and more people the opportunity to live in ways consistent with our deepest needs. If we can understand those needs, and practice what it takes to meet them, we can find the strength to grow, and perhaps also to bring about the kind of changes that must be made if the planet is to survive.

Community develops quite naturally, then, out of ecofeminist ideals. The many and varied forms that our communities take, from Northern Mozambique to Eastern Ontario, from Ata to Mattaposett, evolve according to the myriad factors which influence any group choosing to live and work together in harmony with the Earth. Both the commonality of principle and the diversity of practice are characteristics of the ecofeminist movement, as indeed they are of the natural universe itself. By honoring both, we in our communities can help to build the kind of future we dream of for ourselves and for the Earth.

(First published in **Healing The Wounds: The Promise of Ecofeminism.** Philadelphia: New Society Publishers, 1989.)

Jacqueline Froelich.

Bioregion As Community: The Kansas Experience

Except for tiny pockets of affluence, every bioregion since the advent of civilization has in some way been a hinterland, an area to be exploited by institutions and forces that have no stake in what happens locally. It is the classic story of empire, whether that empire is driven by renewable or non-renewable resources. It is the dialectic of the center and the periphery, the city and the wilderness. In this sense, the problems of the Great Plains are no different from those of the Pacific coastal forests, which are being mined for export, or the Brazilian Amazon, which is being destroyed forever by mechanized greed.

The central paradox of localism is that local economic and cultural problems are almost always extra-local in origin and, by definition, not amenable to solution at the local level. Eventually they require unified political action, a bioregionally federated social and cultural resistance movement willing to test its resolve in a struggle for survival. Yet while these local problems cannot be solved at the local level, that is the only place they *can* be solved. Without a local population whose roots are firmly planted in the land and its history, there is no preventing the destruction of the locality for profit by extralocal forces.

Because the lines of conflict between center and periphery are never clear cut, most, if not all, of the local population complies in its own destruction. The rules of the game require each actor to exploit a common resource to survive, so the exploited become the exploiters. The Kansas farmer who is mining groundwater and soil at a rate that will assure that he will not have a farm to pass on to his children is doing so because his only alternative would be to voluntarily suffer economic collapse now rather than later. For agriculture, participation in an international market economy means ruin for the land.

Only when the decisions that affect everyday life are made by those most directly affected does the notion of local control have any meaning. Those who advocate the politics of place must bridge that gap between the world of the hinterland and the world of the self-governing local community. If people have lost the ability to understand and control their own lives and places, then the task and meaning of bioregionalism is political, and is the same everywhere. In this age of industrial empire, we must develop locally specific and bioregionally appropriate ways to increase political, social, economic, and technological independence and self-reliance. We need to increase mutual aid, self-help and self-regulation within the local community and bioregion and develop a renewable energy-based, environmentally appropriate technology capable of being produced, understood, maintained, and controlled at the local and regional levels through democratic means...

...But the problems of this or any other region cannot be addressed without first involving people in the process of personal, cultural, institutional and technical change in the place where they live, in their own backyards, streets and towns. Without that, there can be no bioregional movement for change. It is the central paradox of localism and the central problem of bioregionalism. People must be firmly rooted before they will fight destruction that comes from beyond their boundaries. Community is the beginning and end of bioregionalism. Before the bioregion can become a community, the experience of community must become a familiar and cherished condition of everyday life."

— **Gary Coates and Julie Coates, from Co- Evolution Quarterly,** *Winter, 1981.*

BIOREGIONALISM / WESTERN CULTURE / WOMEN

Marnie Muller

Bioregionalism begins to tap the very heart of Western historic tradition by re-asking the question: "What is our place in the universe?" Bioregionalism does this by squarely challenging the error of hierarchical thinking as it looks at:

1. the historic dogma of the male God's dominion (read *oppression*) over the heavens and the male (white) human's dominion (oppression) over the Earth;

2. the secular, Ptolemaic system of anthropocentrism, whereby all of nature revolves around the human race;

3. the more "liberal" concept of benign (read *paternalistic*) stewardship whereby humans "take care of" the Earth.

As if that was not enough in itself, bioregionalism has also begun to challenge the very innards of historic Western tradition by examining the error of body/mind dualism. This dichotomy has been woven into the very fabric of Western culture for hundreds of years, and it will be difficult to realize all the ways it has affected and lobotomized us. However, bioregionalism, with its emphasis on in-corporating (literally) the sensual, the spiritual and the mental in our relationship with our Earth means that healing is occurring—that mind and body are beginning to grow together once again. Praise to all of us in our efforts toward this healing, for it is with this healing that our Earth will become less tormented. Another error of thinking underpinning Western culture which bioregionalism challenges is the "Trash your homeplace, there's always a new frontier" mentality.

In light of bioregional self-criticism, I ask that we all regard these errors of thinking in depth, in order to see how they affect *not only* how Western culture relates to *the earth* but also how it relates to *the female*. In the interest of bioregional self-criticism, I suggest that we explore in earnest how these two areas are vitally intertwined and how, in order to deal with the treatment of Earth, we must also deal with the treatment of Women.

Hierarchical Thinking

For thousands of years we have been assured that God is male; that the human male has dominion over the human female; that the human female came from the human male; that the human male has dominion over the female *and* children; that the human male has dominion over the female, children *and* animals, plants and the Earth itself. This opinion has been the basis for overt physical, political, spiritual and psychological oppression for centuries. Finally, a number of males today have begun to "catch on" (many females have known for *quite* some time), to realize that by this system they, too, are entrapped. They have begun to realize the perverseness and pervasiveness of this system, as some people in the white population have begun to get a glimmer of the oppression directed towards peoples of color. Still, realization is only a first step. Pervasiveness is insidious when it comes to actually changing an age-old system.

Body/Mind Dualism

By historically divorcing "mind" from "body," Western culture was able to do away with a number of truths. This was accomplished by drastically reducing the human powers of perception and declaring them to be false. Our perceptions (not deceptions) had told us that the Earth was alive, that we were part of this functioning process...that the food we ate and the air we breathed united us with this process…that our children were born of this process…that the Earth turned from this process. Stars beckoned us. Waters lapped us. Sunlight fell on us. Music/sound pulsed through us.

Western culture untied us from this "process"—from sensual reality. (By "sensual," I mean all the aspects of our being which allow us to experience fully, with all our senses, the creation around us.) Western culture began to emphasize mind and "spirit" and to denigrate the sensual. The sensual became "other"—it was a source of enticement, temptation, sin, blame—something to be suppressed. Because the culture was dominated by male patriarchal concepts which identified the male with "mind," the female was then identified with "sensual," "flesh," "dark." With suppression came oppression. Objectification and use of the female and objectification and use of the Earth occurred. Perception of the full presence of the female and of the full presence of the Earth was obscured because of this objectification.

The Homeplace

In bioregional thought, the homeplace is sacred. In Western culture, it is the place "to get away from;" the homeplace is the place where chores need to be done, where children are, where the elderly need to be cared for. In a wider context, the homeplace is boring, should be used up so that new frontiers can be moved towards. At best, it is used as a retreat.

Throughout cultural history, the female is associated with the homeplace. It is here where we, as bioregionalists, most need to look. Whether male or female, we need to allow our homeplace to be resacralized. Our shelter (whether nomadic or stationary) is our place from which we go out and to which we return. It is our membrane—something to be cared for, nurtured with energy, loved. Sometimes we have a shelter with someone else—a partner or friend. Sometimes we have children—sometimes we have elders with us—in our shelter. It is a place to be in, to relax in, to prepare food in, to repair when necessary. It is situated in a wider place—a homeplace of Nature—a place to know…to find out about water, animals, plants, trees, soil, wind currents, seasons, migration patterns. Reconnecting with our homeplace allows us, in a safe way, to begin reconnecting with our inner selves. In turn, we then connect or reconnect with other humans.

In addition to Western culture's treatment of the Earth and of the female, we also need to look at Western culture's treatment of the *child*. Our homeplace will not become "breathable" again until we do this. Western culture treats the child as though s/he is not really all the way there. It is as though the culture's bounds of reality have become so narrowed that no longer can the full presence of the child be acknowledged. Within the child's psyche, there is so much crossover between the "sensual" and the "conceptual" that in order to acknowledge and rejoice in the full presence of the child, we as a culture would have to "un-atrophy" our powers of perception and reincorporate the "sensual" into our lives. A step in our own healing process is to recognize and nurture in children the gifts of "being" we are attempting to reclaim for ourselves.

As we bioregionalists truly begin to locate ourselves in the universe, let us, as females and males, begin to locate ourselves in relation to each other. Then we can mutually begin to work together on an equal basis to reform the values of our human culture as it affects ourselves and our homeplace, Earth.

(First published in **Raise the Stakes**, No. 10, Summer 1984.)

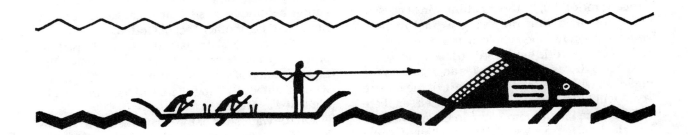

EARTH DIET, EARTH CULTURE

William Koethke

The energy an organism feeds upon defines it within the cosmic web of energy flows. What each species feeds upon within the life of the earth describes the parameters of its behavior and physical identity. The wolf, for example, is physically structured so that it can catch and eat deer. Its social life is structured so that it can hunt in packs, therefore enabling the wolf to catch deer that it could not catch individually.

What one puts in one's mouth is a fundamental spiritual, cultural and political act. The nature of the energy one feeds upon either puts one in balance with the cosmos or it puts one in disharmony with the cosmos—an organic state of disease.

How Much of the Planet's Life Does Your Cadillac Cost?

In the recent past of our two million year family history, some have abandoned the natural culture of the human family and a disease has broken out in the form of empires. The patriarchal empire is a fundamental ecological imbalance, a fundamental sexual imbalance, a fundamental population imbalance and a fundamental mental imbalance (wherein a living organism confuses its identity with its accumulation of dead material objects).

The basic nature of this planetary disease is a cyclic swelling and collapse of populations who make increasing material demands upon the declining planetary fertility. The legacy of Empire can be traced through China (the great forests and soils gone), Indus Valley (entire semi-arid ecosystem gone), Tigris-Euphrates (forests, soils gone and one-third of the arable land salinized), Mediterranean (soils, forest gone and North Africa, a rock pile), Europe (natural forest ecosystem gone, acid rain preparing a final *coup-de-grace*)—and now, the whole planet through the agency of the world-wide industrial empire.

When a disease agent invades an organism the organism will attack and eradicate it, or the disease agent will kill the host and then die itself, or, there will be some kind of remission. In China we see a late stage of the disease that has achieved some

remission at a very low level. The forces of the planet-cosmos have guided the Chinese social body into a highly simplified, artificial and probably temporary balance wherein they live on their own excrement. The culture of empire was finally forced to observe one natural energy cycle. When there was nothing left alive, the people began creating soil from their own feces. Historians agree that the Chinese could not have survived without the use of "nightsoil."

So, what we choose to put in our mouth enhances the life of the planet, balances with it or runs a net deficit. It takes the planetary life between 300 and 1,000 years to build each inch of topsoil and "civilization" has been running a net deficit since it began. Once balance was lost, the warrior cult of empire began dipping into the fund of planetary fertility. Since then, its explosive boom and bust cycles have been financed from the death of the living things of the planet.

Within the Industrial Empire, the media of communication frame the beginning of the end of the last cycle as "acts of God." In the most ecologically devastated areas of the planet, where there is no ecological margin left—Ethiopia, East Africa, Central America, etc.—there are masses of people and few living things— topsoil—and any perturbation becomes a crisis that is called a drought, flood, famine or other "act of God."

As the ecological devastation frames the picture of numerically exploding "societies in crisis," the great question of the next century arises: "How can we live without killing the Earth, and ultimately ourselves as well?"

On the watershed of the San Francisco River we know of six distinct cultural forms that have occupied the area and each has addressed the question in a different way. Each cultural form was integrated with or isolated from the life of the earth by diet. These cultures were the Pleistocene—Pit-House People; the Kiva People (Anasazi-Mimbres-Mogollon-Pueblo); the Apache foragers; the Spanish village—planter-herders; the Texas cow herders and the present cow, timber, industrial axis.

The Human-Planet Metabolism

The Pit-House People lived thoroughly within the cyclic metabolism of the San Francisco watershed. There are two moisture cycles on the watershed. One of the "rainy seasons" begins around the first part of July with the incoming thunderstorms that come with air currents off the Gulf of Mexico—these last until Fall. In late Fall and Winter, weather comes from the Southwest, from the direction of the southern tip of Baja California.

These winds bring winter storms and moisture. From March until July a mini-drought or dry season occurs. Each of the two seasonal rain periods have their own characteristic species of grasses and herbs known as "cool season" and "warm season" plants. As the summer plants seed out and become brown, the cool season plants germinate and begin some growth. They lie dormant over December and January and then grow again to seed out in May and June.

The animals have their own cycles of migration and reproduction as well as the birds. Many of these cycles climax in the fall in the Chaparral country, that life zone where the pinon-juniper forest meets the ponderosa pine forest at 6,000 to 7,500 feet elevation. This area, the Chaparral, features an abundant mixture of oak and manzanita also. In the Fall many things ripen: the pinon nuts, yucca, bananas, grapes, acorns, berries, grass seeds and many others. At this time the animals migrate

"On The Mattawa," anonymous block print.

to the Chaparral to get fat before the winter. Skunks, raccoons, squirrels, deer, bear, elk, peccary, turkey, mountain sheep and others are followed into the Chaparral by the coyote, cougar, ringtails and bobcat.

It is in this Chaparral region that one finds most of the shallow depressions and other artifacts of the ancient Pit-House People. No doubt they foraged widely, but they were in the Chaparral each fall for the big harvest.

The metabolism of the planet was their metabolism. In wet cycles more deer ate more acorns and the deer fat kept the Pit-House People fueled against the cold-damp. We have no record of these peoples' human culture but anthropologists studying tribal foragers calculate that they had exceptional health and each person averaged 500 hours "work" annually to sustain themselves; plenty of time to sing and dance—and tell coyote stories.

The Mayan Adaptation

The Pit-House People were in the area in the dim past and until 100-500 A.D. We don't know if the Pit-House clan were the grandmothers and grandfathers of the Kiva People (Anasazi era, 500 A.D. to pueblo present), but chances are good that they were. There was, though, one essential difference: the Mayan Adaptation; that is, Mother Corn and her Sisters—beans, squash and chiles.

The Mayan Adaptation brought in a new metabolism with the Kiva People. The Kiva People shared the Feathered Serpent cosmology with the Maya-Aztec and were in a sense the suburbs of Copan, Uxmal and Teotihuacan.

Corn needs reasonably flat land, while squash and chiles especially need periodic watering, so the Kiva People put up their stone house villages near the live water streams in valley bottoms. This is the riparian habitat. It is the other area on the watershed of explosive fertility that resonates with the Chaparral. Beaver dams, great meadows, willow thickets, cattails, black walnut, grapes, berries, arrowleaf potatoes, birds, animals and more abounded. From their agriculture-forager-hunter metabolism these people of the Mimbres pottery designs created a rich, complex and beautiful human culture, the equal of any on the planet. Not only did they participate in the planetary metabolism by eating from what was offered by the earth, but their very culture was a dramatic expression of that life.

Whether it is a mid-Winter ceremony to divine the fate of the bean seed for next season, the kinship communicated with the deer in the Deer Dance Ceremony, the Green Corn Dance, the Snake Dance or any of the other ceremonies too numerous to mention—they are the life of the earth in human dramatization, as the present Kiva People, the Pueblos, demonstrate.

*

But—there are questions. Anthropologists who study agriculture-forager-hunter people worldwide say individuals of those cultures each average 1,000 hours "work" per year and that their health is not as good as the forager-hunter and

---

The Parasites

I believe Western European culture will never endure in the Americas. I believe it is only a passing phase like the hoola hoop or the skate board. I also believe that the peoples living in the Americas will become American; that they will have to in order to survive in America. That means that a truly *American* culture will evolve—is evolving—in the Americas, a culture which is not a European import, nor an adaptation of a European import. That means that the sons and daughters of immigrants who strove for over four-hundred years to possess the Americas will be possessed by the Americas; the descendants of those who tried to conquer and subdue the Americas will be conquered and subdued by the Americas. It means that the stubborn land the pioneers cleared and cursed will be loved, respected, and revered by the great-grandchildren of pioneers. And the native creatures of that land will also be loved and fostered, including the original American human: the Indian.

— Wilfred Pelletier and Ted Poole, *from* **No Foreign Land: The Biography of a North American Indian**. *Toronto: Random House of Canada Limited, 1973.*

many die sooner.

On this watershed, there was a tremendous concentration of Kiva People, in excess of thirty thousand. Questions exist from archeology. Did they deforest the area for firewood and building materials? Did they denude the area of wildlife? Did they bring the life of the land to the edge so that when the dry cycle came on there was no margin left? Did they too precipitate "acts of God?" The present Pueblos have not. But why did the Anasazi disappear so mysteriously during one era? We don't know and if any grandparents in the Pueblos do know, they are not telling. What we do know is that the Athebascans (Navajo-Apache) filled the vacuum.

The Roving Harvesters

The invading masses from 16th Century Europe found a people on this watershed that they called Apache. According to ethnobiologists Morris E. Oppler and Edward F. Castetter, about 50% of the Apache diet was meat and the other half made up of non-meat sources—true forager-hunters.

These two scholars say that the people "moved with the seasonal change of weather, and followed the wild food harvests as they occurred.... When colder weather came he [sic] removed to a lower altitude; in Summer he [sic] was in the highlands again. When the mesquite and screw-bean ripened or a certain animal's fur or flesh was at its best at a particular time, the Apache was present to share in the harvest."

The San Francisco watershed was the home of the northern clan of the Chokonen (Chiricahua) tribe. In the last days, Chihuahua was Elder of the northern clan and Cochise was Elder of the clan centered around the Chiricahua and Dragoon Mountains to the South.

On the West of the Northern Chokonen, were the White Mountain bands and to the East, on the headwaters of the Gila River, were the Bedonkohes of which Geronimo was a member.

Kaywaykla (who was one of the handful out of all the local bands to survive the genocide of the Empire) was from the Chihinne band, of which Victorio was a leader in the last days. The Chihinnes were centered Northwest of the watershed near Ojo Caliente. Kaywaykla says that sometimes they migrated in Winter to the bottom of the Barranca del Cobre, the deep canyon system leading West off the Sierra Madre Occidental in Mexico. There, they could watch sea lions play in the river and eat tropical fruit off the trees in the canyon bottoms.

He says (by translation): "My people spent their Summers in the mountains of New Mexico, carefree, untrammeled. They migrated to Mexico in the Fall, living off the land as they went, killing game, harvesting fruit, and giving thanks to Ussen for the good things He had given. They knew the land of jungles and of tropical fruit. They knew the people whose land they crossed. They were on the very best of terms with Cochise and his band. They penetrated the fastness of Juh, Chief of the Nednhi, and were received as brothers. When they in turn came to us we gave freely of our best."

The Chokonen were foragers and hunters, but could be keen planters when the occasion arose. At their camps, if the area was appropriate, they scattered seed which would help feed them next cycle. Of all the groups of omnivore humans, the Chokonen reached toward the maximum nutrition of the watershed. Whether lambsquarters (more

---

I believe that anyone now living in America or anyone who wishes to come to America can belong here. When I say "belong here," I mean that it isn't necessary to buy land and "own" property in order to belong someplace. How can you buy something you've already been given? Besides, the land is living; how can you butcher it up and offer the cuts for sale without killing it? And the land is sacred. You don't live off it, like a parasite. You live in it, and it in you, or you don't survive. And that is the only worship of God there is. When you buy land you are dispossessed by the act of purchase. The whole transaction is a lie that says, "This is my land. It belongs to me," when the truth is that you belong to it.

Those who belong here know this. They've always known it. And they're increasing in numbers. The people who *belong* in America are coming home.

— Wilfred Pelletier and Ted Poole, *from* **No Foreign Land: The Biography of a North American Indian**. *Toronto: Random House of Canada Limited, 1973.*

calcium per volume than cow's milk) or cattail roots (ground to flour, it equals rice or corn nutritionally) or any of the other dozens of food sources, their nutrition was superior.

Diet is Politics

The Chokonen were democrats. They practiced as pure a form of democracy as is known. All leaders served by popular assent and, in addition, decisions were made by consensus, that is, all must agree to a decision, not just a simple majority. The diet was the basis, and the knowledge transmitted through human culture, its empowerment.

As Mark Twain said, "Tell me where you get your corn pone and I'll tell you what your opinions are." In Chokonen society, no one controlled another's food supply. With the profound knowledge of the natural world transmitted by culture, each Chokonen could secure their food independently.

This contrasts with the cultural forms of the Kiva People. The diet of the Mayan Adaptation requires villages because crops must be worked and land apportioned. Food, land, and social power created a mixture that resulted in a social hierarchy where power is (as in the Pueblos today) based upon merit, birth, membership in tribal organizations and age.

The Pit-House People, being small groups, no doubt functioned along the lines of the Chokonen with emphasis on family politics, age, experience and wisdom.

The agriculturalist Kiva People who lived in pueblos show an increasing centralization of power compared to the forager. In the same manner, the people who ate a rice diet of Asia show the tendency. To grow rice in a populated country there must be a centralized power to administer the irrigation systems, as anyone who has irrigated from a community ditch readily understands. This centralist tendency must have existed also in the irrigated empires of the Indus Valley and the Tigris-Euphrates Valley of Sumeria.

In the present diet-ecology-social form on the San Francisco watershed, food is almost entirely shipped in by diesel truck. Now, people work 2,000 hours annually and need constant medical attention. This diet is refined and produced by mass industrial production.

The raw food material for the diet comes from industrial agriculture on a mass scale. Mass production requires the organization and control of a large mass of tractable people by huge social institutions over which the mass of people have little or no control. It is freedom and an organic life traded for Cool Whip.

What one eats empowers whatever or whoever produces it. Ham and eggs for breakfast requires domesticated animals which require fences and the European farm system, which requires hierarchs to administer the many plots with many farmers—as in monarchical Europe. Now, with technology shaping society, diet is even more simplified than the Swiss farm.

There are ten basic food plants, plus cattle, swine, sheep and fowl, feeding civilization. No longer can we forage over the hills for the widely varied diet our physiology demands. We get the simplified food that is easily adapted to mass machine harvesting. Further, our conditioned taste in food changes according to the changes in the technical processes of machinery used to produce it.

Few children would eat "old-fashioned" hand churned ice cream when the industrially produced skimmed milk or hydrogenated vegetable oil with a chemical ester flavor developed from coal tar is available. (The new "ice cream" has the proper "mouth feel.") With the machine process, civilized people are conditioned to food that is the most technically efficient to refine.

What one eats determines one's ethical relationship to the cosmos and shapes and determines power relationships within each culture.

The Coming of the New Order of Reality

The Pit-House People, the Kiva People and the Chokonen saw the Earth as a secure home, and they felt and practiced a kinship with the life around them. The Chokonen, finally, were confronted by strange invaders who were qualitatively different than any native culture they had been exposed to. The invaders lived in the strange mental world of the Judeo-Christian-Muslim tradition where life was bad (a veil of tears and suffering), and death was the portal to good (Heaven). Matter, the planet, living things and one's body were of the Satanic realm, while pain, suffering and death for the Holy Cause were good—and would be rewarded in Heaven. Curiously, at the same time, these people were exploding out of Europe in a colonial expansion, bent upon stealing any gold, goods, land or resources anyone else in the world might have.

The Spanish immigrants on the watershed were few in number because the Athebascan tribes had not yet been exterminated. The invaders set up a village agricultural-herder dietary regime. They settled on the most fertile areas, the riparian habitats in the valley bottoms. The Spanish diet was basically the Mayan Adaptation diet borrowed from the Mexican Indians but they also exploited the fertility of the Earth for surpluses, to trade for a few industrial products. They nonetheless were close to a food self-sufficient cultural style. Social power in their communities was based on private property, age and social status.

The Spanish began the desertification of the watershed by overgrazing with cattle, sheep and goats. They accomplished much of the destruction of the riparian habitat by grazing it out, clearing and burning. They also greatly altered the hydrology of the entire area by beginning to kill the beavers because they interfered with irrigation systems.

In the time of the Chokonen, there were beavers from the tops of the mountains of the Mogollon Rim, down the San Francisco and Gila Rivers, all the way to the Gulf of Mexico. Now, there is only one strong colony on the San Francisco drainage and a few weak remnant groups. Along with the beavers, riparian habitat (with minor exceptions) has been destroyed from here to Yuma, Arizona.

In the 1880s, the Texas cow herder group invaded with vast herds of cattle. Hungry for profits and free range grazing, they dealt the grass cover a blow from which it has never recoverd. They translated the biomass of grass into a diet of industrially refined sugar, white flour, lard, beans, beef, and canned tomatoes and peaches purchased with the profits from cattle ranching.

If the price of beef went down, they reacted by expanding the herds and increasing the grazing pressure. They attacked the most vulnerable point of the ecosystem: the grass cover over the soil. As the grass went, the topsoil followed. Next came the arroyo cutting and the meandering rivers began to flood, tearing out the meadows, tremendously widening the river courses and filling them with gravel, in a re-enactment of the 10,000-year-old story of "civilization."

Finally, the modern regime of the colonial-industrial economy took hold. Now, the process of desertification on the watershed is so advanced that when the San Francisco River floods, the Federal government will no longer provide disaster aid because what seems like a disaster has occurred so frequently in recent years it has become a normality.

Now, the people of the watershed are fed by the industrial metabolism. The diet is shipped in from the metropolitan centers of industry. The diet is bled from the life of the land. Topsoil, the reservoir of fertility of the land, maintains itself in a dynamic cycle by feeding upon the organic matter that falls upon it. This continuous cycle is the gauge of the health of the planet. The present logging system bleeds the Earth of what is topsoil in potential. The "raw resources" (biomass) are traded with the industries in the center of colonial power for industrial products and for the food that makes up the present diet.

Many cycles and ecological systems on the watershed are now reeling—the hydrological cycles, the fire cycles, the weather cycles, the vegetational cycles, and the animal abundance and inter-mix cycles, to mention a few.

Ham and eggs for breakfast and the European farm system have ecologically destroyed Europe. The transnational food company propagandists have caused the Japanese (and other societies) to choose the white bread of empire, thus empowering U.S. agribusiness and the transnationals—and cashiering the small Japanese rice farmer. Throughout the world-wide industrial empire, the mutant relationship with the Earth expands as the planet dies.

Will a cultural and spiritual balance and personal empowerment flow from dietary choices for us? They will if we stop empowering the white sugar-flour crowd by our choices. An average Chokonen could run fifty miles a day and up toward a hundred if need be; they didn't eat white bread and baloney!

Get together. Speak for the plants and animals that feed you and for all the other living beings. Inform others about the Earth diet on your watershed, its nutritional superiority and its ecological fragility.

Learn the food plants on your watershed and in your bioregion. Create culture by telling your friends about them. Observe the principles by which they thrive. Gather their seed. Help them spread. Help increase the fertility.

(First published in **Fifth Estate**. Detroit: Spring, 1987.)

THE COUNCIL OF ALL BEINGS

Pat Fleming and Joanna Macy

Some twenty-five of us are gathered at a riverside wilderness site in New South Wales, Australia. Last night we shared stories from our experiences which awakened our concern—even anguish—over what is happening to the natural world in our time. Although we come from different backgrounds, we have this concern in common and it has brought us here to work together. We want to strengthen our courage and commitment to take action to heal our world.

We took time to honor that intention as we first sat down together last night. It has called us to experiment with new ways of healing our separation from nature which is at the root of the destruction of the forests, the poisoning of the seas and soil.

This morning we engaged in a number of group exercises to help make us more conscious of our embeddedness in the web of life. They helped us *remember* our bio-ecological history, as our species and its forebears evolved through four and a half billion years of this planet's life. They helped us relax into our bodies, into our intuitive knowings, and our trust in each other. Now, after clearing up after lunch, we assemble to prepare ourselves for the promised ritual of the Council of All Beings.

Instead of beginning right away, we receive from our co-leader Frank an invitation to disperse and go off alone for an hour. *Find a place that feels special to you and simply be there, still and waiting. Let another life-form occur to you, one for whom you will speak at this afternoon's Council of All Beings. No need to try to make it happen. Just relax and let yourself be chosen by the life-form that wishes to speak through you. It could be a form of plant or animal life, or an ecological feature like a piece of land or a body of water. Often the first that occurs to you*

is what is right for you at this gathering.

Even before I sit down quietly on the warm sand beside the river I have a sense of the "being" that waits to emerge in me. It is Mountain.

Brmm, brmm...the drum calls us back. It summons us all back to take time to make our masks and to explore further together our various life-forms. In companionable silence our hands reach for paper, colors, paste-pot. Under the rustling trees are sounds of cutting, folding, breathing.

Brmm, brmm...the drum calls us once again, this time to enter the ritual ground and convene as the Council of All Beings. Wearing my Mountain mask of earth, stone, leaves and grasses, I move heavily and slowly toward the ritual ground. The water of the stream that borders the site is cool, washing away the old, preparing us for the new, the unknown. As we gather in a large circle I look around at all the assembled Beings—such an array of forms and colors, some brash, some shy and subtle. An air of uncertainty, yet expectation hangs between us.

Frank briefs us first on the structure of the ritual. I recognize a blending of different native traditions of our planet's peoples. Through fire and water, we will ritually cleanse ourselves and the ritual ground. To acknowledge the full breadth of our concerns, we will invoke and invite into our circle the earth powers and beings that surround our lives in this space and time: the powers of the four directions and the beings of the three times. Then as the Council proper begins, we will, as the life-forms we have assumed, speak spontaneously, letting be said what needs to be said.

These utterances, we are told, will fall into three stages. From the perspective of the other life-forms we will speak spontaneously among ourselves. We will say why we have come to the Council and be free to express our confusion, our grief and anger and fear. Then, after a while, to the signal of a drumbeat, five or six of us at a time will move to sit in the center of the circle to listen in silence as humans. We'll each have the opportunity to shift between human and nonhuman roles. And lastly we will have the chance to offer to the humans (and receive as humans) the powers that are needed to stop the destruction of our world.

Now with the slow beat of drum and the lighting of fragrant leaves, the Council ritual begins. An abalone shell with burning sage and cedar passes from hand to hand; we inhale the sweet pungent smoke, waving it over our faces. We acknowledge our kinship with fire. Next a glass bowl of fresh water comes round the circle. Each dips into it to annoint the head of the next person, acknowledging our need for cleansing and refreshment.

As the four directions are invoked, we turn to the East, to the South, to the West and North. Drawing on the ancient lore of the Medicine Wheel, we all face in each direction, arms upraised, as one of our number evokes in turn and aloud the meaning it can hold. "We invoke and invite the power of the East...the power of the rising sun, of new beginnings, the far-sightedness of eagle..." As Mountain I feel special kinship with the North, "powers of stillness and introspection, of waiting and endurance..."

After each invocation, we all join in with a simple, deep, two-tone refrain: "Gather with

us now in this hour; join with us now in this place."

Frank, as the ritual leader, now helps us invite the Beings of the Three Times.

Spontaneously and all intermingled from around the circle comes the murmur of randomly spoken names: first, those who have gone before; then the beings of the present time; and, lastly, beings of the future time.

After a moment of silence, a silence for the generations we hope will come after us, we chant again the refrain that has followed each invocation.

"Gather with us now in this hour; join with us now in this place."

Now we are ready to speak as a Council. We sit and take our masks. We ease out of our solely human identification; we settle into the life-forms that have come to us and that seek expression.

We hold a roll-call of the assembled beings. One by one around the circle, speaking through our masks, we identify ourselves: "I am wolf and I speak for the wolf people." "I am wild goose and I speak for all migratory birds." "I am wheat and I speak for all cultivated grains."

We meet, Frank says, having donned his mask of prickly stalks and leaves, *because our planet is in trouble. We meet to say what is happening to ourselves and our world. I come to this Council as weeds. Weeds, a name humans give to plants they do not use. I am vigorous, strong. I love to thrust and push and seed—even through concrete. Pushing through paving I bring moisture and life. I heal the burned and wounded earth. Yet I am doused with poison now and crushed, as are creatures who live in and through me.*

In acknowledgment we all reply, "We hear you, Weeds."

I am black and white cow, fenced in a paddock, far from grass, standing in my own shit. My calves are taken from me and, instead, cold metal machines are clamped to my teats. I call and call, but my young never return. Where do they go? What happens to them?

"We hear you, cow."

The shells of my eggs are so thin and brittle

now, they break before my young are ready to hatch. I fear there is poison in my very bones.

"We hear you, wild goose."

One by one they speak and are heard. Rainforest. Wombat. Dead leaf. Condor. Mud. Wild flower.

I know that it is my time to speak out.

I am Mountain. I am ancient and strong and solid, built to endure. But now I am being dynamited and mined, my forest skin is being torn off me, my top-soil washed away, my streams and rivers choked. I've a great deal to address to the humans today.

"We hear you, Mountain."

The drum beats again, announcing the next stage of the Council. It summons humans to enter the circle to listen. Five or six of the beings put aside their masks and move to the center. Sitting back to back, facing outward, they attend silently as the Council continues. When the drum beats again after several more beings have spoken, they return to the periphery to be replaced by others; and the process continues until each of us will have had the chance to listen as a human.

Hear us, humans, says Weeds. This is our world, too. And we've been here a lot longer than you. For millions of years we've been raising our young, rich in our ways and wisdom. Yet now our days are numbered because of what you are doing. Be still for once, and listen to us.

I am Rainforest. Counted in your human years I am over a hundred thirty million years old. If I were one of your buildings, you would take precious care of me. But instead you destroy me. For newsprint and cheap hamburgers you lay me waste. You destroy me so carelessly, tearing down so many of my trees for a few planks, leaving the rest to rot or burn. You push needless roads through me, followed by empty-hearted real-estate grabbers who purport to own me. You cause my thick layer of precious topsoil to wash away, destroying the coral reefs that fringe me... Your greed and folly shortens your own life as a species. When you leave me wasted and smoldering, you foretell your own death. Don't you know that it is from me that you have come? Without my green world your spirit will shrivel, without the oxygen my plant life exhales, you'll have nothing to breathe. You need me as much as your own lungs. I am your lungs.

Oh, humans, as Clean Water I was a bearer of life and nourishment. Look at what I bear now that you've poured your wastes and poisons into me. I am ashamed and want to stop flowing, for I have become a carrier of sickness and death.

Brmm, brmm...the drum sounds into the circle. The humans in the center, looking relieved to be leaving, return to the wider circle and resume the masks of their other life-form. A half-dozen others move to the middle as humans and sit close together, some holding each others' hands as they listen.

I feel myself beginning to boil inside and know again I must speak.

Humans! I, Mountain, am speaking. You cannot ignore me! I have been with you since your very beginnings and long before. For millenia your ancestors venerated my holy places, found wisdom in my heights. I gave you shelter and far vision. Now, in return, you ravage me. You dig and gouge for the jewel in the stone, for the ore in my veins. Stripping my forests, you take away my capacity to hold water and to release it slowly. See the silted rivers? See the floods? Can't you see? In destroying me you destroy yourselves. For Gaia's sake, wake up!

Look on me, humans. I am the last wild Condor of that part of the Earth you call California. I was captured a few days ago—"for your own good," you tell me. Look long and hard at me, at the stretch of my wings, at the glisten of my feathers, the gleaming of my eye. Look now, for I shall not be here for your children to see.

"We hear you Dolphin, we hear you Rainforest...we hear you Mountain, Lichen, Condor..."

One by one our stories pour out, filled with pain, with anger, and, occasionally, with humor. We all report how rapidly and radically humans are affecting our lives and our chances for survival. Yet the words carry, too, a sense of kindred spirit, for we are all of the same Earth.

When the flow of expression begins to subside, our ritual leader Frank, taking off his mask as Weeds, comes into the center of the circle. It is the first time in the ritual that we hear someone speak as a human.

We hear you, fellow beings. It has been painful to hear, but we thank you for your honesty. We see what we're destroying, we're in trouble and we're scared. What we've let loose upon the world has such momentum, we feel overwhelmed. Don't leave us alone—we need your help, and for your own survival too. Are there powers and strengths you can share with us in this hard time?

No other signal or instruction is needed to shift the mood of the Council. The grim reports and chastisements give way to a spontaneous sharing of gifts.

As Slug, I go through life slowly, keeping close to the ground. I offer you just that, humans. You go too far, too fast for anyone's good. Know carefully and closely the ground you travel on.

Water says,

I flow on and on. I deal with obstacles by persistence and flexibility. Take those two gifts for your lives and your work for the planet.

I, Condor, give you my keen, far-seeing eye. I see at a great distance what is there and what is coming. Use that power to look ahead beyond your day's busy-ness, to heed what you see and plan.

"Thank you, Slug...thank you, Water...Condor," murmur the humans.

One after another the beings offer their particular powers to the humans in the center. After speaking, each leaves its mask in the outer circle and joins the humans in the center, to receive empowerment as a human from the other life-forms.

I feel Mountain wanting to speak through me again.

Humans, I offer you my deep peace. Come to me at any time to rest, to dream. Without dreams you may lose your vision and your hope. Come, too, for my strength and steadfastness, whenever you need them.

I take off my mask and join the group of fellow-humans in the center. Hands reach out to pull me in close. I feel how warm and welcoming is the touch of human skin. I am beginning to gain a fresh recognition of our strengths. For all the gifts that the beings offer are already within us as potentialities, otherwise we would not have been able to articulate them.

The last of the beings gives its blessing. Frank has taken up his mask again and speaks:

I offer you our power as Weeds—that of tenacity. However hard the ground, we don't give up! We know how to keep at it, slowly at first, resting when needed, keeping on—until suddenly—crack! and we're in the sunlight again. We keep on growing wherever we are. This is what we share with you—our persistence.

We thank him and pull him into our midst. A wordless sounding arises. Grasping hands, we stand and begin to move outward in a circle, laughing and humming. Sheila leads the long line of us back in upon itself, coiling gradually tighter and closer around ourselves into a group embrace. It is the ancient form from this land's aboriginal tradition known as a "humming bee." The close intertwined embrace, cheeks against shoulders, skin on skin, feels good, as the humming of our throats and chests vibrates through us. It is as if we are one organism.

The hum turns to singing. Someone takes the drum. To its rhythm some move and dance, leaping and swaying and stamping the ground. Others move off among the trees and down to the waterside, to be quiet with themselves and what has happened.

Later, as the sun sets, we reassemble to release the life-forms that we have allowed to speak through us. A fire has been kindled in the growing darkness. One by one we come forward with our masks and put them in the flames, honoring the beings they symbolized and letting them burn. "Thank you, Condor." "Thank you, Mountain."

Tomorrow the circle will meet again, to speak of the changes we as humans will work for in our lives and in our world. Then we will make plans for action, hatch strategies, concoct ways of supporting each other. Right now it is good simply to rest upon our ground and watch the masks curl and crackle as they catch fire.

(From **Thinking Like A Mountain: Towards a Council of All Beings**, New Society Publishers, 1988.)

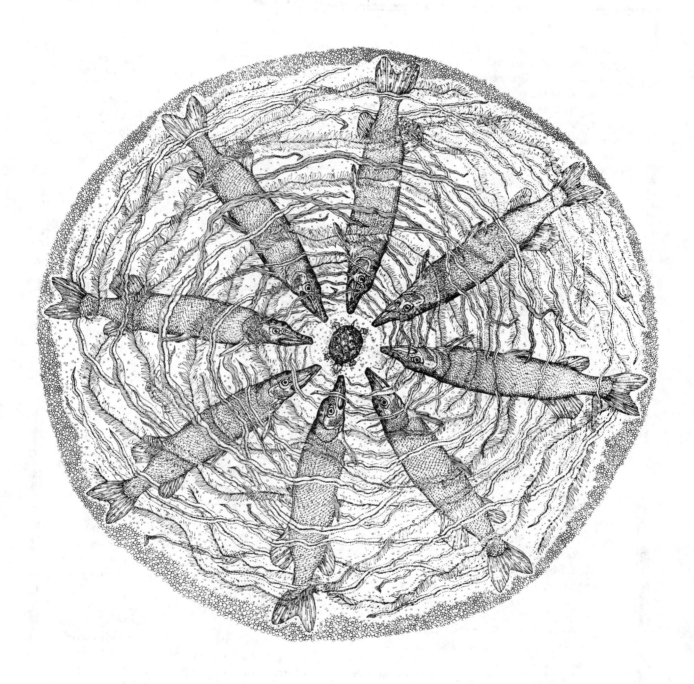

"Eco-mandala, Pikes and Turtle," by Jacqueline Froelich.

Part Four

REINHABITATION AND RESTORATION

"...the salmon were telling us, what was good for them was good for us. Both species benefit from healthy watersheds and an extended sense of commonality. Ladies and gentlemen, they were saying, please, let's get serious about this business of coevolution." — *Freeman House*

Engaging in the work of restoring the earth to good health, "removing the human-centered barriers to the earth healing herself," in turn begins the process of reintegration of human and non-human life. To know one's life-place in detail, the native plants and animals, creeks, rivers and seasonal changes, the healthy places and the not-so-healthy places, is to have a finger on the pulse of one's own life.

"How can they not listen to a Green Cities Program?" asks Peter Berg in his inspiring and practical essay on how to go about reinhabiting the city. The contrast between what can be done, as is shown in the article on Maxworks—the revitalization of an abandoned slum area in Chicago— and the gray reality of most urban areas is astonishing. Activities like recycling, permaculture, neighborhood struggles, industrial reclamation, organic gardening, housing, recycling research, neighborhood economics, parks, alternative energy, tree planting, and graywater use, bring together nature, culture and community in urban spaces. And a coalition of 18 local groups in New York point the way in lobbying for a Green City program that could be adopted by groups in other cities, towns and smaller munipalities.

The significance of water is poetically relayed by David McCloskey. This is followed by "To Learn The Things We Need To Know" in which Freeman House shares his community's experiences with watershed restoration. While this article can be used as a preliminary guide to salmon enhancement, what is equally important is the emphasis on the need for local people to be involved in such work. To do the work of rehabilitating the ecosystem in which one lives is to actually transform our social and economic systems.

Preservation and restoration are inseparable, says Jamie Sayen in "Taking Steps Toward A Restoration Ethic." This essay stresses the need to "re-wild" damaged land, and that there is no alternative if we want to prevent the collapse of the biosphere. He calls for a social, economic and political culture that brings together human and ecological values. Bill Mollison reiterates the call for the formation of small, responsible communities involved in permaculture and appropriate technology. He feels that "the only response is to gather together a few friends and commence to build the alternative, on a philosophy of individual responsibility for community survival."

Providing more of a vision of what is being called for, Starhawk finally takes the reader into a world of cooperation and harmony with place, testing the idea of bioregionalism as it might actually be realized.

Getting Over The Distance Between Us

Sometimes I think it's true that territory
Is only how far we're willing to go
To get to the girl or boy next door.
Geography really all we have to talk about.
I want you the names of three rivers, I say.
She mentions softly two ranges of mountain.
Over the hugest most western rock, I complain.
She answers with ocean, tides, storms, miles of sand.
I'm reminded of the fault between us.
Of the ups and downs of differently shifting plates.
The tendencies of continents to drift apart.
She is unmoved.
Though again and again I fold my maps, go home
To be among familiar birds and flowers
She knows what latitude and longitude
I'm set on. What long-sought passage.
The trail of abandoned lives and furniture
That follows the heart of discovery.
Another life. Another country.
It always begins at the border.

— *Jerry Martien*

GREEN CITY: An Introduction

The way we live in cities today is probably the greatest threat to our survival. Cities unconscionably consume resources and spit out horrendous waste. The green city movement does not face this reality by turning to the countryside. It recognizes that most of us live in cities and will continue to do so for some time. It faces up to the reality that cities are basically anti-nature; but instead of writing them off, it looks to ecologize them. Green city sees the city ecologically—in the context of its bioregion and the world.

Another important aspect of green cities is the affirmation of urban life. Beyond the crass recognition that most of us live in cities and will continue to do so, green city thinking accepts social organization in cities as being part of social evolution; thus part of nature.

The focus on practical everyday actions was wonderfully evident at the Green City conference in Chicago, 1989. In the city itself we saw urban gardening as *slum busting*. And the people at the conference represented actions on recycling, permaculture, neighborhood struggles, industrial reclamation, new jobs in the city, organic gardening, community gardens, housing, recycling research, developing neighborhood economics, preservation of parks, peoples' architecture, alternative energy systems, tree planting, graywater use, and more than we could recount. There is simply too much here to even attempt a summary. A unique Chicago example, however, is too outstanding to go without special mention: beyond Chicago's "magnificent mile" lives "Maxworks."

To envision a green city while living in the wasteland of a neglected, decaying inner-city neighborhood is quite a feat in itself; to actively work towards such a vision against overwhelming odds is indeed a daunting prospect. But that is exactly what a small, dedicated community is doing in the area around Maxwell Street in Chicago, and the result is a project known as Maxworks. To use the term "project" in describing Maxworks does not do justice to the people whose collective vision and energies have created a self-empowered, self-reliant community.

Maxworks operates out of what was an abandoned three-story warehouse in an area where entire city blocks have been neglected to the point where it is no longer feasible for the owners of the buildings to pay taxes. Decaying buildings are simply allowed to deteriorate and are then abandoned. Amidst these conditions, Maxworks obtained an abandoned warehouse and turned it into a neighborhood recycling center, research (tire recycling), and publishing center (*Things Green* and another newsletter), hostel and residence. Inside, floor to ceiling, are three floors of clothes, books, machinery parts, and household items of every description. Also there are some primitive sleeping spaces on raised platforms wherever there is room. Outside, the yard is divided into collection areas for paper, lumber, glass, scrap metals, tires.

The Maxwell Street area has had a weekend market for over one hundred years. Today it is primarily an open-air recycling market spread out on hundreds of makeshift tables occupying several city blocks. Within this stands the Maxwell area's "blues tree:" an old tree where people have been gathering every Sunday for over a hundred years to sing and play the Chicago blues. Inspired by this linkage of nature and culture, Maxworks is involved in neighborhood tree planting. A "Rose of Sharon" growing amid the garbage and rubble of a vacant lot is truly an affirmation of life. In the wasteland of a decaying Chicago neighborhood, the people of Maxworks are green urban pioneers. (You can contact Maxworks Co-op at 717 W. Maxwell St., Chicago, IL 60607—visitors welcomed.)

— **Kathryn Cholette, Ross Dobson, Kent Gerecke, Marcia Nozick, Roberta Simpson, Linda Williams,** *from* **City Magazine,** *Vol.11, No.1 Summer/Fall 1989.*

A GREEN CITY PROGRAM FOR SAN FRANCISCO BAY AREA CITIES AND TOWNS

Peter Berg

The San Francisco Bay Area is unique in so many ways that its most common characteristic is probably diversity. Differences in natural characteristics range from Pacific tide pools to redwood forests, from flat, bird-filled marshes to the abrupt rise of Mount Diablo from where the Sierra Nevada Mountains can be seen more than a hundred miles across the Central Valley.

A diversity of people matches that of the bioregion. Inhabitants generally pride themselves on being tolerant, but the truth is that if they weren't, they would probably be miserable. Italian Catholics go to school with Chinese Buddhists, surviving hippies rent apartments in the same buildings as prosperous yuppies, Latinos speak Spanish to Filipinos, and recently arrived Southeast Asians who don't speak each other's languages raise children together and build strong communities in formerly destitute downtown areas. Thousands of immigrants from foreign countries and just as many from the rest of the United States stream in constantly to find opportunities for both work and self-expression. Who can blame them? The Bay Area is one of the most naturally-endowed and enlightened life-places on the planet.

There are growing cracks in the surface of this benign picture however, and they can eventually grow to be more devastating than anything that could emanate from the San Andreas fault. Here's the problem: *No large urban area in North America is sustainable at present. How can the Bay Area expect to* absorb the additional two-thirds of a million people that are predicted to arrive by the beginning of the twenty-first century without losing its livability?

Cities aren't sustainable because they have become dependent on distant, rapidly shrinking sources for the basic essentials of food, water, energy and materials. At the same time they have severely damaged the health of local systems upon which any sensible notion of sustainability must ultimately depend. Watercourses have become dumps for everything from petrochemicals to sewage, nearby farmland is continually lost to housing developments, soil and watertables are poisoned by seepage wastes from garbage buried in landfills, fossil fuel emissions increasingly mar the purity of air, and the small refuges for wildlife and native vegetation that still remain are constantly reduced or threatened.

These problems are worsening at a faster rate in the San Francisco Bay Area than in many other urban centers. In addition, the social benefits that make cities livable, such as a sense of community and wide civic participation, are more typically eroded rather than strengthened as the

> *"What would it take to establish a positive outcome for the seemingly overwhelming problems of cities? What features of city life should be addressed and in what ways? How would an alternative approach for the future look and feel?"*

megalopolis that surrounds the Bay continues to grow.

The situation is critical, yet there hasn't been a comprehensive movement to create a saving alternative. There isn't a single realistic plan in operation to ecologically redirect and thereby advance the quality of life for any sizable urban area in North America.

What would it take to establish a positive outcome for the seemingly overwhelming problems of cities? What features of city life should be addressed and in what ways? How would an alternative approach for the future look and feel?

*

First it's necessary to understand that the nature of cities has already changed tremendously in just the last few decades. In 1950 about two-thirds of North Americans lived in cities or towns of 25,000 or more, but by 1986 the proportion had jumped to 75% of an overall population that had itself increased significantly. To accommodate this tidal wave of new residents, the sheer number and size of cities has grown very rapidly. Mexico City is the most dramatic example, almost doubling its population from eight to 14 million betwen 1970 and 1980. Since then it has swollen to over 20 million to become the most populous city that has ever existed. The movement of people from the countryside into cities is one of this century's strongest demographic trends, one that promises to continue into the future. Urban-dwelling, once the rarest way for people to live, is fast becoming the dominant form of human inhabitation on the planet.

The San Francisco Bay Area's population grew from 4.6 to 5.2 million between 1970 and 1980, and is around 5.8 million at present. About 6.5 million people are expected to live in the region by the year 2000. That means that the rate of population increase in only 30 years will have been more than an astonishing 40%.

But while the size and number of cities is growing so drastically, there hasn't been an appropriate-

New York Green City Program

A more recent Green City Program has come forward in New York. The New York effort is in the form of a platform for action which is put out by *Environment 89*—a coalition of eighteen local groups such as the Environmental Action Coalition, the Green Guerillas, Neighborhood Open Spaces Coalition, and Transportation Alternatives. The program of Environment 89 is also endorsed by a further 115 New York groups.

The Program for the Future of New York is summarized in a one page pamphlet. The seven points of the New York environmental platform, offered as a "blueprint for debate about our common future," are reproduced from the pamphlet below.

This program has multiple applications. In 1989 it was used to lobby and influence politicians running for office, was part of the ongoing action orientation of New York environmental groups, and was also a guide for a major New York Green City conference in the Spring of 1990.

THE CITY MUST PROTECT AND EXPAND ITS PARKS, GARDENS AND OPEN SPACES

• acquire for the Parks Department privately owned natural sites in city and any city-owned natural sites not in Park Department
• create a continuously accessible, public waterfront
• build esplanades and greenways that link major park systems
• widen sidewalks where possible and plant trees in all neighborhoods
• protect and expand community gardens
• manage natural sites to provide habitats for wildlife and native plants
• provide convenient open spaces for farmers' markets to encourage a regional food system
• raise operating park budget from current fiscal crisis level to at least one per cent of total city budget
• make city planning criteria of 2.5 acres

ly direct change in the way people live in them. City-dwelling is still imagined as a special and privileged condition that is supported by a surrounding hinterland with rural workers to provide necessities. The fact that city living is now the norm for the vast majority of North Americans hasn't really penetrated popular awareness. The vast scale of ecological damage that is directly attributable to the ways cities presently function (for instance, roughly 40% of the non-agricultural pollution of San Francisco Bay is simply the result of run-off from city streets) still isn't fully recognized. The demands for resources that cities make on their own bioregions as well as on faraway locations are becoming hundreds of times greater while means to supply them are drying up, but this urgently important issue still hasn't had an impact on the core of municipal policy-making.

There needs to be a profound shift in the fundamental premises and activities of city living. Urban people have to adopt conserver values and carry out more responsible practices in wide areas of daily life. Municipal governments need to restructure their priorities so that long-term sustainability can become a feasible goal. With such a large portion of the population removed from the land and from access to resources, ways to secure some share of the basic requirements of food, water, energy and materials will have to be found within the confines of cities.

Cities need to become "green." They must be transformed into places that are life-enhancing and regenerative.

*

There are dozens of sustainability-oriented groups in the Bay Area who, taken together, represent a sizable reservoir of good ideas and willing hands. Planet Drum Foundation has brought together representatives of these groups to develop proposals for an over-arching program of changes that could be supported by the general public in order to prevent further deterioration of the region and lead in the direction of greater

---

per 1,000 people a reality
• press for stronger State and Federal support of their NYC sites and activities.

NEW YORKERS MUST HAVE CLEAN, HEALTHFUL AIR TO BREATHE

• implement controls needed to meet federal standards for minimally healthy air
• change transportation, development and land use policies to cut auto use dramatically
• encourage use of mass transit, bicycles and walking; limit official car and parking privileges
• close down antiquated apartment incinerators and phase out dependency on city incinerators
• expand testing program for less polluting fuels and begin purchasing alternate-fueled vehicles to reduce emissions from buses and other moving sources
• retain low-sulfur fuel requirements to reduce pollution from power plants and heating systems of buildings and reduce pollution from industrial sources
• renew multi-billion dollar program to buy new subway cars and buses and rebuild system in 1991
• hold bus/subway fares at one dollar to encourage ridership
• plant trees and maintain existing ones to reduce carbon dioxide levels as part of Global ReLeaf effort to lessen greenhouse effect

THE CITY MUST ENSURE ABUNDANT CLEAN, HEALTHFUL WATER

• practice water conservation: upgrade infrastructure, improve and enforce building codes, mandate low flow fixtures, speed up metering, and increase water conservation education
• enforce laws, like the Federal Clean Water and Coastal Zone Management Acts, to preserve and protect rivers, wetlands, waterfronts, and coastal waters for public open space and water dependent uses
• safeguard city watersheds: purchase development rights solely for watershed protection, acquire land, and vigorously use watershed regulation authority
• halt city schemes for non-water-dependent development in the water that are environmentally unsound, including the use of landfill, platforms or floating structures
• create city policy to test for lead in water and begin to remove lead pipes when hazards are identified

self-reliance.

A series of "Green City" meetings, held at San Francisco's Fort Mason Center in 1986, brought together groups and individuals from specific fields of interest who were asked to contribute suggestions and visions. Over 150 representatives attended in person and an equal number added recommendations to written reports of the sessions. The range of participants was usually much broader than any one of them would have predicted, and for most it was a first opportunity to meet their fellow "greeners." At the Recycling and Re-use meeting, for instance, there were not only representatives of some city and county recycling agencies but also a well-rounded showing from private re-use businesses, citizen groups opposed to waste, youth employment agencies, and professional scavenger companies. The Urban Wild Habitat meeting was one of the largest and included nature society members, urban gardeners, defenders of open space, native plant experts, animal-tenders, teachers, environmental

writers, the founder of the citizens' group that helped secure the Golden Gate National Recreation Area and even the director of Golden Gate Park. Other meetings were held on the subjects of transportation, urban planting, renewable energy, neighborhood character and empowerment, small businesses and cooperatives, sustainable planning, and celebrating life-place vitality.

Each session began with a description of the current situation from each participant's point of view. Not surprisingly, these accounts portrayed more dismal overall conditions than are usually acknowledged in political rhetoric. Renewable energy advocates complained of no significant gains in using alternatives to fossil fuels since oil resumed a low price in the late 1970s. Neighborhood representatives related how high-rises and chain stores are crowding out the last remnants of unique small businesses and block-scaled social and family life. Community gardeners spoke of losing land to developers because city governments lacked the will to protect it or ensure the

THE CITY MUST CONSERVE ENERGY

• promote co-generation and conservation-oriented utility pricing
• retrofit offices and homes for energy efficiency and renewable energy sources
• improve mass transit, bicycling and walking, while eliminating commuter toll discounts and parking subsidies
• plant trees to cool city
• amend zoning and building codes to encourage use of natural ventilation and daylight, prohibit sealed buildings, and include energy conservation

THE CITY MUST BE RESPONSIBLE FOR ITS GARBAGE, SEWAGE AND TOXIC WASTES

• recycling everything physically possible (60-85%) by 2005; reduce and clean waste stream by limiting such materials as non-recyclable packaging, styrofoams, batteries, tires and household toxics; and then dispose of whatever residue remains in the most environmentally benign way
• set up exchange facilities for reusable trash
• build holding tanks to contain sewer over-

flow during storms, rebuild sewers to curb beach wash-ups, develop new policies for sewage overflow problems
• use new sewage treament funds to reduce pollution rather than build new infrastructure for inappropriate development
• reduce toxics in sludge to use as compost to improve soil
• enforce federal, state, and local "right-to-know" laws for work places and industries
• help residents get low-interest loans to remove damaged asbestos
• require industry to improve pretreatment of waste, and hospitals and other medical facilities to dispose safely of their toxic medical garbage
• clean up hazardous waste sites

THE CITY MUST ENSURE ENVIRONMENTALLY SOUND DEVELOPMENT

• plan development based on the carrying capacity of natural systems, the city's infrastructure, and needs for a livable city
• require disclosure of environmental permit requirements at the beginning (not end) of development process, and insist on full compliance with the laws and environmental goals that underlie them

acquisition of substitute space. Sustainable planning proponents detailed the failure of residents' influence on growth-dominated municipal planning processes. Transportation analysts unhappily forecast a doubling of the capacity of existing freeways and even the addition of another deck to the Golden Gate Bridge unless people began using alternatives to automobiles.

Next the attendees were asked what alternatives were possible, at which point the outlook brightened considerably. Practical examples of many positive choices already exist in communities scattered throughout the Bay Area. If all of the potential alternatives were happening at optimum levels in every city and town, the decline of the region could be halted and actually turned around.

*

A Green City Program for San Francisco Bay Area Cities and Towns is a full account of all the areas of sustainability that were covered in the meetings.

The real heart of the Green City Program lies in the question, "What can cities do to promote...?" Here the values and practices of a new kind of urban resident are matched with needed alterations in municipal policies to create a more livable future. Transforming the outlooks of people alone won't be enough to do the job; there must also be changes in city administrations to reflect self-reliant values. Cities and towns that are serious about sustainability can carry out significant large-scale public projects (refitting all municipal buildings to use some form of renewable energy, for instance) while also encouraging extra-governmental changes.

The popular will that can move governments in this direction can be generated through activist groups who organize Green City programs for their own communities. Invitations to join the program's planning process shouldn't be restricted to previously active veterans, but should include a wide range of interested people. These

---

• strengthen planning capacity and responsibility of local Community Boards by providing staff, technical assistance, and access to information

• reinstate a Comprehensive Planning Process supported by environmental groups and citizens that mandates least environmentally damaging alternatives for meeting city-wide needs and then equitably site remaining necessary projects where they do least harm

• mandate full disclosure and analysis of all public subsidies for development as integral components of environmental impact analysis

• require careful analysis and disclosure of all impacts from development; shape development to avoid harmful environmental impacts, including displacement of residents and businesses, shadows and wind created by new buildings, loss of open space, increased pollution, and impact on resources needed to achieve environmental goals

• limit building heights in and adjacent to parks and historic districts

THE CITY MUST PROVIDE ENVIRONMENTAL EDUCATION FOR ALL AGE LEVELS

• urge the New York City Board of Education to establish strong environmental education policy, including the appointment of a full-time Environmental Education Coordinator

• conduct intensive media campaigns about NYC environmental problems and programs, increase environmental coverage on WNYC and WNYE, negotiate with cable TV companies for city-wide channel to monitor city's ecology

• help schools acquire or use natural sites for outdoor nature study and gardens and provide school camping sites within the city

• provide innovative, informal environmental education for adults through workshops conducted by city departments with environmental responsibilities; provide environmental information for non-English speaking New Yorkers

• train teachers to teach about the city environment in a multi- disciplinary manner

(First published in **City Magazine**, *Vol. 11, No. 1, Summer/Fall, 1989.)*

days, most individuals, citizen organizations, businesses and labor groups are aware of urban decline and care strongly about some aspects of sustainability. Under a Green City umbrella, they can begin to care about all of them.

Green City groups can develop a platform for change that is most appropriate for their particular city or town. Once a platform is made public, it will become a powerful tool for influencing boards of supervisors, town councils, elected officials and candidates for office. (How can they explain *not* endorsing a Green City?) Local initiatives and bond issues could be drafted so that voters would have an opportunity to show their support and approve carrying out specific proposals. Eventually, Green City groups could link together to carry out bioregion-wide initiatives that aren't currently possible because of the separation of county jurisdictions.

The San Francisco Bay Area has been a leader in arousing ecological consciousness. Its residents have rallied to preserve natural features and oppose despoilation of the earth in ways that inspire people in the rest of North America and throughout the world. If we will now begin to establish well-rooted Green City programs, by the twenty-first century we can create a model that will save this great Pacific Basin life-place and show a positive direction that others can follow to rescue their part of the planet.

(From **A Green City Program**, by **Peter Berg, Beryl Magilavy, Seth Zuckerman**. San Francisco: Planet Drum Books, 1989.)

Mandala by Rob Messick.

On Permaculture And Community

The organic farming movement is part of the new revolution in self-sufficiency in country and town. The global village community is in the throes of its formative years, and should produce, over the next decade, the most remarkable revolution in thought, values, and technology that has yet been evolved.

I see no other solution (political, economic) to global problems than the formation of small responsible communities involved in permaculture and appropriate technology, for both individual and competitive enterprise and "free" energy have failed us. Society is in a mess; obesity in the west is balanced by famine in the third world. Petrol is running out, and yet freeways are still being built. Against such universal insanity the only response is to gather together a few friends and commence to build the alternative, on a philosophy of individual responsibility for community survival.

I believe that the days of centralized power are numbered, and that a re-tribalization of society is an inevitable, if sometimes painful process. The applied theories of politics, economics and industry have made a sick society; it is time for new approaches. We live in the post-industrial world, and have an immense amount of sophisticated information and technology which enables us to exchange information while living in a village situation. Permaculture is a basic technique for such an evolution, and like all biological, wholistic systems, is within the reach of every person.

Permaculture both conserves and generates the fuel energies of transport systems, and would enable any community to exist comfortably on very restricted land areas. Supplemented with the appropriate and available technologies of methane and alcohol fuels, dry distillation processes, and wind, wave, water or solar energies, it would provide the basis of a sustainable and regionalized society. Combined with community cooperation, permaculture promises freedom from many of the ills that plague us, and accepts all the organic wastes of the community it serves.

Thus, a permaculture system integrated with human settlement provides an inexhaustible energy system, fueled by the sun and developed by the community.

In moving towards such a safe society, all we have to fear is fear, for in the end the only security lies within ourselves, the only safety in having friends, good neighbours, and a meaningful society.

— **Bill Mollison**, *from* **Permaculture Two: Practical Design for Town & Country In Permanent Agriculture**, *Tasmania: Tagari Books, 1979.*

TO LEARN THE THINGS WE NEED TO KNOW: Engaging the Particulars of the Planet's Recovery

Freeman House

The Mattole River runs coastwise south to north for 64 miles through a wrinkle in the North American crust formed as the Pacific plate collides with it and dives, pushing up the King Range. Just to the north is Cape Mendocino, California's westernmost point, where the Japanese and California ocean currents meet. Under the sea near the mouth of the Mattole, three fault lines meet to form the Triple Junction, the most seismically active spot in the state. The coast road from San Francisco to Portland takes a major detour around this rough terrain; it's an hour from any major highway to most parts of the Mattole. Redwoods grow in its fog-washed headwaters, a rich mixture of Douglas fir and hardwoods elsewhere. Of the 2000 or so people living here now, some two-thirds of them have migrated here in the last twenty years as large sheep and cattle ranches have been subdivided into homesteads.

In the late seventies, a few people began to observe that the native Mattole king salmon population was diminishing in an alarming way. In recent memory it had been the local custom to gather the few large fish it took to make a winter's supply from a migration that arrived each November and December in seemingly limitless numbers. Now only the hardiest of outlaws was gaining occasional protein this way. The Mattole run was one of the last purely native "races" of salmon in California, largely because the river was so remote that the state Department of Fish and Game (DFG) had never gotten around to stocking it with hatchery fish. Salmon runs play a large and dramatic part of the spectacle of life in valleys where salmon run. Their value as food only begins to justify the depth of feeling that some people have for them. People who wouldn't dream of eating them get moon- eyed at spawning time and will sit quietly in a drizzle for longer than is reasonable in order to see one jump. It became vitally important to some people in the Mattole valley to attempt to reverse the decline. It was important in terms of maintaining this most visible celebration of the mosaic of wild life in the valley, and it was important to maintain this remnant of genetic diversity for the health of all Pacific salmon. The creature response was to take it on, to attempt to puzzle it through, to learn whatever needs to be learned in order for the people who lived in the valley to do what was necessary to make the king salmon population viable once more.

The few people who undertook this challenge made up for their small numbers with a large name—the Mattole Watershed Salmon Support Group. They were flying in the face of the common wisdom of the time, which was laced with despair. In the two decades between 1950 and 1970, something more than three quarters of the Douglas fir and redwood trees which held the slopes in place had been cut for timber. A disastrous amount of bare soil had been exposed to a disastrous amount of rainfall. Starting in the flood year of 1955, huge amounts of hillside began to slide into the river system, a process which continues as much as twenty-five years after the original disturbance, as root wads rot and cease to lend their tensile strength to steep slopes. Deep pools and channels in the river had filled up with silt; the river jumped its banks, taking out whole stands of riparian growth which had shaded and cooled the water.

The clean gravels that salmon require for spawning and the deep pools the young fish needed to grow in were gone, and anyone with eyes for it could see the destruction in the new broad and cobbled floodplains where farmland had been in the lower stretches of the river. This was the source of the despair: the processes that had been cut loose by the too-rapid deforestation of the basin were apparently too huge to be engaged by humans with fragile limbs and frugal means. Most people were willing to ride out their assumption that nothing much could be done. If we were willing to make fools of ourselves, we would be given the opportunity, but not much else.

The salmon group worked from the assumption that no one was better positioned to take on the challenge than the people who inhabited the place. Who else had the special and place-specific information that the locals had? Who else could ever be expected to care enough to work the sporadic hours at odd times of the night and day for little or no pay?

Working symptomatically, we discovered a low-tech decentralized tool in the streamside incubator used previously in British Columbia and Alaska, which treated the problem of silted-in gravels by imitating the ideal natural situation. These incubator systems—or hatchboxes, as we were quick to call them—fed filtered water from the client creek through select clean gravels in a box the size of a pickup truck toolbox and were located in a creek-neighbor's yard. Cheap to build, without moving parts or external sources of power required, the hatchboxes proved to be relatively trouble free. They could accomodate as many as 30,000 fertilized eggs and consistently deliver a better than 80% egg- to-fry survival rate—compared to less than 15% survival in the mud-stricken river.

If we were to maintain the native adaptations of the populations we were hoping to enhance, we would have to take our eggs from native stock in the wild, rather than accept eggs from another watershed or from homogenized hatchery stock. It was around this idea that we first began to encounter official resistance to the notion of locals and non-professionals dealing directly with nature. It was difficult for DFG to break precedent and allow non-licensed civilians to put a net or a trap in fresh water, a procedure heretofore strictly forbidden to non-agency personnel; and even more difficult for some (but not all) agency-employed biologists to accept the possibility that non-credentialed locals might be able to handle some of the field work that had been their province only. There was one point in our negotiations when one of the more stiff-necked wildlife managers was insisting that we needed a fisheries biologist to drive any truck transporting live fish. Our quest for legitimacy finally took us to the office of then Secretary for California Resources, Huey Johnson. Huey took a chance on us. A year and a half after we had first approached the state, we were ready to put away our briefcases and put on chestwaders.

When they leave the Mattole for the open sea in the late spring or early summer of their first year, it takes as many as 200 king salmon to make up a pound of salmon flesh. When they return as adults after spending three to five years in the Pacific, one fish often exceeds twenty pounds and an occasional one may approach forty pounds of muscle, will, and utterly exotic intelligence. We had arrived at an agreement with the state which allowed us to capture twenty female salmon, each one carrying three to five thousand eggs, and enough males to fertilize them. The spawners run up river in mid-winter, preferring the obscurity of muddied, rising water, the obscurity of night. A trap and weir close off the river, but only temporarily. Once the waters rise to a certain point, the structures must be moved out of the channel or they will be washed away. Once trapped, the salmon must be moved to safety and held until the eggs are ripe and ready for fertilization.

To enter the river and attempt to bring this strong creature out of its own medium alive and uninjured is an opportunity to experience a momentary parity between human and salmon, mediated by slippery rocks and swift currents. Vivid experiences between species can put a crack in the resilient veneer of the perception of human dominance over other creatures. Information then begins to flow in both directions, and we gain the ability to learn: from salmon, from the landscape itself.

The first thing we learned from salmon was the importance of the watershed as a unit of perception. If salmon organize themselves so clearly by watershed, wouldn't it make sense for us to organize our efforts similarly? Salmon are not only creatures of unique watersheds, adapted so that

Watersheds

Spring, seep, or glacier, creek, stream, river or "kicking horse" blasting to the sea, deep pools underground, marsh, estuary, confluence, delta or tide-flat, lake, sound, inland sea and the ocean deeps—these are only some of the many faces of the waters.

One's watershed address is crucial because the waters give life to the land. Reacquaint yourself with your local stream or river--often it's like going back in time, to the forgotten part of town. Fish or run your river, find the headwaters, hike the divide, follow its life-course through the valley, sail the bay....

In orienting each other toward your common watershed address, the basic question is: which way do the waters flow? For watershed both joins and divides the rainfall, snow, and runoff, establishes directions, apportions the waters, and reveals the basic lay of the land.

Watershed provides a significant frame of reference because it represents a whole and distinct life-context. From high edges to low centers, there are many linked habitats and evolving communities. In Ish River bioregion, for instance, there are many different habitats: salt water (surface and deep), salt-fresh estuaries, beaches of different types (sand, mud, or cobble, exposed or protected), floodplains large and small, thick lowland forests unique in the world, prairies, plateaus, highland forests, alpine communities, and so on, many of which are differentiated one from another by localized differences in topog-

generation after generation responds to the timing and flow of utterly specific rivers and tributaries—but they are also dependent on watershed processes in general. During their reproductive time in fresh water, salmon live at the top of the aquatic food chain, but at the bottom, so to speak, of fluvial and geological processes. The success of incubation depends on the availability of river bottom gravels free of fine sediments. The survival of juveniles depends on the presence of cold deep pools cut down to bedrock.

In the Pacific Coast Range, new mountains are still rising out of the ocean bottom at the rate of two to four meters per millenium, and the soft sea silts have rarely had time to metamorphose into competent rock which might stay in place against the winter storms which are washing most of the uplift back to sea. A ten year storm combined with any one of the frequent earthquakes which informs this coast can cause a landslide which will change the course of the river and alter the pattern of salmon reproduction for several human generations. Combine these conditions of the fundament with a ranching technology that requires a few hundred feet of dirt road for every head of stock; with a timber economy that makes it cheapest to build a road to every tree and remove all vegetation from the slopes; with a homestead ethic that can rationalize miles of benchcut road to protect the privacy of each and every American home, and you have a recipe for the kind of catastrophic impacts we were observing.

To nurture the health and natural provision of the wild salmon population, the salmon were telling us, we were going to have to understand them as an integral part of the habitat, and that habitat extends all the way to the ridgelines above us, and includes the human settlements. In order to address the aquatic habitat, we would need to keep the topsoils on the slopes where they could grow forests and rangeland ecosystems, meat and vegetables, and out of the streams, where they killed fish. We would need to attempt to reduce the amount of silt entering the riverine system each year to below the amount which winter flows were able to flush out. Above all, as humans, we needed to learn to take our meat and wood in ways that didn't cancel out the potential for natural provision and other relationships within our own habitat. Finally, the salmon were telling us, what was good for them was good for us. Both species benefit from healthy watersheds and an extended sense of commonality. "Ladies and gentlemen," they were saying, "please, let's get serious about this business of coevolution."

Bioregionally, there might be a number of ways to define "your" part of the planet—physiographic areas, the ranges of species of plants and animals, climatic zones, human language groups. In terms of psychological comfort, scale and appropriateness enter into the equation. Efforts to define and embrace ecological responsibilities, either in individual or social terms, can be most successfully undertaken in the context of specific places. The human organism demands, finally, that its intuitions and ideas become embodied through physical perception, and the landscape surrounding generally offers us our only proof of our immersion in biospheric life. In our case, the range and requirements of a particular race of salmon had defined a context for our efforts, and the 306-square-mile watershed of the Mattole offered a scale in the range of the possible. If the experience of the whole place remained beyond the perception and understanding of any one person, the drainage divided itself into more than sixty tributaries, many of which were home to groups or individuals interested in the demands of stewardship, and interested too in the possibilities of an identity extended beyond parcel boundaries.

The attempt to engage ourselves with a salmon run shifted almost at once from a symptomatic, technical-mechanical approach to a systemic, multi-leveled, ecological approach. Focusing on the crisis of another species had boomeranged into the need to take a close look at our own social organizations and economic activities. This latter was no new insight, of course. The same conclusions had been reached by everyone from the United Nations to Earth First! The difference was the conviction that, through engaging the fundamental processes of a particular place, we might discover the appropriate models for our own activities and organization. Adopting the conceit that our restoration and enhancement projects would hasten the process of watershed recovery, those same projects might be the very means by which we learned what we needed to know in order to live integrated lives in living places.

What easy rhetoric! What facile promises! The long list of skills required for the task quickly turned our leap of consciousness into a scramble for data. But to my surprise and pleasure, much of the expertise we thought we lacked would be found among the two thousand plus people already living in the watershed. Some of my fondest memories are of whole days spent once a month by twelve to twenty people, training ourselves for the initial job of inventorying salmonid habitat.

A consulting biologist living on Blue Slide Creek gave us lectures on Odumesque energy budgets that were full of sunlight, nearly understandable, and wholly inspirational. A self-trained naturalist gave us descriptions of mychorrizal relationships so rhapsodic that some of us fell in love. When the information we needed wasn't available in the neighborhood, we never had to go far to find a helpful technician: biologists from the

---

raphy, aspect (sunlight or shade), microclimates, soil types, and, above all, the way in which the waters flow through. Feel the river systems as veins pulsing in your hands, arms, legs, the land circulating its life through you.

Human habitation, too, largely depends on rivers, floodplains, deltas and estuaries. Agriculture on precious alluvium or loess (like the Palouse); ports are trans-shipment points; cities and core regions at major confluences of regional rivers, and so on.

Watercourses also sculpt the land, inscribe a special history into the face of the landscape itself. Landforms and water courses go together. If rivers are knives, then glaciers are plows. River means "to rive" as well as to run, to cut down into, incise the landscape's own memory into its living face. Water in all its forms carves out the curved face of the land, gives it character. Character is how we are carved out by the world, how we come to a consistent form of action.

Imagine rivers as the current between mountains, sea, and sky. Watersheds thus represent not only a unity of landscapes from high edges to low centers, but also a temporal wholeness as well- -the hydrological cycle. Rivers serve as that part of the continuous air-ocean-sky-earth-air recycling of the waters above and below—the great hydrological cycle which medievals saw as emblematic of "the wisdom of God"—most apparent to us. The waters in all their forms and phases represent the gift of life as a series of transformations or "give-aways." Water cycles are the very symbol of the intricate crossings of this earth and that sky.

— **David McCloskey**, from "Coming Home: On Naming and Claiming your Bioregion," 1986.

DFG, a geomorphologist from the Forest Service, and most especially geologists and hydrologists from Redwood National Park, that planet-class laboratory in landscape rehabilitation only a hundred miles away. The agencies proved rich in this kind of talent, and were sometimes cooperative to the point of dipping into small public relations budgets to send their people our way during working hours. Often, too, the scientists showed up on weekends, anxious to share and test their ideas in the field.

Most of the skills we needed were gained more by experience than training or education. For all the headiness of ecological relationships and hydrological theories, for all the stretched mental landscapes of geological time, when it comes right down to engaging watershed recovery processes, you'll most often find yourself with a shovel in your hand or in conversation with a backhoe operator. The great days of the worker-owned tree-planting co-ops were past, diminished by hostile legislation, but some of the workers were still around, and no one is better fitted to organize a large-scale treeplanting or to take on the risks and intricacies of a government planting contract.

As the physical effort grew, with crews engaging in salmon enhancement and habitat repair and erosion control and reforestation, the need arose for a new sort of organization based on watershed priorities. This structure would need, on one level, to serve the interests of various factions among the human community interested in engaging recovery, including groups organized around specific tributaries, groups organized around jobs, land trusts, and schools and civic groups devoted only peripherally to land-based issues. The larger need, however, was to invent a process for developing a shared perception of the real ecological parameters of the riverine watershed, to make long range plans, to make consensual decisions about projects and, increasingly, to take positions on complex issues.

Which should be approached first—the accumulated sediments choking the estuary, or the new sediments being introduced upstream?

(*Answer so far: both.*)

If habitat recovery can't be monitored, how many additional fish should we be introducing?

(*As many as we can without violating our general guideline of closely imitating natural processes.*)

Knowing that less than ten percent of the original forest complex remains uncut, should we

risk assuming a high moral ground we have no way of implementing? Call for a moratorium on the logging of ancient forests and risk alienating the largest private landowners in the watershed?

(*Yes.*)

The Mattole Restoration Council was formed to serve these ends, a consensual council with thirteen member groups at this writing. Monthly meetings rarely manage to remain serene deliberations on the ecological parameters of the basin, however. The Council has, over the years, arrived at a position which recognizes the need for localized ecological reserves, based on the perception that genetic diversity is more site-specific than is generally assumed, and on the exact knowledge of how little of the original forest and range complex is left. At the same time, the Council embraces a vision of the most desirable future wherein productive lands stay in production: forests continuing to produce timber and fisheries, rangeland continuing to provide forage, stabilized agricultural lands producing farm products.

The need for reserves outrages industrial timberland owners, and the desire for an economically productive landbase over which local residents maintain some control makes environmentalists jumpy. Often the Council finds itself in the ambivalent position of monitoring and resisting the tendency of industry and government agencies to harvest every mature tree at the same time that it is participating in a statewide attempt to invent a set of sustainable and restorative forest practices. Either one of these processes will eat up a lot of volunteer time, and they present themselves over and above the Council's stated goals of supporting a certain level of active rehabilitation work, of attempting to meet contract deadlines and, importantly, of developing and distributing the baseline information we need if we are to engage our watershed in a manner which restores it to previous levels of health and productivity.

The process of researching the biotic and geological realities of natural places is likely to surprise anyone undertaking it for the first time. Our own experience has led us to describe watersheds and other natural areas as unclaimed territories, so sketchily are they documented. When the DFG first opened its files to us in 1980, we were disappointed to find how scanty the salmonid habitat data for the Mattole River was, but not surprised once we came to the realization that two counties with a combined area the size of Delaware were being monitored by a single biologist. But if we were to approach the restoration of native salmon populations in any sort of systematic manner, we would have to do it without historical baseline data, and in order to understand the current situation we would need to generate the data ourselves. Later, when we needed to understand just how much old growth forest remained in the watershed, we encountered a similar situation. Antagonistic theories and counter-theories about how much ancient forest was left were getting a lot of press space, but when we took a closer look, *no-one knew what was out there.* (A little later, the U.S. Forest Service found itself with the same problem.)

In both these cases, we were able to find some support for finding out, and we were faced with the choice of hiring professionals to do the surveys, or to train local residents. Either option would cost out about the same, the added local knowledge balancing out the cost of training amateurs in survey techniques. We went with the locals, reasoning that, as a watershed population, we would have gained an array of skills that had a value beyond the data we would collect.

Even when the information you need is available, it will almost always be in the wrong context if you are filling in the map of a natural area. No wonder so many find themselves alienated from planetary processes when all the information for their part of the planet is filed by township and range, rather than river and mountain. The Mattole watershed, for instance, extends into two counties, two jurisdictions of the DFG, and overlaps with about half of a Bureau of Land Management holding. Research the distribution of a species and you'll find it laid out for the state of California, in an amalgam of ranges and townships, rather than intertwining complex of habitats. Try to find out who lives in the Honeydew Creek drainage. You'll find the owners listed alphabetically, rather than by where they live. And so on.

By spending the time to reorganize biotic, geologic, and demographic information into a watershed context, we are ritually reanimating a real place that had become totally abstracted. Our maps of salmonid habitat, of old growth distribution, of timber harvest history and erosion sites, of rehabilitation work, our creek addresses for watershed residents, become, when distributed by mail to all inhabitants, the self-expression of a living place.

*

The hatchbox program is entering its tenth year, and it has not been the quick fix our early naivete allowed us to hope for. The salmon population turned out to be even more diminished than we had guessed. If we aren't yet able to put a number on the volume of Mattole topsoil that is delivered to the Pacific each year, we do know where it's coming from, and where in the river it is tending to settle out, jamming up biological and hydrological processes. Thousands of trees have been planted, thousands of tons of rock moved to armor gullies and streambanks. A whole generation of elementary school kids has released a lot of salmon into the wild as part of each of their eight school years. Some of those kids have gone on to attend a recently established watershed-based high school where they learn, among other things, local appropriate land use techniques. There is no end in sight, but the prospect is now one of ever-deepening experience, rather than one of ever-diminishing possibilities. Our long, slow systematic look at the landscape has revealed the tremendous vigor with which nature heals itself, and some of the wonderful logic and time sense of natural succession is now available to us.

It is part of the process of recovery that we gain a new and deeper perception of home. Before this we lived on parcels, on acreages; now we are invited to live in watersheds and ecosystems, rivers and streams, mountains and valleys. But our emerging identities, fragile and unsure, are bruised and buffeted by forces which reside both within and without our chosen region of effect. The success of state agencies in appearing impermeable; the seeming venality and single-mindedness of industrial resource extractors; the demanding tedium of the court system—together they combine to make a clamoring immediacy which threatens to obscure our purpose (which is transformative) and divert our energies toward the perpetual claims of crisis response.

But it is also part of the process of recovery that we learn the things we need to know to live in places. Our crisis response becomes more effective as we come to know more about our particular places than *they* do. But it is likely that our most important and effective contribution to the solution to the puzzle of humans on the planet will be to develop resource related industries which are *restorative*, which tend to improve air and water quality, biodiversity, and soil fertility, as organic gardening and farming already tend to do. Two examples are emerging in our own Alta California backyard.

Along the northern coast of California, salmon fishing has been a major source of protein and income as long as humans have lived here. By the late 1970s, the combination of a growing fleet and dwindling salmon runs had most fishermen casting about for a new occupation. For the last ten years, the number of small one and two person trollers had kept growing and among the new members of the fleet were younger fishermen who were to become leaders in an exercise in consciousness-raising for the industry. In a very short time, these notoriously independent operators were to learn a new and reciprocal relationship to the resource which would allow them to continue in business.

In the past, the very independence of fishermen had worked against them. As individuals, they tended to be the best and only source of local knowledge about aspects of the salmon life cycle. But as a political entity, fishermen were most likely to do little more than to lobby the government for the least amount of regulation, and to fight the annual fight for the best price they could get for their catch. As the catch decreased each year, the fleet was seized by a mood of deep pessimism. It seemed to many as if the Pacific salmon was doomed to the same sort of depletion as had eliminated the Atlantic salmon as a commercial species. Some argued that no course of action was available but to cut their losses by taking all the fish they could until the fishery was gone.

Nat Bingham had spent a winter on Big River nursing a batch of hatchery eggs through California's first streamside hatchbox, and he had been impressed by the results. Bingham began to argue that if the fishermen would involve themselves in the fate of the freshwater habitats of salmon, in the watersheds critical to the reproduction of the fish, then it might be possible to imagine a sustained fishery.

One by one, local marketing associations began to line up behind Bingham and the other Young Turks, sometimes by margins of no more than one or two votes, to tax themselves toward a fund that would be invested in salmon *enhancement* and habitat repair projects—often run by the fishermen themselves. Today, Nat Bingham has been president of the Pacific Coast Federation of Fishermen's

Associations for seven years; and that group has spearheaded a Salmon Stamp Program which generates in excess of one million dollars per year for salmon enhancement work in California. In 1988, the salmon fleet had its largest catch in over 40 years. A good part of the credit for that must go to small salmon restoration programs conducted up and down the coast by fishermen's groups and watershed groups alike.

In those same watersheds, natural processes are deeply engaged by yet another set of workers, the loggers. If the commercial fishery was able to develop restorative relationships to its work, mightn't the timber industry? The answer, of course, is yes, and always has been. Though seemingly rare, the presence of small- to medium-sized timberland owners managing for sustained yield *and* wildlife and watershed values is as much a constant in the history of timber production as the more noticeable (and widespread) operators who try to translate whole biomes into cash.

One logger on the neighboring Eel River has taken the notion of sustained yield one necessary step further. Jan Iris of Wild Iris Forestry in Briceland, California, starts with land cut over in the last forty years and has as his goal restoring forests to their previous diversity and productivity—steady-state, climax, mixed species Coast Range forest. In the process, it looks like he will be able to make an acceptable income as a timber producer, while rarely harvesting an old growth redwood or Douglas fir, both now rare enough that every harvest is now the object of contention. Since it comes at a time when loggers have lost large numbers of jobs due to automation and stand to lose more if the larger mills fail to retool for smaller trees, this innovation has important implications for a widespread regional economy.

At the edge of the once great temperate rain forests, California Coast Range forests exhibit a wider range of species than their neighbors to the north. The incidence of the valuable redwood and Douglas fir is low compared to the incidence of Coast Range hardwood like tanoak, madrone and chinquapin. The latter woods have rarely found their way to market due to the long term hands-on care required to cure them for lumber. Iris has begun to manage timber for small landholders by selecting mature hardwoods and harvesting them in such a way as to release the young conifers which have been kept small by the shade of the great hardwoods. Second and third generations of hardwood trees are also left in situations where they will growth straighter and more quickly than if harvest had not occurred. There follows a two year curing process capped off by a period in a climate- controlled kiln which represents the largest part of Wild Iris's capital outlay. The Wild Iris has had to endure a couple of lean years, but has found a demand for their product which exceeds their rate of production. Now local building-supply operator Bob McKee has invested in a six-headed molding machine and has begun to mill tanoak flooring, another local economic turnover.

Iris can see a future with "an operator up each little watershed" with restorative practices as their goal and their reward. "It doesn't always have to be cut, cut, cut, chop, chop, chop. You may cut trees in the morning and do stream rehab in the afternoon. A lot of things need to be done."

What is striking about these innovators is not so much that they gained their analysis and inspiration from personal engagement in restoration work—although that is the heart of my argument for environmental restoration as a transformative process for humans. (Iris gained his insight into the relationship between silviculture and soil erosion through time spent in stream rehabilitation work in the seventies.) More importantly, these are clear models, right in our midst, of ecological restoration translated into cultural and economic sustainability.

*

It is inevitable, for several reasons, that ecological restoration will take its place on the national agenda of the United States. The very flesh and blood of evolution, which is wild ecosystems, may already be so severely diminished that the evolution of large plants and animals can no longer proceed. Most experts agree that this potential exists; biologists Michael Soulé and O.H. Frankel claim we have already reached this point. By the time that experts agree as to how much habitat is enough habitat, it is likely that restoration of wild systems will have become not only an appropriate human activity, but an essential one.

This nation has never given much credence to the appropriate, but is very good at responding to threats. To the degree that ecological restoration is interpreted as a matter of survival, to that degree the U.S. will respond. In that this time-frame coincides with a time when there will be no undisturbed habitats left to isolate and preserve, this effort must spill over into "resource areas," human-occupied, which make up over three quarters of the planet.

There is no tradition of extended liability for ecological damages. The historical perpetrators are not going to be hunted down and fined. Rural areas will not be able to generate the funds necessary to restore themselves and will always need to appeal to one public agency or another. There will be more Superfunds. But if a national effort at ecological restoration is considered in the context of cultural transformation (and as a pathway to it), it may be possible to limit public costs to a single generation or less, by which time restorative economies should have begun to pay for themselves and consumer appetites will have begun to adjust themselves to biospheric realities.

The people want it and the talent is available. There is an enormous psychic need on the part of North Americans to engage their continent once more, physically and culturally, evinced on the one hand by a surprising explosion in the sales of stuff like backpacks, hang gliders, canoes, scuba gear, and mountain bikes; and, more to the point, by a proliferation of in-place grassroots restoration groups. The Hudson River. Papago reservations in the deepest Sonoran desert. Inner-city kids working on weekends to find rare prairie grass specimens in Chicago vacant lots. The Land Institute in Kansas blurring forever the distinction between prairie restoration and appropriate agriculture. Make a list of your own.

At the same time, a body of expertise is growing willy-nilly at the leading edges of what used to be called the life sciences. Loosely organized around the banner of conservation biology, more and more young scientists are dedicating themselves to the maintenance and restoration of specific ecological systems. The science of ecological restoration is less than fifty years old and has for most of that time been a study conducted in reserves isolated from human habitation, but not from the wind and water- borne effects of the surrounding human economies, nor from the wild phenomena of animal migration, distribution of seed from exotic sources, and occasional human predation. Rallied by papers such as those found in the two volumes of *Conservation Biology* (Soulé and Wilcox 1981, Soulé 1986) and by iconoclasts in the field like Daniel Janze, academic and field scientists have begun to organize themselves around pro-active groups like Conservation International (established 1987) and professional groups like the Society for Ecological Restoration (established 1989). This movement recognizes the need for the application of the principles of ecological restoration to the agro-ecosystems, but has made little systematic effort to ally themselves with the multitudinous grassroots organizations who need its expertise.

It is an indication of the environmental movement feeling its way toward ecological activism that some of its most effective leaders are advocating ecological restoration as a national undertaking. With surprising consistency, one hears a misspent military budget proposed as a source of funding, and the Civilian Conservation Corps (CCC) of the thirties as a model of organization. It is appropriate to demand a piece of the military budget for the job—both to give credence to the enormity of the task, and as recognition of the true nature of security. But the use of the CCC as a model is inappropriate. The CCC was raised as a response to massive unemployment during the depression and activities were selected, in part, for their non-controversial nature—treeplanting, building park infrastructures, firefighting. Large numbers of workers were moved great distances.

The use of CCC as a model for the current discussion gives rise to the likelihood of seeing the unemployed of Michigan and Louisiana put to work restoring natural systems in northern California, thus ignoring the potential of restoration work to teach local inhabitants the things they need to know to live integrated lives. If the nation embraces a massive effort in ecological restoration which disregards its potential for social transformation, then, no matter how many trees are planted, species enhanced, or people employed, it will have missed its real goals.

One clear function of any ecological restoration movement is to treat symptoms of habitat decline which are "other" than human, i.e., diminution of species and genetic diversity, deforestation, soil erosion. I am arguing that an equally important goal of any restoration movement is to provide individuals and inhabitants the clear experience of themselves as functionally benign parts of living systems. The cumulative effect of these experiences is the transformation of social and economic institutions. As the true nature of environmental decline becomes apparent to more and more people, the desire for social transformation will become more widespread. In the best of all possible worlds, governments will attempt to serve these desires.

Thinking about national approaches to ecological restoration can be seen as an opportunity to broaden the scope of our search for organizational models. One good place to search is in the organization of nature itself. I would like to suggest three principles which we might keep in mind as the mandate to engage in recovery grows:

1. *Approach the planet as the planet reveals itself.* Ecological restoration must be approached contextually, bioregionally, within the boundaries of natural systems like ecosystems and watersheds. This is a fairly obvious principle sometimes obscured by the fact that we do most political things entirely in the context of abstract political boundaries. The absence of alligators cannot be treated in the state of Washington, nor the need for redwoods served in Arizona.

2. *Human populations of natural areas are necessary participants in local ecological recovery.* Ecological restoration deals with real plants and animals in real time in real places. Real places are not uniform, but break down immediately into a wonderul array of microsystems and microclimates, each of which mediates and modifies tendencies toward eccentric behavior on the part of living things within them. These behaviors are the very expression of recovery, and information about them generally resides nowhere else but in experience of locals. This vernacular science combined with the generalized monuments of legitimate biology, geology, and so on combine to create the most effective (and cost-effective) strategies for site-specific habitat repair. You can't treat the fish population in Bear Creek without knowing its current status. Given only one choice, will you mount a three year study or drop by and visit with the avid fisherman who has lived for fifteen years directly above the banks of Bear Creek?

3. *Natural regions exist in time.* One pass through with a government crew isn't going to do the job. The resident will remain in place after the government has come and gone. If the restoration program has been structured so that problems are defined and decisions made by inhabitants with the counsel of technicians, and if much of the work has been performed by local people, especially young people, then a population will remain whose identity has been extended to include their habitat. They will have the skills to maintain equi-

librium with the changes inherent in natural succession. They will have the will to defend the place against further violations. And they will begin to invent the styles of resource development appropriate to the long range survival of their places, and thus of themselves.

They will have become participants in the planet's recovery.

(First published in **Whole Earth Review**, Winter 1989- 90.)

"Transformation," by Daniel O. Stolpe.

TAKING STEPS TOWARD A RESTORATION ETHIC

Jamie Sayen

"This is the irony of our age: hands-on management is needed to restore hands-off wilderness." — *Reed Noss, landscape ecologist.*

Since there is nowhere enough wilderness to permit the full mystery of evolution to flourish, we, as a culture, must begin the daunting task of restoring vast tracts of damaged land to a condition where they can begin to re-wild themselves. To speak of ecological restoration by humans of ecosystems and species damaged by humans is to speak in paradoxes. Enter at your own risk. Bring a healthy dose of humility and recognize that you are attempting work that only Mother Earth can properly do. Be not deterred by the apparent absurdity of the task. The alternative is the collapse of the biosphere.

The only option left to us is to begin to live by an ethic that 1) preserves all remaining wildlands; 2) opposes all abuses to global and local ecosystems, including "mitigation;" 3) restores, in an ecologically appropriate manner, large tracts of lands that have suffered from human development; 4) restores human culture to natural succession; and 5) aggressively advocates the above points.

The newly-formed Society for Ecological Restoration and Management (SERM) held its first meeting in Oakland in January.... The SERM conference offers hope for a responsible restoration movement. If SERM avoids becoming mired in bureaucracy, it can become a progressive force in the environmental movement.

At the 1988 Restoring The Earth conference, Michael Fisher, Sierra Club executive director, said the "highest priority" of restoration environmentalists is the preservation of the remaining 10% of wilderness on Turtle Island. "Restore the 90%," he said, "but not at the expense of the 10%."

Fisher is rightly concerned that restoration will be used by mitigationists to justify the destruction of the 10%. He also fears that attention to restoration could distract activists from the fight to preserve wildlands....

Preservation and restoration are inseparable. The values at the heart of the preservation movement—the intrinsic value of wildness and biodiversity—are at the heart of an ecologically responsible restoration movement. Preservation is the preventive medicine of restoration....

> "There is no such thing as reforestation.... We can't fix nature.... We can put back pieces and allow nature to heal herself." — Chris Maser, forester.

The search for appropriate restoration techniques leads to the realm of paradox. In *Conservation and Evolution*, O.H. Frankel and M.E. Soulé write of "our abysmal ignorance of biological processes in complex ecosystems." With humility and patience, we can gain insights into the mysteries of nature, but our ignorance remains the dominant factor in our efforts "to save the world."

We must not, however, use ignorance as an excuse for inaction. We must act, but—to avoid the pitfalls of *hubris*—we must act with acknowledgement of our limits. All the restorationist can do is remove the human-created barriers to the natural healing process and guard against the creation of further barriers. As Don Falk, of the Center for Plant Conservation, in Jamaica Plain, Massachusetts, said: "It is ourselves we are trying to manage, not nature."

This attitude rejects the analogy of the ecosystem to a machine. Even a complicated machine can be understood by the human mind. It can be taken apart and reassembled to working order. In contrast, no one can ever fathom the mysteries of natural systems. Numerous conference speakers acknowledged that systems reconstructed by humans are always biologically impoverished relative to similar natural systems, and are always more susceptible to invasions by exotics.

Efforts to recreate or replicate damaged ecosystems can never succeed. Even if we knew all the parts (down to site-specific soil microbes and mycorrhizal fungi), we wouldn't begin to understand the web of relations. Furthermore, an undisturbed system today is quite different from what it was 100 or 1000 years ago. It may have the same appearance, but changes caused by climate, disturbance, succession, adaptation and evolution change it in ways no historian, archeologist or ecologist can ever fully know.

The goal of restoration, therefore, must be natural recovery. Remove the destructive forces; restore as many native species, communities, and functions as possible. Collect data on patterns of species and communities, but don't get bogged down with useless data. Restore natural processes—the spirit of the place--not some static, idealized, pre-settlement condition.

Since the goal of restoration is the health of a system, not merely of any one species, a holistic view is required. Freeman House of the Mattole Restoration Council says his community's effort to restore salmon in the Mattole River revealed that it was not enough to supplement the salmon population, that the whole habitat must be restored.

Though we cannot know exactly what conditions prevailed in ecosystems before they were damaged, we can identify many critical components. Native and exotic species can be identified (the exotics, at least). In his superb "Recipe for Wilderness Recovery" (*Earth First! Journal* 9-86), Reed Noss lists sources helpful in determining pre-settlement conditions: ecological literature, historical narratives and photographs, early land surveys, analysis of sediments and mapping, analysis of packrat middens, and study of old growth remnants and of live and dead plant materials.

At the conference, Gary Nabhan described how analysis of packrat middens has helped identify pre-settlement species for Sonoran desert communities going back 20,000 years. By studying the pollen, insects, and small vertebrate bones found in packrat middens, and comparing this inventory with currently existing species, restorationists can begin to reconstruct elements of pre-settlement conditions. Of course, these inventories will neces-

"Wilderness"

Wilderness is the raw material out of which man has hammered the artifact called civilization.

Wilderness was never a homogeneous raw material. It was very diverse, and the resulting artifacts are very diverse. These differences in the end-product are known as cultures. The rich diversity of the world's cultures reflects a corresponding diversity in the wilds that gave them birth.

For the first time in the history of the human species, two changes are now impending. One is the exhaustion of wilderness in the more habitable portions of the globe. The other is the world-wide hybridization of cultures through modern transport and industrialization....

To the laborer in the sweat of his labor, the raw stuff on his anvil is an adversary to be conquered. So was wilderness an adversary to the pioneer.

But to the laborer in repose, able for the moment to cast a philosophical eye on his world, that same raw stuff is something to be loved and cherished, because it gives definition and meaning to his life.

— **Aldo Leopold**, *from an essay entitled "Wilderness" in* **A Sand County Almanac**.

sarily be incomplete, and often difficult to date with precision....

One of the thorniest problems facing a restorationist is the issue of "exotic" genetic stock. Often, species replanted are native to an area, but the genetic stock is non-native (i.e., has grown in a different environment with different species). Constance Millar, a forest geneticist, gave a talk entitled: "Restoration—Disneyland or Native Ecosystem: Genetic Guidelines for Restoration." Her thesis was that the genetic nature of introduced stock has a profound impact on existing communities.

She explained that Redwood National Park, while still in private ownership, had been aerially reseeded with three native species: Sitka Spruce, Coast Redwood, and Douglas Fir. The seeds had come from Oregon and Washington, and each had been grown in isolation from the other two species. Thus, they were not adapted to the site or the biological conditions of the Park. They were exotics, and the result was the genetic pollution of the native stock. "They were apparently real," she said, "but were not functionally real...."

Disturbance is another critical factor in any restoration effort. Disturbance (a natural process) differs markedly from disruption (from human activity). Chris Maser, noting that humans disrupt natural disturbances, clarified this distinction: "Nature always allows healing. We don't."

When disturbance and disruption are scrambled together, how do we identify the dynamics of the natural disturbance regime for the system under study? How do we reintroduce natural disturbance? How do we restore a natural fire regime? How do we bring in disease?

The issue of disturbance is further complicated by habitat fragmentation and preserves (or restoratation projects) that are too small to survive natural disturbances. The Yellowstone fires revealed that even a large National Park is far too small to absorb the impact of a cataclysm like last summer's fires.

There is pressure on restorationists working with a tiny fragment to minimize disturbance. James MacMahon, a shrublands restorer, observed that "Restorationists tend to prevent at all costs disturbance to their projects." We need more and larger preserves so that we don't feel compelled to control natural disturbance....

Mycorrihizae, or "fungus roots," are critical to the health of soils, plants, and trees. They are espe-

cially important to the survival of transplants. They promote rapid growth and increase drought resistance. They weather mineral grains and extract nutrients for their root hosts. They protect their hosts from pathogens.

Clearcuts and herbicides are death to mycorrhizae, and the fungi recover only very slowly. One cause of tropical rainforest decline is the rapid loss of mycorrhizal fungi after cutting.

Though plants can be grown by artificial means, without mycorrhizae, they become addicts, forever dependent on artificial nutrients. Studies have shown that two plants without mycorrhizal fungi interact very negatively, while plants with "fungus roots" interact very positively. Trees in old growth forests, with root systems linked by mycorrhizae, communicate with each other....

Mycorrhizal fungi may be highly site specific, which would imply that genetic adaptations are more local than previously suspected. If this is true, we must save every microenvironment to save biodiversity.

*

What is the relationship of restorationists to a restoration project? Are we outside the ecosystem, tinkering to repair it? Or are we working to restore human culture into a restored ecosystem? The role of humans in the ecosystem is one of the most divisive issues in the environmental movement.

Despite the malignancy of modern human culture, we are a species related to all other species. The quest to eliminate the malignant elements need not become a mission to eliminate our species. Humans have been a natural part of the system for 99% of our history. Modern human culture, Chris Maser said, is "separating human values from ecological values." Until we have a social, economic and political culture based on a "biologically sustainable system," he said, our crisis will worsen.

Stephanie Kaza suggested that the two challenges facing restorationists are repair work and establishment of a new way of relating to the planet. Without the latter, she said, restoration work is "emergency triage...."

In the introductory chapter to *Conservation Biology: The Science of Scarcity and Diversity*, Michael Soulé writes: "Many of the authors also appear to be suggesting that the perennial reluctance of scientists to discuss matters of ethics may imperil the very organisms and processes they hold most

Wilderness for Science

The most important characteristic of an organism is that capacity for internal self-renewal known as health.

There are two organisms whose processes of self-renewal have been subjected to human interference and control. One of these is man himself (medicine and public health). The other is land (agriculture and conservation).

The effort to control the health of land has not been very successful. It is now generally understood that when soil loses fertility, or washes away faster than it forms, and when water systems exhibit abnormal floods and shortages, the land is sick.

Other derangements are known as facts, but are not yet thought of as symptoms of land sickness. The disappearance of plants and animal species without visible cause, despite efforts to protect them, and the irruption of others as pests despite efforts to control them, must, in the absence of simpler explanations, be regarded as symptoms of sickness in the land organism. Both are occurring too frequently to be dismissed as normal evolutionary events....

In general, the trend of the evidence indicates that in land, just as in the human body, the symptoms may lie in one organ and the cause in another. The practices we now call conservation are, to a large extent, local alleviations of biotic pain. They are necessary, but they must not be confused with cures. The art of land-doctoring is being practiced with vigor, but the science of land health is yet to be born.

A science of land health needs, first of all a base datum of normality, a picture of how healthy land maintains itself as an organism....

The most perfect norm is wilderness.... Paleontology offers abundant evidence that wilderness maintained itself for immensely long periods; that its component species were rarely lost, neither did they get out of hand; that weather and water built soil as fast or faster than it was carried away. Wilderness, then, assumes unexpected importance as a laboratory for the study of land-health."

— **Aldo Leopold**, *from "Wilderness" in* **A Sand County Almanac**.

dear."

In the next two decades we could lose the ability to recover 4000 species in the wild in North America. Over 1000 are critically endangered now. Don Falk said that the fates of over one-fifth of the flora in the U.S. are of concern.

As Jasper Carlton has said, "America is dying." To avert this death, we must work for an Endangered Ecosystem Act, a Biodiversity Act, and a National Biological Preserve System, which system could begin with the lands now mismanaged by the U.S. Forest Service. We must overturn local, state, and federal tax breaks and subsidies for developers.

Finally, we must be guided by an ethic of humility, which acknowledges "our abysmal ignorance." Can-do optimism is a prescription for furthering the destruction caused by what conservation biologist David Ehrenfeld has aptly called "the arrogance of humanism."

Instead of attempting to control evolution or create ecosystems, we should work to restore the possibility of the evolutionary dance. We must rely upon the resiliency of Mother Earth, not on our species' cleverness.

The ultimate goal of restorationists should be to put ourselves out of business.

To join the Society for Ecological Restoration and Management, send $25 to SERM, 1207 Seminole Highway, Madison, WI 53711 (608-263-7889).

(First published in **Earth First!** May 1, 1989.)

Tee-shirt design for NABC III held in the Mish bioregion, by Alison Lang.

FANTASY OF A LIVING FUTURE

Starhawk

You are walking the dogs up on the hill they call La Matria, the Mother's Womb. Below is spread a sparkling panorama of the city, a living tapestry of rainbow colors on a warp of green. Toward the west, the Maiden's Breasts thrust their twin peaks up into a clear sky. All during Sunreturn Moon, fireworks lit the sky there, celebrating La Purisima, the festival of the conception of the Virgin. The streets were filled with processions, the Catholics and the Pagans dancing together without arguing about which Virgin they were celebrating, and everyone else in the city, it seemed, joining in just for the fun of it.

Now it is Fruit Blossom Moon, no fog, and the winter rains have turned the hillside green, dotted with the orange of a few early poppies. Three cows graze the hillside; the dogs are used to them and ignore them. You smile a greeting at the young girl who watches them; she is sprawled on her back in the sun, not working too hard. The cows are the project of the kids from your own child's school; the neighborhood market collective buys their milk and cream, and with the money and their own labor, they are constructing what you believe must be the world's most elaborate skateboard run.

Atop the hill stands a circle of stones. You pause for a moment, feeling the energy of the city, the hill, the sky all converge here, remembering the bonfires and the dancing and the rituals. On the Jewish New Year, they blow the shofar, the ancient ram's horn, here. On the Winter Solstice, you climb this hill at dawn to welcome the newborn sun.

To the east stretches the bay. The air is so clear today that you can see all the way to Coyote Mountain in the distant hills. Great

flocks of pelicans and seabirds wheel and dive around the fleets of fishing boats, their bright-colored sails plumped out by the breeze. Among them sail the great ocean-going trade ships, their huge sails spread like wings. No need today to switch to the solar batteries; the wind is strong.

You call the dogs and head down the winding, processional way, reveling in the scent of the blossoms from the apple trees that line the walkway. You glance into the gardens of the houses on the hill; it would be a great day to double-dig your tomato bed and plant out the seedlings. The dogs run ahead as you follow the road down, past the park at the bottom of the hill. Sidewalk cafes line the park; you spend pleasant hours there watching the kids play on the slides and swings, taking your turn, as do most of the neighborhood adults, on playground watch.

Now the walkway narrows as you turn down your street. On your left are the front gardens of the old Victorian houses. On your right, a low greenhouse structure lines the roadbed where trolley cars and electric autos run on the one-way street. The greenhouse is the neighborhood waste treatment plant, where banked rows of water hyacinths are aquacultured to purify wastes and generate clean water and compost.

You pass another small park, where a group of older people sit conversing under walnut and almond trees. Like everyone else on the street, they are a mix of races. Africa, Asia, the Americas, Europe, all contribute to their heritage, and you smile with pleasure, for to see a group of elders who embody the Four Quarters is considered extremely good fortune. "Blessed be the elders; blessed be the Four quarters that complete the circle," you murmur as you pass.

There are several elders' houses on the block: equipped with elevators and intercoms, the older people can live independently in a suite of rooms with someone always on call; some take turns cooking and baking, some pool together and hire local teenagers to cook and clean. In your own house, each of you cook once every two weeks. Once a week, you eat out at friends' or go to restaurants. On another night, you go to the neighborhood dining club, where, for a fixed membership fee, a collective provides a good organic meal. The dining club is a place to meet, talk, socialize, do informal business, and talk politics.

The fruit trees that line the sidewalks are very old now, planted years ago as an attempt to provide free food for the hungry. Now, of course, no one goes hungry. The very thought is barbaric, amidst all this abundance. No one lacks shelter, or care when sick, or a chance to contribute to the work that sustains abundance.

You open the door to your collective house. The dogs run in. Your computer sings to you: someone has left you a message. One of your housemates calls to you to tell you the news.

"The ship's in! The Chocolate Consortium called—they want everyone who can to come down there and help unload."

All thoughts of gardening disappear. You hop on your bicycle and speed down the path that winds past houses, shops, and parks to the docks.

The ship is in from Central America: one of the great winged traders, carrying your long-awaited shipment of cocoa beans and cane sugar. You greet your co-workers from the Truffle Collective and say hello to your friends from the other collectives in the consortium: the Candymakers, the Bakers, the representative from the Ice Cream Consortium, the Chocolate Chip Cooperative. Together, you unload the heavy sacks, count the inventory, and examine their other wares: the finely crafted hammocks, the innovations in intelligent crystal technology in which Central America leads the way. The ship will return laden with fine Sonoma wines, precision tools from the East Bay foundries, artichokes from Santa Cruz, and, of course, a load of state-of-the-art skateboards from the City.

You have arranged this deal yourself and it has been a complicated one. Your work collective is part of an extensive tradeweb, involving the households of your members, your sister collectives in the Delta graingrowing region and the Wine Country, your lover, who works in an East Bay steel mill, where the worker cooperatives pride themselves on producing the finest alloys in the cleanest, safest plants in the country, your exlover, who is a computer genius, and your housemate's brother, who repairs and maintains ships. You can resort to currency if you need to: the City's money is good anywhere, but you prefer to trade when you can. Fortunately, with a few exceptions, everybody loves truffles. The Tofu and Tempeh Consortium won't touch sugar products, but many of the soybean growers have voracious sweet tooths, so it all works out.

The work is hard but you enjoy the physical labor as you all talk and joke together. It's a nice change from the candy kitchen and the computer terminal. The smells and the staccato sound of Spanish remind you of the winter you spent visiting the Cooperativa de Cacao, where the beans come from. You remember the lush fields of corn and vegetables, the sturdy children, the trees you helped plant to hold the slopes of the mountain, the doorways open to the mild nights and the people calling out as you took an evening stroll. The visit cemented the friendships that established your trade contacts.

Finally, the whole shipment is packed away on electrotrucks that will take it back to the factory. The captain invites you and your friends up to her cabin for a cold drink. After you ritually exchange compliments and computer software, you invite her and her compañeros to spend the evening with you. The moon will be full tonight; your ritual circle will meet up on the hill and guests will be welcome. You will dance to the moon and then head downtown, for it is Chinese New Year and the dragon will dance through the streets. There will be fireworks, parades, and celebrations.

You bicycle home. In the last hour of daylight, you have time to pull a few weeds and turn the compost. Your household, like most of the city's living groups, grows much of its own food, providing all its salad greens, most vegetables, many fruits, nuts, and herbs. Your housemate feeds the chickens and milks your goat. You can shower, soak your sore muscles in the hot tub, chat with your child, and relax before dressing for the celebration. It's been a long day—but a good one. Now for some good food, and you'll be ready to dance all night in the friendly streets aglow with moonlight.

(From **Truth or Dare: Encounters with Power, Authority, and Mystery**. San Francisco: Harper & Row, 1987.)

Mimbres pottery design.

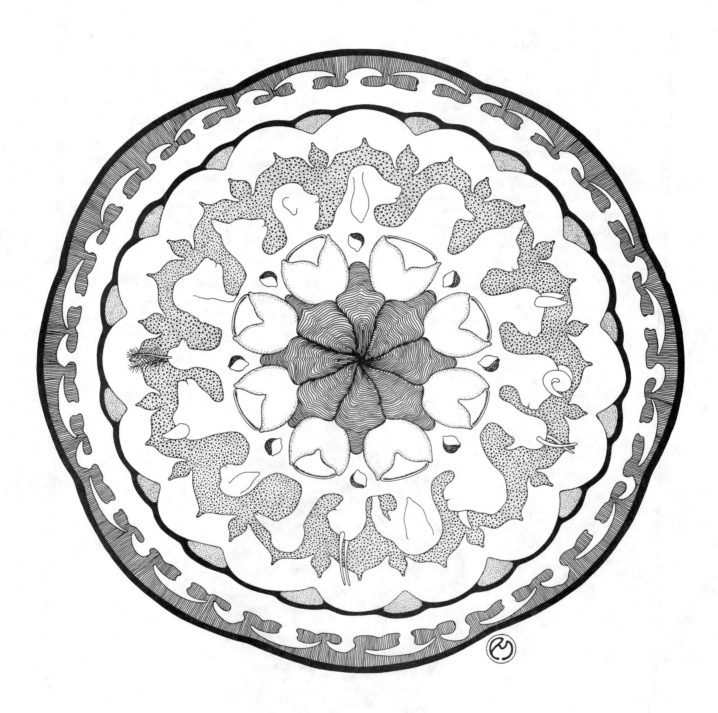

Design by Rob Messick.

Part Five

SELF-GOVERNMENT

"Active bioregionalists don't merely raise their hands to vote on issues but also find ways to interact positively with the life-web around them. They work with neighbors to carry out projects and build a culture together." — Peter Berg

If bioregionalism is a relatively new word, the many modes of thought and experience from which it draws its full meaning have deep roots in history. And, while the political change implied by the bioregional goal of ecologically sustainable, human scale governance—the dismantling of centralized structures—may be clear, the ways by which we work toward that goal, the day-to-day *practice* of bioregionalism, are many and diverse. For bioregionalists organize across a wide spectrum that includes local, regional and continent-wide political work; justice for native peoples and peoples of color; the creation of local economic and trading networks; the development of sustainable agriculture systems; and the education of a new generation. The rich mix of traditions that informs this work ranges from Western anarchism and the contemporary vision of the future known as the Fourth World, through the practice of consensus used by native peoples, Quakers and anarchists alike, to the wisdom of the modern feminist movement.

Bioregional politics is the politics of scale, of decentralization, the politics of cultural autonomy and *self*-government. By extension, it is also the way by which we can most clearly see the reality of empire—how Western Civilization has emerged on the backs of indigenous peoples and at the expense of viable local cultures and local ecosystems. The bioregional project, in this regard, is to establish the conditions for the re-emergence of sustainable local communities that might form the nuclei of new worlds.

Michael Zwerin's *Devolutionary Notes* distinguishes "states" from "nations" and points out the commonality among the world's Native peoples and, for example, southern French farmers: occupation! While warning of the dangers of nationalism, his voice is one among many through history which has spoken up for a radical scaling down of contemporary government. To this, Leopold Kohr adds the succesful experience of Switzerland's canton system, and Murray Bookchin outlines what he calls "municipal libertarianism": the taking back of power by local councils and townships according to a long tradition that has included the French and Spanish revolutions in Europe, and the town democracies of New England in the United States.

The Fourth World movement—made up of communities, indigenous peoples and small nations—is one of the "sister" movements to bioregionalism, advocating the small scale in all human endeavors. The term was first used by indigenous North Americans. According to the Haudenosaunee—or Iroquois—the Native peoples are keepers of crucial knowledge which they have to impart to the world: the knowledge that, when people cease to respect and express gratitude for the things that support life, then all life will be destroyed. We have much yet to learn from Native peoples everywhere.

Peter Berg's "Growing A Life-Place Politics" is a fundamental piece, sketching the full range of activities needed to become self-governing in both cities and rural areas. He advocates watershed-scaled governments—"socialsheds"—in turn forming bioregional congresses and wider alliances. It all comes down to meeting our needs in a genuinely sustainable manner; bioregional self-sufficiency, he points out, would go a long way toward easing the strain on the rest of the planet.

Doug Aberley pursues the topic of sustainable development, outlining "the means by which the existing structures of governance and development may be replaced by those based on bioregional principles." And Bill Mollison, from Australia, adds further wisdom from yet another "sister" movement: permaculture. His practical suggestions for the development of extended families, villages and trusts are inspiring, the motive force being "to identify areas where resources (water, soil, money, talent) leak from the region," and then set about plugging up those leaks.

The LETS System (Local Exchange Trading System) represents a tried and tested way to further plug leaks of money from a given community. Inventor of the system, Michael Linton, and Tom Greco—a Fourth World activist—explain how "green dollars" can work for your community, too, even when "the system" is *not* working.

One of the key ways in which this diverse array of thought and practice has come together has been through the bioregional congress, organized both regionally and—biannually since 1984—on a continent-wide scale. Drawing activists together from Canada, the U.S., Mexico and beyond, the North American Bioregional Congress (NABC) was begun following the success of OACC (the Ozarks Area Community Congress). David Haenke's contribution to this phenomenon has been profound, and here he passes on advice as to how to go about organizing your own congress. *Sustaining* bioregional groups is Caryn Miriam-Goldberg's contribution, and Caroline Estes speaks in detail about the consensus process, used with a high degree of success at all three NABCs to date.

Finally, through the eyes of Ernest Callenbach in *Ecotopia Emerging,* we get a glimpse of how things could be *really* different...

Self-government. Bioregionalism. Welcome Home!

Ecotopia Emerging...

And so the group sought a shared vision they could hope to transmit to the people at large: a vision of a society that would take long-term care of its natural resources the way a responsible farmer takes care of productive fields. A society that would protect members of the human species but also all others. A society that would arrange its institutions to encourage people to respect each other and work with each other, rather than working against each other. A society that recognized the unbearable fearfulness of uncontrolled hazards to life— whether they were nuclear or chemical. In short, a society that would feel safe and free, a society that an uprooted, exploited people could learn to call home....

DEVOLUTIONARY NOTES

Michael Zwerin

Balkanization, until recently an unqualified perjorative meaning the proliferation of many small, uncontrollable States hostile to each other, has become whether we know or like it or not, the tide of our times. The United Nations more than doubled its number in a generation as colonies broke away from empires. Now, nations which consider themselves *internal* colonies are exercising increasing pressure to escalate the Balkanization process still further.

Documents...I am flooded with documents I have in front of me, documents claiming that the Peoples Republic of China oppresses its Tibetan minority, Yugoslavia its Croation minority, Ceylon its Tamils. Soviet Russia is accused of suppressing its Georgian minority. These are all Socialist states.

Then there are documents of outrage against the Spanish occupation of the Basque Country, Norwegian occupation of Lapland, French occupation of Corsica. There is one document praising Greenland for having voted to end Danish occupation. ("Greenlandic" will become the principle language of Greenland.) A northern California back-country press is printing "Alta Libre" posters, calling for autonomy from southern California. There are groups advocating a State of "Superior" to be cut loose from northern Michigan, Minnesota and Wisconsin; an "Ozarkia" independent of Missouri and Arkansas; a state of "Cascade" free of Oregonian occupation. Welsh and Scottish autonomists call for an end to English occupation. People in power in Quebec want to secede from Canadian occupation. Indian nations call for an end to American occupation. These are not Socialist States.

Why, then, do all these documents shout the same message?

Occupation. Occupation is the imposition of rule by aliens. Occupation can take political, sociological or cultural form. States occupy nations.

Nations should not be confused with States. A Nation is an organic social, economic and geographical unit with common history, language and mores...a clan or a collection of clans. States are artificial political assemblages, constructed, as

Charles de Gaulle said of France, "by strokes of the sword." States have been superimposed over Nations. Nationalism's triumph was once considered "progress." However, nationalism is now a reactionary word in dispute. We should find another word to describe the new progressive struggle of nations.

What about "Nationism?"

Look at Europe. There's a Nationist map under the map of European States. Not too far under, covered but not quite buried. It is not an official map. It has no legal boundaries. On English maps, Wales is only twelve English counties, thirteen if you include Monmouthshire which some do and some don't. Catalonia exists only as a vaguely defined district of Spain. There is no Basque postal system. There is in legal fact no Basque Country. Brittany is a nation with a proud history, beautiful language and a culture of its own. There is no Breton Minister of Cultural Affairs. Brittany does not exist. Brittany is only five French Departments. The Lapps do not elect their own parliament. Lappland does not show up on maps of Scandinavia. Corsica exists merely as two French Departments. None of these Nations exists. And yet they do exist. How is this possible?

Dylan Thomas, Welsh poet famous for his English poetry, wrote to a friend in 1933, "It's impossible for me to tell you how much I want to get out of it all. Out of the narrowness and the dirtiness, out of the eternal ugliness of the Welsh people. I am sick. This bloody country is killing me."

That was before ethnics were "in," as a cover of *Time Magazine* proclaimed a few years ago, before cities ceased being unqualified lights of our culture, before they began to choke on their effluents and numbers, before the quality of life we are losing became possible to ignore. We can imagine Thomas today, writing in Welsh perhaps, certainly re-examining his Welshness. History is running backwards. We search for what we once discarded.

The Croatian Liberation Front is right wing. ETA in the Basque Country is Marxist. Catalonian autonomists tend to be anarchists. American Indian autonomists look like hippies. Very confusing. Why do all their documents read the same? The Ethiopian monarchy repressed the Eritrean Liberation Front as being dangerous left-wing "Separatists." (States take the position: "If you want to separate from us there must be something wrong with *you*.") The succeeding Ethiopian left-wing revolutionary government only stepped up the battle against the Eritreans. The reactionary Shah told the Kurds they should become good Iranians and forget about Kurdistan. The revolutionary Ayatollah Khomeini tried to tell them the same thing.

The Kurds conducted a war against Iraq in the mid-seventies. The Iraqis, supported by the socialist Soviet Union, said that the Kurds were an outpost of American imperialism supported by the CIA through the reactionary Shah of Iran. The

The Swiss Example

The basis of the success of Switzerland is not that she is a federation of three nationalities, but a federation of twenty- two states, the *cantons* which, far from uniting her unequal national blocks, have *divided* them into so many small pieces that no single federal unit has a sizeable preponderance over any other. By this, the essential precondition of every well-functioning federation was created: a pattern which furnishes harmony and manageability by ensuring the physical and numerical balance of all participants on a small enough scale to enable even a weak central authority to execute its decisions.

The greatness of the Swiss idea is thus the smallness of the cells from which it derives its guarantees. The Swiss from Geneva does not confront the Swiss from Zurich as a German to a French confederate, but as a confederate from the Republic of Geneva to a confederate from the Republic of Zurich. The citizen of German- speaking Uri is as much a foreigner to the citizen of German- speaking Unterwalden as he is to the citizen of Italian-speaking Ticino. Just as there is no intermediary Prairie government between Wisconsin and Washington, so there is no intermediary government between the canton of St. Gallen and the Swiss federation in the form of a German-speaking sub-federation. The power delegated to Berne derives from the small member republic and not from the nationality.

For Switzerland is a union of *states*, not of *nations*.

That is why it is important to realize that in Switzerland there live (in rough numbers) 700,000 Bernese, 650,000 Zurichois, 160,000 Genevese, etc., and not 2,500,000 Germans, 1,000,000 French, and 500,000 Italians. The great number of proud, democratic, and almost sovereign cantons, and the small number of the individual cantonal populations, eliminate all possible imperialist ambitions on the part of any one canton, because it would always be outnumbered by even a very small combination of others which at all times would be at the disposal of the federal government....

One final point should be made with regard to the small unit as the only workable basis of social organization. It underlies not only all successful *federal* government, but *all* government, federal as well as centralized. In other words, it represents not only *a* principle of government, but *the* principle of government, and politics—however incredible this may appear to the politicians of failure—cannot disregard it any more than physics can disregard the principle of gravity.

— **Leopold Kohr,** *from* **The Breakdown of Nations.** *London & New York: Routledge & Kegan Paul, 1957.*

Shah said the Kurds represented progressive nationalism in their valiant struggle against the imperialist Soviet Union and *their* reactionary outpost, Iraq. The Kurds, ducking, said it was all the same to them.

"That's right," we used to say, "and that's left." It used to be so easy. Why are all these people on the left and the right doing and saying the same thing?

Contemporary events will become increasingly confusing if we continue to try and classify them as right and left. Left and right as we know them did not exist before the growth of the Nation-State. Left and right is now ceasing to have any meaning whatsoever. We might try and look at the world with another perspective. A horizontal perspective. Big and little.

OPEC, the oil-exporting cartel, is a group of small States working together, working rather well together. By left and right criteria, they ought to be mortal enemies—Saudi Arabia, Iraq, Iran, Libya, Venezuela, Algeria, Indonesia, Nigeria—every hue from white to black, from red to green; Catholics, Protestants and Moslems together having one thing in common. The small weakling who has been beaten up by the big bully down the block ever since he can remember has finally found himself a big gun.

Alexander Solzhenitsyn is called a reactionary by the progressive Soviets and a liberal by the reactionary Americans. He supports organized religion and supported the American involvement in Viet Nam. Surely he must be a reactionary. But Solzhenitsyn calls for a return to traditional values, roots, the family, for a new type of nationalism and this is now considered—by Jean-Paul Sartre among other radicals—the progressive struggle. Perhaps Solzhenitsyn should be viewed simply as a little guy who took on the big State and seems to have got away with it.

The North American Indians occupying Wounded Knee some years ago appealed to Finland's Lapp community for aid. "The Lapp nation will do all it can," replied a spokesman, "But our situation is so bad that the possibilities for action are limited."

On the Larzac Plateau in southern France (known as "Occitania" on the map of nations), 100 farmers have been resisting French occupation by refusing to sell their land to the French army, which says it needs more room for maneuvers. Little Feather and a delegation of North American Indians visited the Plateau. A member of the Pit River tribe reacted to the militant atmosphere he found there: "The situation of the Pit River Tribe is identical to that of the people of Larzac, and we ought to be part of the same struggle." Janet Mat Cloud of the Nisqually tribe said: "I didn't think that I would find people in France with the same problems as we have, and who want the same things as we do for our children. Our struggle is for our children. It is for them that we fight to get our land back, just like the people of Larzac are fighting to keep their land for their children. Our children are not made for factories."

What does the Lapp situation have to do with the Indian situation? What do Indians have in common with southern French farmers? Occupation!

(From **Devolutionary Notes,** San Francisco: Planet Drum Foundation, 1980.)

...Ecotopia Emerging...

The Survivalists, recognizing that traditional American politics tended to work from the top down, expended a great deal of effort in encouraging popular participation in their new movement. They had worked out a federation network structure that fed people's ideas, needs and perspectives upward to the party's central committee. Like mushroom spores so light they can float through the air for miles, Survivalist ideas had penetrated every town and city and neighborhood in the Northwest. In some places party chapters were set up to cover a whole small town. In larger communities there are a number of neighborhood organizations. Sometimes people who had started working together for other purposes gradually developed a political identity and began to call themselves Survivalists. In other cases new groups formed, brought together by the usual techniques of meetings, pamphlets, posters, leaflets. But always, as Vera Allwen said in one of her broadcasts, the emphasis was on the direct and personal....

BIOREGIONALISM AND THE GREENS

Bioregionalists, ecofeminists, community activists, spiritual healers, earth-guided poets and curious people of all walks of life are raising hope for the evolution of new attitudes and new ways of relating to the earth and to our fellow beings.

…Greens in the United States are working today in many different spheres and using many different approaches. Some people are focusing their attention on specific issues of local and regional concern. They are working to curb the excesses of industrialism and to head off the social and ecological disruptions rooted in our present way of life. This current is basically oppositional in nature, embracing political methods such as community organizing, lobbying for legislative reforms and a variety of direct nonviolent efforts to protest or obstruct especially threatening policies and projects.

The second major current is reconstructive in its approach. It includes a wide variety of efforts to create living alternatives to our present ways—a wealth of experiments in cooperation and local democracy—both in the community and the workplace. It includes the development of alternative technologies and the raising of bioregional awareness. For a Green movement to develop and to grow in North America, there will need to be a merging of oppositional and reconstructive strategies that allows these two currents to support and strengthen each other.

Issue-orienting politics without an alternative vision can be politically limiting and personally frustrating. Many people are uncomfortable with the way things are, but are not motivated to act on their beliefs because they see no other way. Others might choose to work on a particular issue of concern, but are easily exhausted as each small victory reveals new complications. One might work for many months to block a particularly devastating project or to achieve a particular reform in the system, only to find that new injustices crept in the back door while your attention was focused on one small piece of the problem. The ecological crisis cannot be simply controlled within the limits of the existing system. In fact, some Greens believe that reformist efforts merely forestall the impending collapse of the industrial economies, a collapse which may need to occur before the real work of reconstruction can begin.

It can be equally limiting to work to create new institutions without actively seeking to understand and oppose the injustices of our present ways. Such efforts can be slowly bought off and accommodated into the service of the present system. One can point to food co-ops that have become more involved in elaborately marketing their goods than in fully challenging the limitations of the existing food supply system. A once-vibrant alternative energy movement in New England has become tied to the ecologically-devastating vacation home industry, as solar builders have drifted toward affluent resort areas in their search for steady employment and the freedom to experiment. Should healthy food and solar-heated homes become the luxury goods of an affluent minority seeking to purchase an ecological "lifestyle?" How can a Green sensibility guide us toward a better way?

The West Germans have borrowed a phrase (originally attributed to the ecologist René Dubos) that has become a slogan for the worldwide peace movement; "Think globally, act locally." Local ecological problems, local symbols of the military- industrial complex, and local attempts to create alternatives in housing, food distribution and other basic needs all offer a focus for local activities that carry a global message. By working primarily on the local level, Greens are demonstrating the power of people to really change things and creating the grass roots basis for a real change in consciousness.

— *Brian Tokar, from* **The Green Alternative: Creating an Ecological Future.** *San Pedro: R. & E. Miles, 1987.)*

GROWING A LIFE-PLACE POLITICS

Peter Berg

The most obvious conclusions sometimes disguise the most mysterious situations. Ask city dwellers where their water comes from, for instance. Most will answer with something like "The faucet, of course. Want water? Turn the tap handle." But the faucet is only the last place water was, not where it came from. Before that it was in the plumbing, and before that in the mains. It got there from a reservoir, and from an aqueduct connected to a storage lake. "So tell me the name of the lake and I'll know where the water really comes from." Finding out the name and, even better, walking on the shore of that lake is definitely a start toward acquiring a sense of care and gratitude. But even that lake is just another place where water was. It got there as runoff from rain or snow that fell from clouds. Where do clouds come from? Evaporated ocean water? Two weather systems meeting? Whatever forces are involved in making any particular cloud, the source of every particle of water in it remains a deep mystery. If anything can be said about the ultimate state of water, it is probably that it doesn't begin or end anywhere but is constantly cycled through one form and location to another.

Here's another easy observation: We all live in some geographic place. And here's the accompanying mysterious and very critical situation: the places where we live are alive. They are *bio*regions, unique life-places with their own soils and land forms, watersheds and climates, native plants and animals, and many other distinct natural characteristics. Each characteristic affects the others and is affected by them as in any other living system or body. And bioregions are all different from each other. Not just "mountains," but Appalachian Mountains or Rockies. Not just "river valley," but Hudson or Sacramento.

People are also an integral part of life-places. What we do affects them and we are in turn affected by them. The lives of bioregions ultimately support our own lives, and the way we live is becoming crucial to their ability to continue to do so.

Knowing that water is always cycling has a lot of practical value (regardless of how frail our sense of every station in the cycle may be). It means, for example, that simply dumping water that is dirty with sewage or chemicals won't really get rid of those pollutants. They'll just be carried along to the next station wherever it happens to be, to the water intake of a town downstream, perhaps, or through the ground to later seep into a well. Since water that we've used has a good chance of quickly becoming someone else's, limiting what goes into it and treating it before sending it along becomes a realm of social responsibility and reciprocity. That's the basis of what could be termed "water cycle politics," and it's serious business. Most town, city and country governments have official departments to oversee water supplies and sewage, and questions of water quality and use can arouse some of the most serious public debates.

What's the practical response to knowing that we share in the lives of bioregions? If what we do degrades them, how does that fit with our concepts of social responsibility and reciprocity? What is a life-place politics?

Rootstock

It's probably best to begin by looking at the actual conditions that exist where some people live. Doing this may run the risk of over-particularizing, but at least it won't deliver the kind of over-generalization and abstraction that can turn political thinking sour with ideology.

Right now I'm in a clearly defined sixty-mile-long watershed that empties into the Pacific Ocean on a fairly remote stretch of the northern Caifornia coast. I've been teaching Shakespeare's Sonnets ("When I consider everything that grows...") at the small high school my daughter attends here, work-learning about fruit trees from a local master pruner, and helping with some community projects. A borrowed cabin provides heat by woodstove and light by kerosene lamps. Water comes from the same creek that later flows through salmon-rearing tanks tended by self-taught homesteaders who are trying to bring native fish back up to their historical levels of population in the river.

Living here has never been especially prosperous. Fifth-generation families still cut and haul firewood, maintain excellent gardens and home-can everything from cherries to salmon. So do many of the new settlers. Much of the work that requires more than one person's labor is carried out on an informal exchange or volunteer basis that is held together with good-willed neighborliness. (People's skills and the services they can make available are wide-ranging and sometimes astonishing.) A volunteer fire department garage is the most visible municipal institution in the nearest town, a small post office is the only sign of a distant national government. If police are ever called, they will come from the county sheriff's office two mountain ridges and an hour and a half away. "Folk anarchism" wouldn't be a bad term for the social ethos that guides generally respectful relations between this valley's residents. Most of them are here because they like it that way.

"You make it sound too idyllic," remarks my pruner friend. "I live here but I'd move *there*, the way you're describing this place. You've left out the mentality about doing anything you want to on your own land even if it means destroying it. How about bickering over water rights or the other personal grudges that can go on for years?"

There's all that, but a visitor who has any inter-

est in reversing the degradation of life-places couldn't help but be struck by seeing the rootstock for sustainable inhabitation in the future that exists here. Plentiful local renewable wood for heating fuel, good water from springs and creeks, natural building materials, varying but workable soil, and some natural provision of food from fish are native resources. Human resources include broad skills, a spirit of informal mutualism, serious work on natural preservation and fishery enhancement projects, and a growing ecologically-centered culture.

Actually achieving a workable harmony with natural systems in this valley is another matter, however, and much more difficult than it would appear to be to a casual visitor. For one thing, it would require acceptance of a political perspective that is different from anything that most people here (or elsewhere) have known.

"Restore natural systems, satisfy basic human needs, and develop support for individuals: those are the most fundamental requirements for sustainability and should be the goals of watershed-scaled bioregional politics."

Let's start with the place itself, which hasn't been treated very well over the last century since settlers arrived and native inhabitants suffered extermination or removal. Cattle and sheep over-grazing (with forest-burning to create larger pastures) and brutal logging have scarred most of the hills. Subsequent erosion carried away vast amounts of soil, caused huge landslides and filled the formerly pristine river with gravel bars. A sustainable future would first of all have to be based on a local commitment to restore and maintain the river, soil, forests, and wildlife that ultimately support inhabitation here.

Next would come developing means for meeting human needs in ways that are both sustainable and self-reliant. Current food production, although more evident than in some other places, is really only minimal. Even hay for animals often comes from outside the valley. Energy needs, now partially met with local wood, could be completely filled by using alternative techniques and other renewable sources such as solar and micro-hydro power. Gasoline is presently one-fifth more expensive here than it is just outside the valley. Nearly all manufactured goods are carried or shipped in from outside. There are a few health practitioners, but complicated cases (or even ones requiring eyeglasses or dentistry) have to travel outside the watershed limits for care. And public transportation is non-existent.

Finally, there is the problem of earning a living in a place where there is little regular employment. Income from the present boom in marijuana cultivation (which also exists in many other deeply rural areas) is in perpetual jeopardy from law enforcement zealots. Even if marijuana became legalized, the most effective long-term economic solution would be to build on other existing activities that are more boom-and-bust proof and compatible with restoring, rather than further depleting, natural systems—natural enhancement projects, education (especially in sustainable fishing, forestry, grazing, and farming practices), visitor services, and local crafts and culture. The internal need for cash can simultaneously be reduced through community undertakings that "make money by not using money"—some large commonly-held farms, tool and machinery sharing co-ops, labor exchanges for new improvements like refitting homes for energy efficiency, a local currency or system of credits for trading goods and services, a transportation sharing system, and other formal ways to heighten social interdependence.

Restore natural systems, satisfy basic human needs, and develop support for individuals: those are the most fundamental requirements for sustainability and should be the goals of watershed-scaled bioregional politics in the valley. Achieving these is already a concern among some of the people, and their numbers could easily grow in the future. Even so, those who have been involved the longest feel they won't see full fruition in their lifetimes. How many generations might it take to restore the valley? (For that matter, has it really ever happened anywhere else before?) How self-reliant in regard to food, energy, manufacturing, education, and health can this place ever become?? How much continuing outside support is needed, and under what terms should extra-watershed support be secured? As for increasing social interdependence, what political means can enable all the individualistic and differing personal beliefs that exist here to coalesce in formal co-operation without losing the free-souled spirit that the valley nurtures now?

Closer to hand, there are plenty of issues that need immediate attention. There should be a moratorium on logging the few stands of first-growth trees that still remain. A full recycling program should replace hauling away unsorted garbage from the local dump. A valley-wide alternative energy plan should be mapped out and put into action. Watershed education, although featured at the small high school, should be a concern of the larger elementary and junior high schools and should be offered to adults as well. There's a lot to keep everyone busy before politics can be largely framed by the principles of restoring natural systems, filling human needs and developing support for individuals.

Evolving Watershed-Scaled Governments

Growing the politics for a life-place has to be based on the reality of living there, and it's necessary to remind ourselves that no facts are established without evidence. Someone has to do something that is consistent with the vision of fitting into on-going natural processes before any reasonable person will support the vision.

No outside agency proclaimed that salmon enhancement should begin in the valley, for instance. A desire to see past numbers of salmon running the river again led a few people to investigate how this might be accomplished and inspired them to commit time-consuming labor (with frustratingly numerous false starts and mistakes) that eventually led to some small success. They communicated their vision to other people, involved them in the project, and consequently increased their chances for success. Now that more neighbors are involved, the threats to restoring salmon—such as loss of fish habitat through further logging, overgrazing, overfishing, and stream destruction—are becoming more widely exposed and understood issues. If it becomes a generally shared ethic, "Don't do anything that could hurt the spawning cycle" could lead to profound changes here.

Bioregional politics originate with individuals who identify with real places and find ways to interact positively with the life-web around them. Involving close-by watershed neighbors creates a "social-shed." This seed group is and will remain the most important unit of bioregional political interaction.

Several socialsheds of neighbors working on a wide variety of different projects (co-ops, community gardens, renewable energy, bioregional education, recycling, and many others) can easily join together to form an organization for the broader local community. In effect, it would be a watershed council, rightfully claiming representation for the closely shared place itself. A watershed council is the appropriate forum for directly addressing present inhabitory issues and also for stating new objectives that are based on the principles of restoring natural systems, meeting human needs and supporting individuals. It can effectively contend with the closest institutions of government (town, city and county) to secure positions. These established governments may be arbitrary units in bioregional terms, with unnatural straight-lined borders or control over a patchwork of different natural geographies, but their policies hold for parts of real life-places and must be dealt with while the council presses for eventual self-determination in the watershed.

Whole bioregions are usually larger than one watershed and are overlaid with equally arbitrary and even more powerful governments—several counties, state(s), national departments and agencies—too many, in fact, to serve as practical institutions for resolving bioregion-wide problems. Rather than seeking to influence anything higher than local governments, watershed councils must band together to form an independent body in order to represent their entire bioregion. A council from the valley, for instance, while holding positions on town and council issues, would also join with similar northern California (Shasta bioregion) groups in a federation or congress.

Watershed councils and bioregional congresses have, in fact, sprung up in parts of North America reaching from Cascadia in the Pacific Northwest to the Lower Hudson estuary in New York. One might ask (as even the environmentalist establishment does) whether these new groups are really necesssary. Couldn't the goals of sustainability be reached through existing forms, and wouldn't it be better if those forms were made to work rather than cranking up something that is probably going to be seen as unacceptably radical anyway? And how about places other than remote valleys—areas that are more populated or nearer to metropolitan centers?

It goes without saying that creating a new political framework is difficult and that it will inevitably be seen at first as too radical (with some justifica-

tion, considering the snaggy, frustrated and boilingly ambitious types it may attract). The only reason to bother is to gain something that is absolutely necessary but can't be achieved through existing means. The question becomes: Is there any other way to preserve life-places? Aside from immediately local ones, governments and dominant political parties aren't open to accepting sustainability as a serious goal. They seem barely able to hear outcries against obvious large-scale destruction of the planetary biosphere from merely reform-minded environmentalists now, and aren't likely to take bioregionalists seriously until the District of Columbia itself becomes totally uninhabitable. Government has forfeited defense of life-places to the people who live in them. Watershed councils and bioregional groups are necessary to secure inhabitory rights.

Is sustainability really necessary? Rather than reviewing all of the colonialist, resource-depleting and environmental horror stories of the twentieth century that continue in the present and which without opposition will definitely extend in a compounded form into the next century, let's simply look at who we want to be. Do we want to degrade ourselves by participating in the degradation of humanity and the planet? And don't both of these processes begin where we live? *Un*sustainability simply isn't a lifesome alternative. Struggling for sustainability is necessary if we want to achieve it, like freedom.

As for abstracting from the situation in a northern California valley to other places, won't that be committing the same error that earlier was said to turn political thinking sour with ideology? Frankly, yes. No two life-places are the same, for one thing, and the differences between back-country, rural, suburban, and city environs are enormous. Are there any similarities? Yes to that, too. Every site of human inhabitation is part of some watershed or other and exists within a distinct bioregion. The goals of restoring natural systems, meeting human needs and supporting individuals that are appropriate in the valley apply wherever else people are living. The problem lies in searching out how human activities in any lifeplace are ultimately rooted in natural processes and discovering how

> *"Unsustainability simply isn't a lifesome alternative. Struggling for sustainability is necessary if we want to achieve it, like freedom."*

to fit into them.

A more populated rural area, for instance, may share the same watershed as a nearby urban center. This is the case for most of the agricultural country near cities on the Atlantic seaboard stretching from Boston to Atlanta, although the population-dense coastal edge is commonly seen as one long megalopolis and the connection between each city (usually sited on a river or at the mouth) and its watershed of support is virtually ignored. This natural continuity must be restored to our consciousness, and recognizing the differences between whole bioregions that lie within the territory separating the Atlantic Coast and Appalachian Mountains is an important initial step toward developing sustainability in that part of the continent.

In the Great Plains, however, cities are much smaller and often already identify with the country surrounding them. The problem there is that agricultural use of the land has supplanted native features nearly completely. Mammoth farming operations exhaustively mine soil and water and export it in the form of grain and meat to places as far away as the Soviet Union. The Great Plains (like the great valleys of California) is a resources colony for global monoculture and is rapidly being stripped of the basic components of sustainability. Watershed councils and bioregional groups in this increasingly endangered part of the continent advocate restoring the native prairies, non-abusive farming methods and greater diversification to relieve dependency on mono-crop agriculture.

There's tremendous diversity among bioregions, from Sonoran Desert to the Gulf of Maine, from the Great Lakes to the Ozarks, but the schema for growing native life-place politics starting with socialsheds of neighbors, joining these in watershed councils, and proceeding to the creation of bioregional federations or congresses can fit them all.

Green Cities

Cities don't hover on space platforms. They are all within bioregions and can be surprisingly dependent on fairly close sources for food and water, at least. All of them can become more responsible for sustainability by lessening their strain on the bioregions where they are situated. Urban life-place politics can be expressed through Green City programs for whatever aspects of restoring natural places, meeting human needs and supporting in-

dividuals are realistically possible. And there are more ways to do this than a typical city-dweller might think.

Processing urban sewage into fertilizer that can be returned to farm land would reciprocate directly with provision of food, for example. Establishing neighborhood common gardens and orchards would partially relieve the outlying countryside while helping to make a city more self-reliant. Energy demands could be sharply reduced by public projects to retrofit buildings and homes for alternative sources and heat efficiency. City governments can help facilitate starting new neighborhood food cooperatives, and establish centers for lending tools and equipment. (Public libraries for books are an impressive precedent.) Neighborhood- scaled recycling programs could be established. Cities can sponsor urban-rural exchanges to trade labor for agricultural produce. They can create wild-corridor parks so that native creeks, vegetation, birds and other animals can pass through and provide a natural presence. Bioregional arts programs and city- wide celebrations of total life-forms are projects easily begun.

Some of the points in a Green City program may seem similar to current environmentalist proposals but there is a fundamental difference between them. From a bioregionalist perspective, people are *part* of a life-place, as dependent on natural systems as native plants and animals. Green City proposals aren't based on simply cleaning up the environment but rather on securing reciprocity between the urban way of life and the natural life-web that supports it.

On the surface there seem to be few ways to demonstrate bioregional connectedness to city people. They don't see the actual sources for their food, for example, and often don't know where they are. But that doesn't make the life-place link any less real; it just confirms the need to expose it. Since cities are educational, cultural and media centers, the means for exposure are already there. Green City programs can emphasize natural underpinnings by proposing curricula and art that communicate with everyone from school children to theater audiences. They can promote appearances by speakers and cultural groups from outside the city to bring a sense of bioregional partnership. Green City "bioregion reports" could readily become an aspect of daily news. When these and all the other urban informational possibilities are considered, developing life-place consciousness in cities may not be so difficult after all.

North American Bioregional Congresses

What makes sense after the watershed council and bioregional group (now including a Green City program) levels of life-place politics? Representation of these at larger naturally-scaled assemblies seems to follow, and just as there are currently dozens of watershed-bioregion groups, there was in May, 1984, the first North American Bioregional Congress. But the air becomes thinner at this level, and it's good to take a deep breath before climbing up.

The intent of such an assembly should be to extend whatever links have been previously made between groups, make new ones, prepare mutually-felt statements on continent-wide concerns, and decide on an effective course of action that all of the different groups can taken in common.

> *"The continental air is thin because it's difficult enough to understand one's own watershed and then fit it into a larger bioregion, but much more so to think like a continent."*

Some of this was accomplished at the first Congress. Representatives met each other, information was exchanged, there were statements on some positions, and a few working committees were established.

The continental air is thin because it's difficult enough to understand one's own watershed and then fit it into a larger bioregion, but much more so to "think like a' continent." For one reason or other, many attendees at NABC I were basically unfamiliar with bioregional ideas and activities. Some had come to learn what these are. Some others came to represent their own different movements. North America as a living entity in the planetary biosphere was eventually understood and celebrated, but how bioregions interact with each other, what neighboring relationships might be, how groups can assist with real projects in different places, and other matters that presumably should be covered were hardly touched on.

To overcome the thin air, future continental congresses will have to be more definite about their identity and intent. Crucial discussions and decisions should be framed in terms of their usefulness to active representatives of life-places, and there should be more addresses by those who can assist in "thinking like a continent," an array extending from geographers and water basin specialists to story-tellers and poets. A North American Bioregional Congress is an important new political forum, and there is much needed work that it can do. National and state governments persistently maintain destructive policies toward the continent's life-places. A Congress that authentically represents North America can claim authority to initiate beneficial ones. It can confront the problem of arbitrary (and multiple) government power over bioregions. It can select priority issues to bring attention to situations in particular life-places (such as ruinous diversion of rivers in desert Sunbelt areas) and organize exchanges of expertise, work parties and cultural events to support member groups. It can eventually stand as the main voice for a large continent-wide movement.

We've come a long distance from a remote northern California valley to the North American Bioregional Congress, and have picked up new long-term struggles at every level along the way. Restoring the valley will take several generations—the Shasta bioregion several more. How many for the continent? Meeting basic human needs of all its people? Creating means of support for them? They're hugely challenging goals, but undoubtedly worthwhile since they are ways to retrieve the future and offer a definite vision for what is vaguely termed "post-industrial society." Achieving them is the work, the *do*, of bioregionalism.

A Basis For Alliance

There are opportunities for life-place political alliances at all the levels from a local watershed to North America (and eventually with other continents' assemblies). Only a fanatical mind-set would dictate that the basis for these should be to convert everyone else into a bioregionalist, and that would make a travesty of the terms for coalitions. Let's go back to the work of fitting into real natural processes to find more legitimate terms.

Active bioregionalists don't merely raise their hands to vote on issues but also find ways to interact positively with the life-web around them. They work with neighbors to carry out projects and build a bioregional culture together. Put another way, they are the working practitioners of what academics and others term "a paradigm shift." There is a very wide range of ways to express life-place consciousness and no need to exclude anyone's creativity in doing so, but bioregionalists do share a common interest in actually applying their convictions to local situations (in addition to having opinions about more distant ones). Their political activity is an extension of the work they do. They have a hands-on identity that is compatible with the goals of restoring natural systems, meeting basic human needs and creating support for individuals.

Some other groups have a natural affinity for these same goals. Native Americans are an obvious example. Renewable energy, alternative technology and permaculture (sustainable agriculture) proponents can easily share support on many issues. Earth-spirit women's groups, radical conservationists, natural living advocates, and deep ecology adherents envision a similar bio-centric future. It wouldn't even be too difficult for many current environmentalists to fit their causes into a longer-range bioregional perspective.

Less apparent, perhaps, is the basis for alliances with progressive movements that are aimed at affecting policies of existing large government structures and political parties. Disarmament, non-intervention, anti-nuclear, and other movements with a more distant focus than on the immediately local level leave little room for sharing direct support. Bioregionalists don't want nuclear arms or power facilities where they live, of course, and would certainly join with specifically anti-nuclear groups to make those places nuclear-free. Whether or not a watershed council or North American Bioregional Congress should endorse positions of every group or movement that each representative at those assemblies finds deserving is another matter. Some positions will be found in common, but the bioregional movement has its own character and own concerns. Without these it wouldn't be worth much as an ally anyway.

There has been some confusion about the relationship between life-place concerns and "green politics" ever since the first North American Bioregional Congress. A few participants at that event have even stated since that there is no difference between the two. The distinctions are very clear, however, and should be understood so that genuine bioregional goals can be realized.

First of all, green politics attempts to cover a more extensive range of areas, but where there are similarities, bioregional directions are much more definite and specific. This is obvious in a statement of definition from the initial Green Organizing

...Ecotopia Emerging...

As the membership of the Survivalist Party increasingly abandoned hopes of rational government in Washington, Vera Allwen felt as if she were coming to live in the shadow country of Ecotopia, rather than in "the old country," as her associates had now begun to call the United States. Nonetheless, she was startled when a visitor to the Green House announced that he was a representative of the Quebec government and wished to discuss establishing an official diplomatic mission.

"But we aren't a country. You can't maintain diplomatic relations except with countries, surely?"

"We are not particularly concerned with official labels," said the emissary. "Our desire is simply to establish a close relationship. We feel a certain kinship with you, after all, since you are striving to defend yourself against the rest of your country, just as we have been against the rest of ours."

"I can understand that. We might have ideas to share."

"We might be able to help each other."

"That seems unlikely—you're three thousand miles away."

The Quebeçois smiled. "But we are only a few hundred miles from New York. If another oil crisis comes, New York will be needing our hydro power to keep all those air conditioners running."

A few days later, a small building across the street from the Green House was sandblasted down to its original brick. It had once been a corner cafe for warehouse workers, featuring chili dogs, beer and juke-box music. Now the flag of Quebec, bearing four crisp white fleurs-de-lys, flew over its front door...

Planning Meeting:

Green politics interweaves ecological wisdom, decentralization of economic and political power whenever practical, personal and social responsibility, global security, and community self-determination within the context of respect for diversity of heritage and religion. it advocates nonviolent action, cooperative world order, and self-reliance.

Some of the words are the same, but the sense of them is very different. Bioregionalists have a specific direction for "ecological wisdom:" they want to restore and maintain watersheds and bioregions. Those are the places to which they want to decentralize and where they wish to practice self-determination. Their "personal and social responsibility" is to meet basic human needs and create ways to support individuals in life-places. As for extending their goals to "global security...co-operative world order," bioregionalists may well choose to ally with groups and movements which develop effective ways to apply that sentiment, but their own primary effort is to solve problems where they live. (And that may be the best locale for rooting a planetary perspective, after all.)

The most critical difference between the movements may lie with their actual ecological orientation. How much "ecological wisdom" are they really prepared to accept? Bioregionalists answer, "All we can get!" They see their lives as intertwined with ongoing natural processes, part of the life of a place. From their biocentric viewpoint, human society is ultimately based on interdependence with other forms of life. They follow that conviction to make choices about which kinds of work to undertake and to oppose Late Industrial depredations.

It is not established that followers of green politics are similarly committed, and questionable as to whether they will become so. Theirs is a multiplicity of concerns (Ecological Wisdom is only one of ten key values listed), and among many Greens, ecological awareness is limited to an older environmentalist perspective, attempting to reform industrialism instead of aiming to replace it. Some bioregionalists who are also active in green politics feel that they can reach members of that movement and change its direction. No doubt some will be persuaded, but wishful evangelism isn't a good foundation for building coalitions. Truly relevant life-place politics will originate from watershed councils, bioregional groups and the North American Bioregional Congress. When support for the positions of these naturally-scaled groups is sought, Greens may yet prove to be very strong allies regardless of their different emphasis and direction.

The Mystery Remains And We No Longer Deny It

More environmental agencies won't ultimately relieve our situation. They would only be further appendages of a political core that is welded to industrialism itself. We need a core based on the design of Nature instead, from watershed to bioregion and continent to planetary biosphere. Is it self-defeating to avoid established governments other than immediately local ones? Not if we want to anticipate a society whose direction already lies outside those institutions. We need to uncover and follow a natural design that lies beneath industrial asphalt.

What about world spheres of influence, global economies and other international considerations? The whole planet is undergoing the severe strains of the Late Industrial period now: chemical plagues, wholesale mechanical removal of landscapes, disruption of the most major river courses, accelerated destruction of ecosystems, and overnight disappearance of habitats. Couldn't we tame that suicidal appetite by adopting sustainability as a goal? If we become bioregionally self-reliant won't that be a large step toward taking the strain off the rest of the planet's life-places?

*

On a farm in the country or in a city apartment, we're all completely enmeshed in the web of life. We can't know all of the details of all the connections. Bioregional politics doesn't try to overcome the mystery, it is aimed toward making a social transition so that we can live with that mystery. Can we stop tearing the web apart and consciously build a role as partners in all life? We'd better, and we can, by beginning where we live.

(First published in **Raise the Stakes** No. 11, Summer 1986.)

MUNICIPAL LIBERTARIANISM

Murray Bookchin

There's a long history on the part of people living not simply in towns and villages, but even in large cities—capital cities, like Paris 200 years ago, in the early years of the French revolution—who tried to regain their autonomy from the nation state which has really been in existence for about 400 years. People on a local, grassroots level have lost most of their autonomy, their freedom, and have lost even their desire to get involved in politics because they don't feel they can do anything. Most of the power that was enjoyed by people on the local level has been grabbed by the centralized state. But people even in fairly sizable cities like Paris, which had nearly a million people during the French revolution back in 1793 (the heyday of the neighborhood movements in the French revolution), fought to regain that power from the nation state and to form confederations.

Not only in Vermont and in the American revolution generally, but I would say right now even in eastern Europe, there is more and more a desire on the part of people to regain local control. This may take a perverted, very bloody form of nationalism, I'm sorry to say (good ideas often appear in various forms, one cannot guarantee what form they are going to take). But people *are* trying to regain their autonomy.

Right now, in Quebec, a new movement called Ecology Montreal has been formed, one of the main goals of which is to form neighborhood councils. In fact there are two groups now demanding that Montreal neighborhoods—they still have them—be based somewhat on assembly-type organizations, and that power be given to the neighborhoods in the form of councils. So that, when you're speaking of the city council, you're speaking of representatives directly from neighborhoods, who are subject to recall, who are mandated by the people whom they represent, and who are continually subject to surveillance by the people in regular town council meetings. These tendencies exist everywhere.

And let me stress that I don't think you can do it in just one city, or one neighborhood. The most important thing is that the cities interact with each other to form a confederal system. The main challenge now is, first, to make people politically conscious of the fact that they *can* take over their city councils. Second, that they can change their charters. And, most important, that they can confederate. Here in Vermont, for example, the Greens advanced the view that we must establish neighborhood assemblies, link up all the town meetings in a given county, and let the county unit be the confederal basis for that area's communities. The more privileged or well-to-do towns would share their resources with those that are less economically well off, thereby creating a spirit of genuine mutualism—mutual aid—in which we will feel that by helping each other, we are helping ourselves as well.

Now, there's a long tradition in New England and other parts of the United States, in which the town or the village is merely the nucleus for a much larger area, bringing the country and the town together. When town meetings are held in any township, farmers may participate who may live a mile or two miles away, and they're as much a part of the town as the retailers, or artisans, or manufacturers and professionals who live semi-urban lives. So that the farmer and the ordinary workman are all in the same community. Their interests are pooled very beautifully. I've attended I don't know how many dozens of these town meetings and people really think as though they're one people. That creates a new sense of citizenship, something very beautiful, where people are not looking at everything from their own strict economic interests—although there are always those individuals who do.

...We just can't go on the way we're going. I was part of the Second World War era, and I remember a Germany that was nothing but debris. Within five years, once the energy and resources were collected, that whole Germany was literally remade until you didn't find any more empty, or bombed out buildings. This was a stupendous task. So it can be done. We *can* decentralize our cities, we *can* use our land intelligently, ecologically, we *can* have people create new kinds of communities, we *can* bring—as I've seen in New York—gardens into the cities and create new open spaces where before you had nothing but junk and clutter.

Municipal libertarianism is not only designed to decentralize political structures in the city, and ultimately the physical structures of the city as much as possible, but also to maintain control of the people who profess to represent others—their constituents. The most effective way we can prevent power from corrupting representatives is by keeping them at home, number one, and creating another power in opposition to the ever-centralizing nation state: that is the power of people in confederations of communities.

(First published in **Turtle Talk: Voices for a Sustainable Future** by *Christopher & Judith Plant*, New Society Publishers, 1990.)

...Ecotopia Emerging...

The Bolinas Declaration of Independence

We are American people. But we are human beings before we are Americans, and we would still be human beings if we ceased being American citizens. Governments are created to serve people, not the other way around. And so, when institutions have become bureaucratized and rigid, when the laws and applications of the laws no longer protect the people but have instead become a burden and a danger to them, then the people have the right, and indeed the duty, to take the management of their health, their welfare, and their happiness back into their own hands.

"In recent months we have seen the development of an intolerable situation in many parts of the territories which have become known as Ecotopia. Citizens despairing at the ineffectuality of government measures to protect them against the abuses and dangers of the chemical and nuclear industries have been forced to take direct action in self-defense. The citizens' just demands for healthy conditions of life, such as contaminant-free food and water supplies, air to breathe which does not contain dangerous levels of pollutants, freedom from the threat of nuclear plant accidents, and a reduction of the influx of carcinogenic substances into the biosphere, have been ignored or even derided—in government documents which call upon us to sacrifice human life upon the altar of profit. The attempts of our state governments to protect their citizens against the economic and health dangers of the automobile have been overturned by federal court order. Arrogant county bureaucracies and criminals employed by corporations have obstructed citizen attempts to achieve independent, renewable-source energy systems. In a time when experimentation and novelty are essential to our very survival, citizens have been forced into lock-step with out-moded standards.

"Our petitions for redress of these grievances have been met with silence or outright refusal. Now, therefore, we the elected officials of the Town of Bolinas proclaim that a state of civil emergency exists. The people must take the power over their destiny back into their own hands and form new institutions to defend their welfare.

"From this date forward the Town of Bolinas is hereby declared an independent territory in which the laws of the county of Marin, the state of California, and the United States of America no longer have legal force whenever they run counter to duly instituted ordinances of the Bolinas Town Council..."

SPIRITUALISM: The Highest Form of Political Consciousness

The Haudenosaunee Message to the Western World

The Haudenosaunee, or the Six Nations Iroquois Confederacy, has existed on this land since the beginning of human memory. Our culture is among the most ancient continuously existing cultures in the world.

In the beginning, we were told that the human beings who walk about on the Earth have been provided with all the things necessary of life. We were instructed to carry a love for one another, and to show a great respect for all the beings of this Earth. We are shown that our life exists with the tree life, that our well-being depends on the well-being of the vegetable Life, that we are close relatives of the four-legged beings. In our ways, spiritual consciousness is the highest form of politics....

The original instructions direct that we who walk about on the Earth are to express a great respect, an affection, and a gratitude toward all the spirits which create and support Life. We give a greeting and thanksgiving to the many supporters of our own lives—the corn, beans, squash, the winds, the sun. When people cease to respect and express gratitutde for these many things, then all life will be destroyed, and human life on this planet will come to an end....

Our essential message to the world is a basic call to consciousness. The destruction of the Native cultures and people is the same process which has destroyed and is destroying life on this planet. The technologies and social systems which have destroyed the animal and the plant life are also destroying the Native people. And the process is Western Civilization....

The processes of colonialism and imperialism which have affected the Haudenosaunee are but a microcosm of the processes affecting the world. The system of reservations employed against our people is a microcosm of the system of exploitation used against the whole world. Since the time of Marco Polo, the West has been refining a process that has mystified the peoples of the Earth.

The majority of the world does not find its roots in Western culture or traditions. The majority of the world finds its roots in the Natural World, and it is the Natural World, and the traditions of the Natural World, which must prevail if we are to develop truly free and egalitarian societies.

It is necessary, at this time, that we begin a process of critical analysis of the West's historical processes, to seek out the actual nature of the roots of the exploitative and oppressive conditions which are forced upon humanity. At the same time, as we gain understanding of those processes, we must reinterpret that history to the people of the world. It is the people of the West, ultimately, who are the most oppressed and exploited. They are burdened by the weight of centuries of racism, sexism, and ignorance which has rendered their people insensitive to the true nature of their lives.

We must all consciously and continuously challenge every model, every program, and every process that the West tries to force upon us. Paulo Friere wrote, in his book, the *Pedagogy of the Oppressed*, that it is the nature of the oppressed to imitate the oppressor, and by such actions try to gain relief from the oppressive condition. We must learn to resist that response to oppression.

The people who are living on this planet need to break with the narrow concept of human liberation, and begin to see liberation as something which needs to be extended to the whole of the Natural World. What is needed is the liberation of all the things that support Life—the air, the waters, the trees—all the things which support the sacred web of Life.

We feel that the Native peoples of the Western Hemisphere can continue to contribute to the survival potential of the human species. The majority of our peoples still live in accordance with the traditions which find their roots in the Mother Earth. But the Native peoples have need of a forum in which our voice can be heard. And we need alliances with the other peoples of the world to assist in our struggle to regain and maintain our ancestral lands and to protect the Way of Life we follow.

We know that this is a very difficult task. Many nation states may feel threatened by the position that the protection and liberation of Natural World peoples and cultures represents, a progressive direction which must be integrated into the political strategies of people who seek to uphold the dignity of Man. But that position is growing in strength, and it represents a necessary strategy in the evolution of progressive thought.

The traditional Native peoples hold the key to the reversal of the processes in Western Civilization which threaten unimaginable future suffering and destruction. Spiritualism is the highest form of political consciousness. And we, the Native peoples of the Western Hemisphere, are among the world's surviving proprietors of that kind of consciousness. We are here to impart that message.

(From **Basic Call To Consciousness**, Ed. *Akwesasne Notes*, Rooseveltown: New York, 1978.)

The Fourth World Declaration

We are the people of the Fourth World. We represent a broad global spectrum, ranging from ethnic, cultural and linguistic, to religious, economic, ecological and community concerns, many of which have been submerged to one degree or another by the disastrous onrush of giantism of the last two centuries or more. We are united in our determination to defuse the prevailing anarchic crisis of power by seeking to create our own social, cultural and economic patterns as we see fit.

We declare that it is only through small social units which are capable of being subject to the control of their members that the peoples of the world will ever defeat the danger of global wars which giantism has created, and achieve genuine progress and prosperity. It is only by such means that they can resolve the problem of excess human numbers, make effective a proper respect for their material environment so as to defeat the ecological peril, and end the curse of alienation from life and fellowship which now afflicts millions upon millions of people in many parts of the world. Neither we nor our forebears ever desired this development of giantism, very often it was fiercely resisted, it was never accepted and now we proclaim our total repudiation of it.

We assert in its place our inalienable right to live as free, independent, autonomous and self-governing peoples and we denounce the validity of any arrangements, however long-imposed, especially by giant political units, which seek the continued denial of this right.

We further assert our right to operate and control our own schools, hospitals, police forces, banks, industries, commercial trading and transport arrangements, forms of taxation and other matters of community concern as seems best to us without external interference or coercion.

…We call on all the peoples of the world to affirm their membership in the human family and their duty to advance its well-being in terms of peace, freedom and ecological sensibility, by joining with us to establish The Fourth World, a world where power is fully shared by the people in societies which are modest enough in size to do justice to the majesty of the human spirit and to serve the noblest accomplishments and potentialities of its creative genius.

We pledge ourselves to work unceasingly for the liberation of peoples everywhere in these terms.

Long Live the Fourth World!

— **John Papworth**, *from* **The Declaration of the First Assembly of the Fourth World,** *1980.*

STRATEGIES FOR AN ALTERNATIVE NATION

Bill Mollison

We must learn to grow, build, and manage natural systems for human and earth needs, and then teach others to do so. In this way, we can build a global, interdependent and cooperative body of people involved in ethical land and resource use, whose teaching is founded on research but is also locally available everywhere, and locally demonstrable in many thousands of small enterprises covering the whole range of human endeavors.

We know how to solve every food, clean energy, and sensible shelter problem in every climate; we have already invented and tested every necessary technique and technical device, and have access to all the biological material that we could ever use.

The tragic reality is that very few sustainable systems are designed or applied by those who hold power, for to let people arrange their own food, energy, and shelter is to lose economic and political control over them. We should cease to look to power structures, hierarchical systems, or governments to help us, and devise ways to help ourselves.

> "The work of the bioregional group is to assess the natural, technical, service and financial resources of the region, and to identify areas where resources (water, soil, money, talent) leak from the region."

The very first strategies we need are those that put our own house in order and at the same time do not give credibility to distant power-centered or unethical systems. In our present fiscal or money-run world, the primary responsibility that we need to take charge of is our wealth, which is the product of our sweat and our region, not representable by valueless currency.

What follows are some currently successful social strategies that enable a small group or a region to define problems and to solve them locally.

Bioregional Organization

A bioregional association is an association of the residents of a natural and identifiable region. This region is sometimes defined by a watershed, sometimes by remnant or existing tribal or language boundaries, at times by town boundaries, suburban streets, or districts, and at times by some combination of the above factors. Many people identify with their local region or neighborhood and know its boundaries.

The region is our home address, the place where we develop our culture and take part in bioregional networks. Through global associations and "families of common interest", we cross not only the regional but also state and national borders to set up multi-cultural alliances.

Tribal maps often defined bioregions very well, groups occupying ecologies of grasslands, stony deserts, swamps, or mountain ridges. Cities break up into different, often occupational or income districts, each with its own dialect and ecology, consumption spectrum, and morality. The acid test of a bioregion is that it is recognised as such by its inhabitants. Ideally, the region so defined can be limited to that occupied by from 7,000 to 40,000 people. Of these, perhaps only a hundred will be initially interested in any regional association, and even less will be active in it.

The work of the bioregional group is to assess the natural, technical, service and financial resources of the region, and to identify areas where resources (water, soil, money, talent) leak from the region. This quickly points the way to local self-reliance strategies. People can be called on to write accounts of their specialties as they apply to the region, and regional news sheets publish results as they come in. Once areas of action have been defined, regional groups can be formed into associations dealing with specific areas, for example:

- **Food**: Consumer-producer associations and gardening or soil societies;
- **Shelter**: Owner-builder associations;
- **Energy**: Appropriate technology associations;
- **Finance**: An "earthbank" association;

And so on...for crafts, music, markets, livestock, nature study, or any other interest.

The job of the bioregional office is complex, and it needs four to six people to act as consultants and coordinators, with others on call when needed. All other associations can use the office for any necessary registration, address, phone, and newsletter services, and pay a fee for usage.

> *"The very first strategies we need are those that put our own house in order and at the same time do not give credibility to distant power-centered or unethical systems."*

Critical services and links can be built by any regional office; it can serve as a *land access center*, as leasehold and title register, or to service agreements for clubs and societies. More importantly, the regional office can offer and house community self-funding schemes, and collect monies for trusts and societies.

The regional office also serves as a contact center to other regions, and thus as a trade or coordination center. One regional office makes it very easy for any resident or visitor to contact all services and associations offered in the region, and also greatly reduces costs of communication for *all* groups. An accountant on call can handily contract to service many groups. The regional group can also invite craftspeople or lecturers to address interest groups locally, sharing income from this educational enterprise. A regional directory or resource index for the bioregion can then be compiled.

Note that if essential services are listed, deficiencies noted, and leaks of capital detected, then there is immediately obvious a category of "jobs vacant." If, in addition, there is a modest investment or funding organization set up (itself a job), then capital to train and equip people to fill these gaps is also available. When *basic* needs are supplied locally, research and skills will reveal work in producing excess for trade—this excess can be given as information and education to other regions.

Bioregionalism is an excellent concept, given the irrational land use systems and land divisions developed by the present power structures. However, it is rarely an achievable reality unless enough people gather in one area and manage to attract a sufficient number of like people to achieve a viable internal economy and trade infrastructure, together with the community common funds that make such enterprises possible.

And that is the secret of success: assembling sufficient commonsense people in one area. As land titles in a region are bought out and occupied by any group which shares an ethical philosophy, so the shops, markets, processing centers, equipment, and support services for the new economy become worthwhile and available.

An increasing biological resource indicates health in the community. Every bioregion should monitor tree cover, wildlife, seaweed beds, bird colonies, species counts, and productive cultivated land at regular intervals. If these have increased in yield and maintained in species, the area maintains health. If no increase, or a *decrease*, is evident, something is wrong and should be immediately assessed for correction. Every region needs to act as a curator and refuge for some critical life elements of allied regions, so that *absolute* loss of species is unlikely short of global catastrophe.

Extended Families

The concepts of village and bioregion refer to a base or home area, but today many people travel about. Many societies extend as close affinity groups across many nations, thus forming a non-national network. Such groups develop a familial, rather than a competitive or conflicting, inter-relationship. With a common interest and ethical base, cooperative interdependence supplants competition. A "family" of this type, with 1,000 or less members, can ally with like groups to create a tribe, and 20-40 such tribes form a nation. Families, unlike many societies, have child care and the welfare of their members at heart.

Such families already exist in Europe, with small groups living in a scattering of households and locations across many existing national boundaries; some have existed for 18 or more years, and members report individual satisfaction with a larger support group. Families of this kind need to define each adult as an individual, with a right to the essentials of their own space (bed and work space), garden, and occupation. As nuclear family households are a minor part of modern societies (13-18% of all households), households based on friendship, or work affinity, or designed for students, singles, or elderly people, are needed.

In particular, children need a wider alliance and support group than just one or two parents. People can find "aunts and uncles" to take part of the responsibility for children in any such extended family, and if the children have a common fund (like their own credit union) for basic needs, then their care at a basic level is assured. They also have more than one household to relate to, or to visit or dwell in when educational needs change.

As an ideal, groups of 30 or so people could gather in core regions (with some outlying households) and so make travel locally an easier affair. Meta-networking (tribe to tribe) enables such higher-level organizations as travel and accommodation nets to be set up on a global basis, cash to be transferred to areas of need, and larger joint enterprises developed.

Given an extended family, a bioregional network locally, and some form of common work opportunity, any individual is assured of access to resources, capital, cultural exchanges, and good work. We need not only fixed villages and bioregions, but open corridors to other regions, other people, and across nations.

Trusts & Legal Strategies

Trusts in the public interest are the legal basis on which churches, universities and many schools,

A Proposal of Marriage

The bioregional and permaculture movements have been evolving in tandem for ten years or more, each with its own distinctive flavor. Having attended both the North American Bioregional Congresses, and the first and second International Permaculture Conference, I see confluences yet unspoken and divergences of which we might take heed.

Both movements spring from common concerns for a life of equality and empathy with the natural world. Bioregionalism speaks of knowing home and staying put while the permaculture design process begins at the home and works outward. Each movement is decentralized and anarchistic in character, now seeking to strengthen their commitment and widen their influence. Permaculture uses basic ecological concepts, like succession and the stability of species diversity, within a construct of design principles, such as stacking functions and creating edge, to develop sustainable agricultural and cultural systems. Based on natural systems, permaculture tends to be scientific and goal- oriented. It seeks to work natural systems into cultural ones. Bioregionalism began as a cultural endeavor, finding ways to hone the processes of culture in the dynamics of reinhabitation. Acknowledging the patterns which connect mind to matter, civilization to wilderness, bioregionalism works cultural systems into natural ones.

Now as both maturing movements come of age and make plans for their third biennial events, let us find our common grounds and meet the world together.

Bioregionalism and permaculture originally had their humanistic blindspots but have since met and become broadened by the biocentrism of deep ecology. One of the criticisms of permaculture—that it ignores natural wisdom through the wholesale introduction of exotic species—is less and less deserved. Permaculture principles are now used for wilderness restoration and useful native species are increasingly utilized in human-centered designs.

While bioregionalism has been refining ways of knowing home, permaculture has research establishments, some hospitals, many public services, aid programs, and charities rest. About 18-20% of businesses may also be non-profit trusts owned or operated by the charitable trusts that benefit from (are beneficiaries of) them.

It is quite possible, even sensible, to completely replace the bureaucracy of public services with a series of locally administered trusts, as in Holland. In the case of any small country, such trusts can run all public operations, and the "government" becomes simply a way of conveying tax capital back to the regions via local trusts. However, trusts can also self-run via non-profit businesses to become foundations, fully equipped with their own income sources.

> *"Given an extended family, a bioregional network locally, and some form of common work opportunity, any individual is assured of access to resources, capital, cultural exchanges and good work."*

Trusts are formed just to conduct businesses and trade, giving away their profits annually to named beneficiaries. If the beneficiaries are individuals, such gifts are taxed as private income; if the beneficiaries are charitable trusts or churches, the gift is not only not taxable but can be tax deductible to any giver. Trading, or "unit discretionary," trusts are also known as non-profit corporations (not to be confused with for-profit organizations).

Many large companies set up, and to some extent fund, non-profit organizations or even charitable trusts as a means to reduce taxable income, to carry out educational services, or to obtain public goodwill; some businesses tithe to worthy trusts that they believe in (a tithe is usually

---

busily gone about internationalizing. At the recent conference at Evergreen State College in Washington, 600 participants from 10 or more countries heard keynote addresses from Masanobu Fukuoka of Japan, Wes Jackson from Kansas and, of course, the irrepressible Bill Mollison of Tasmania. Permaculture projects are underway in Papua New Guinea, Brazil, the Pyrenees, and India, to name a few.

But some would say that as permaculture has begun to think globally, it has lost some of its ability to act locally. This is where bioregionalism stands most firmly. Though the bioregional ethic runs as an undercurrent through permaculture work and in its design courses, it is not often consciously so. Permaculture designers who would "farm in the image of the forest" may benefit greatly from the woods savvy of the bioregionalist living in place. More than ever, permaculture needs the grounding which is the wellspring of bioregionalism.

Similarly, the kind of agriculture and local economy necessary for a sustainable reinhabitation could well be improved by the permaculture strategies garnered from age-old work found in Bali, Hawaii, or the outback of Australia. Permaculture's collective ex-

perience with economic alternatives and cottage industry innovations would prove useful to any serious bioregional initiative. Bioregionalism is much more than just another back-to-the-land movement; while permaculture is more than just another form of organic agriculture. They are qualitatively greater, I would submit, because they are intrinsically rooted in natural systems.

I am writing with a proposal of marriage, not a smudgepot of two equals becoming One as in "permaregionalism," but rather, in the spirit of mutual respect and mutual aid. Perhaps it is best said in Kahlil Gibran's *Prophet*, where he speaks on marriage: "Give your hearts, but not into each other's keeping, even as the strings of a lute are alone though they quiver with the same music. And stand together yet not too near together; for the pillars of the temple stand apart and the oak tree and the cypress grow not in each other's shadow." In these volatile times where crisis becomes opportunity, it would strengthen us both to watch each other's dance closely and maybe even learn some of the movements.

— **Michael Crofoot,** *from* **North American Bioregional Congress II Proceedings,** *1987.*

Bioregional Economies

The Congress reached consensus on the following statement and strategies.

Vision Statement

A bioregional economy manifests itself through qualities of gift, trust, and compassion. Bioregional economics is a tool for implementing a social agenda informed by relationships, interdependence, and diversity; and is sensitive to the scale of the Earth's systems. Bioregional economics distributes the gifts of Earth to sustain the health and richness of the biosphere in which we live and through which human needs are fulfilled. Decision-making is based on principles of local, democratic self-control and, secondarily, through mutually friendly, cooperative and compassionate relationships between and among individuals, groups, communities, bioregions, federations, and all species. A bioregional economics is expressive of a universe of beings evolving and working harmoniously toward the fulfillment of our individual destinies and our common future. A bioregional economy reflects the oneness of all life.

Sustainability of the bioregion is the hallmark of the bioregional economy. The following principles characterize the quality of action in a bioregional economy.

1. Balance between individual freedom, social equity, and responsibility to the web of life.

2. Respect for the Earth community and responsibility to the future as a context for local decentralized control.

3. Equitable access to the gifts of Earth.

4. Respect for individual freedom within

a tenth of income, but in practice ranges from 5-15%).

It is very wise for any charitable trust to establish a non- profit trading (business) trust to help finance its activities, and this trading trust can refund costs to volunteers, pay wages, and gift profits to the charity or to any other charity. Thus, if the charitable trust is TRUST A, and the trading trust is TRUST B, the system as a whole works as in Figure 2.

Trusts are durable, efficient, easy to administer, and a great public service; everybody should be associated with one! There are several small independent but cooperative Permaculture Institutes and allied groups in existence which have associated non-profit trusts operating businesses to fund them; in this way, many trusts are independent of gifts or grants, and become self- reliant for funds.

The essentials of Trust A are that it holds assets for the public good, does not take risks, and leases or rents to Trust B, which *does* trade and take risks, and has Trust A as one of its beneficiaries. Trust B can duplicate or triplicate itself to accommodate new enterprises and to insulate from risk those successful operations which may later develop. It can also handle financial systems such as leasing and lending units.

Village Development

We need well-designed villages today more than any other enterprise: villages to re-locate those soon-to-be-refugees from sea-level rise, villages to house people from urban slums, and villages where people of like mind can find someone else to talk to and to work with.

An intentional village should have a group ethic acceptable to all who come there. Ethics, if shared, discussed and acknowledged, give unity to groups, villages, and nations, indicate a way to go, and control our use of earth resources. They can be reflected in our legal, financial, domestic, and public lives.

The aims of a sensible village group might be to:
• REDUCE THE NEED TO EARN, by developing food, energy, and shelter self-reliance;
• EARN WITHIN THE VILLAGE IF POSSIBLE, reducing transport and travel needs; thus to recruit people who could fill most essential village occupations, or who are self-employed;
• PRODUCE A SURPLUS from services to others, thus maintaining a strong economy and outreach potential;
• PROVIDE MANY OF THE NON-MATERIAL NEEDS of people, perhaps of children in particular, by devising meaningful work, relevant

community.

5. Attention to scale in relation to ecology, economy, and decentralization.

6. Friendly and cooperative economic relationships.

7. Ecologically prudent design, production and distribution of durable goods (to minimize waste).

8. To engage in the exchange of goods and services by relying less upon taking as much as possible for the smallest possible payment, and to rely more upon giving as much as one is able and trusting that the gift is returned as others are able.

Strategies

(It was noted that the Congress was adopting the strategies, not necessarily the specific examples given here.)

1. Oppose and undercut the dominant system in those areas where it is not in alignment with bioregional principles:
  • boycotts

• divestiture
• socially responsible investment
• live simply/right livelihood

2. Redirect the energies and power of the old industrial/consumerist system into emerging sustainable systems:
  • support revolving loan funds
  • buy locally
  • organize urban/rural partnerships
  • appropriate technologies

3. Establish new sustainable systems in alignment with bioregional principles:
  • intentional communities
  • local currencies
  • be creative!

Committee contact: Susan Meeker-Lowry, 64 Main St., 2nd Floor, Montpelier, VT 05602, USA.

— *NABC Economics Committee*, from **North American Bioregional Congress III Proceedings**, *1989.*

education, and a rich natural environment; and
  • COOPERATE in various enterprises and small associations.

A village can provide PRIVACY in homes and gardens; ACCESS TO TOOLS as leased, rented, or easily accessed equipment from computers to tractors; ENTERTAINMENT from local folk groups to video cassettes; CONSERVATION as a village wildlife, water and forest reserve, and RECREATION in the near environment. It can also provide the BASIC LIFE ESSENTIALS of shelter, food, and energy.

No isolated or scattered group of people can self-provide for the above, but it is probable that about 30 to 200 houses can support these services and basic facilities, especially if there is planning for cooperative funding. What is easy for a group may be impossibly stressful for a nuclear family. It is possible for a group to provide many services, and for many people to earn a living in so doing.

"We need well-designed villages today more than any other enterprise..."

Human settlements vary in their ability to pro-

vide resources, to develop a high degree of self-reliance, and in their alienating or (conversely) neighborly behavior according to population size and function. At about 100 income-producing people, a significant financial institution can be village-based; at about 500, all people *can* know each other if social affairs are organized from time to time.

At 2,000 people, theft and competitiveness are more common, and sects set up in opposition—the "ecumenical alliances" are lost. Perhaps we should start small, at about 30 or so adults, build to 200-300 people, and proceed slowly and by choice to 500, then "calve" into new neighborhoods or new villages.

However, alliances of 200-500 household-size hamlets can make a very viable manufacturing or trading alliance and maintain a safe genetic base. Many tribes of 200 or so confederate to alliances of 4,000-7,000 in this way, share special products by trade, or arrange out-marriages. Thus, pioneer villages can seek alliances with others for the common good.

(From **Permaculture: A Designer's Manual**. Tagari Publications, 1988.)

LETS: The Local Exchange Trading System

Michael Linton and Thomas Greco

Joe cuts firewood. Pat is a welder, and she wants wood but has no money. Joe doesn't want any welding. In a barter system, that's usually where it stops. However, if Joe and Pat are members of the LETSystem, then Joe delivers the wood, and Pat picks up the phone. She dials the LETSystem office and says, "Hi, this is Pat, No. 48, please acknowledge Joe, No. 83, $75.00 for firewood." Joe's account balance increases and Pat's decreases by $75.00. In turn, Joe employs the carpenter, the carpenter gets a haircut, gets some clothes made, buys food from the farmer. The farmer now has a way to pay for a welder, so Pat gets to work again.

And so it goes. The unit of exchange, the green dollar, remains where it is generated, providing a continually available source of liquidity. *The ultimate resource of the community, the productive time of its members, need never be limited by lack of money.*

*

Local Exchange Trading Systems (LETS) is the name of a remarkable tool for building and strengthening local communities. It's a kind of banking system that is fully compatible with traditional currencies. And, like any monetary system, it depends on confidence. Each community exists in the world in a more or less precarious balance between its income and expenditure. Hence the drive to export goods to increase income, and the incentive to shop locally, to keep the money in circulation. From the nation to the province, to the city and the village, we have an appalling history of selling our soul to the export market.

There are two characteristics of conventional money that render it ineffective as a proper support for the convivial community. Conventional money, being universally distributable, has no inherent tendency to remain in circulation in any particular community. Conventional money, which is the essential lifeblood of the economy, derives from agencies external to the community. The combination of these factors causes excessive dependency upon circumstances external to the community and essentially beyond its control.

Communities dominated in this way tend to become of merely geographic significance, having little or no infrastructure that might reflect self-direction.

Local Currency Systems: Benefits

When a community has its own currency, full employment can be available to anyone who wants to work and has a skill or service, of any nature, that is required by that community. It need no longer be the case that there are jobs that need doing and that people who wish to work are are kept idle for want of money. This is a natural consequence of the necessary recirculation of the local monely; in contrast, conventional money will generally drain out of the community to the cheapest available source of labor or goods. A community with its own currency has the capacity to adopt and maintain coherent and relevant directions of development with minimal dislocation by external events.

It generally seems to have escaped notice that money today is essentially a mere promise that value will be given. We are willing to trade in such promises when they derive from governments, one of the least reliable of institutions, but it seems that people are unwilling to go very far in trusting each other as individuals. At the root of the matter lie two fundamental causes—(1) the isolation of the individual from any integral local community, and (2) the failure to take personal responsibility and to assume risk.

It makes greater sense to base a money system on the promises of the individuals who make up the community itself and are the actual producers of value. The promise suggested is not the promise to repay cash to the community for goods received (we know that such promises are too dependent upon external circumstances beyond anyone's control to be reliable) but a promise to make some time or goods available at some future date, which is only jeopardized if the promiser is persistently unwilling or dead.

A Local Exchange Trading System (LETSystem) is a self-regulating economic network that allows its members to issue and manage their own money supply within a bounded system. Essentially, a LETSystem resembles a bank, and being a member of a LETSystem is as simple as having another bank account. Members' accounts hold "green" dollars, a currency equivalent in value to the federal dollar, but no money is ever deposited or withdrawn. All accounts start at zero and members can use "green" dollars only with other members. The system is thus always exactly balanced with some of the members in credit and others in debit. This creates a local recirculatory currency, whose effectiveness is determined by these arrangements:

• There is never any obligation to trade.

• Any member may know the balance and turnover of another member.

• No interest is charged or paid on balances.

• Administrative costs are recovered, in the internal currency, from member accounts on a cost-of-service basis.

LETSystems are self-stabilizing, set-up costs are minimal and the operation can be self-supporting from the outset even at a fraction of its full capacity. Administration is simple and requires no special training.

A LETSystem allows members of the local community to exchange goods and services on a "green" dollar basis when federal dollars are scarce or unavailable.

Essential Characteristics

1. A LETSystem is operated as a non-profit agency whose rights and authority are vested in a TRUSTEE who acts as an agent for the members who are principals. LETS provides a service that allows members to exchange information to support trading and maintains such accounts of that trading as members request.

2. The agency maintains a system of accounts in a quasi-currency, the unit of value being related to the prevalent legal tender.

3. Member accounts start at zero; no money is deposited or issued.

4. The agency acts only on the authority of a member in making a credit transfer from that member's account to that of another.

5. There is never any obligation to trade, but members must be willing to *consider* trading in "green" dollars.

6. A member may know the balance and turnover of another member.

7. No interest is charged or paid on balances.

8. Administrative costs are recovered from member accounts on a cost-of-service basis.

9. Accountability for taxes incurred by members is the obligation of those involved in an exchange, and LETS assumes no obligation or liability to report to taxation authorities or to collect taxes on their behalf. [Barter exchanges *are* considered taxable by the I.R.S.—Editor's note.]

The bookkeeping function of the LETSystem closely resembles that of a credit union whose members can use the currency only in trade with other members. Hence credit transfers between accounts and the issuing of periodic statements are the only necessary accounting procedures. This can be done by hand or computer, as appropriate.

The currency unit used in the system should be recognized as the equivalent in value to the regional legal tender so that valuation between members is customary and the LETSystem can associate accurately with the existing economy. It has to be clear to all participants that the internal currency of the system has no intrinsic value. It is never issued and cannot necessarily be cashed. The distribution and development of LETSystems therefore will generally reflect natural geographic regions and economic communities.

Accounts can be positive: when a member has earned more than spent to date; such accounts are "in credit." Equally, some accounts must be negative: the member has received more than she/he has contributed; in which case the account is considered to be "committed." Clearly, only those accounts in credit risk loss if the currency should devalue. The economy is thus always balanced, the total value of green dollars held in credit being matched by the commitment of the members in debit. The individual member effectively issues money into the community by spending, and redeems it by earning or selling. All transfers from a member's account is on that member's authority and may not be enforced otherwise. Neither can a commitment be invoked. The commitment is to the community as a whole, not to any one person, so no member can ever demand performance from another. However, a member who is reluctant to earn or receive green dollars will find it progressively more difficult to spend them, since this information is freely available to any member from whom she/he might want to buy.

A negative bank account is a private matter, but a negative LETS account is an issuing of promises in a community, and is thus, de facto, a public act. The LETSystem offers a facility, and proposes an ethic, that services can be exchanged on a "cost-to-provide" basis including reasonable profit. It is appropriate that its own service is offered in this way. The constitution of LETSystems as non-profit agencies, paying administrative staff at current market rates, will obviate tendencies to profiteering.

As more goods and services become available for green dollars, businesses will be better able to absorb costs in green, thus expanding their capacity to sell in green. This will eventually raise the applicability of green dollars to that of a full local currency. The effect of a local currency will be to protect local producers from being undercut by imported goods, and thus provide a more stable environment for developng the local infrastructure. This will be of particular benefit to local food producers with ecologically sound farming practices that make price competition with agri-business difficult. Charity groups and service clubs which have found fund-raising difficult during a recession will also be able to raise donations more easily in green dollars. Donors will be comfortable in contributing funds which are more likely to return to them as income, particularly since their other expenditures are not thereby limited.

An organism is defined by its skin, a boundary layer that selectively allows the free transfer of some materials while retaining others. The more complex the organism, the more its activity is related to internal processes than to transfers across the skin. The only skin possessed by a community in present circumstances is geographic and is related to transportation costs. Since the last half-century has seen transport costs steadily decline, most of our communities have been reduced, by excessive dependence on imports and exports, to extremely primitive economic processes. LETSystems are a way to give local communities new skins.

(First published in **Fourth World Review**, No. 26, 1988, with acknowledgements to *Whole Earth Review*, Sausalito, CA.)

Bioregional Education

In his recent book, *The Dream of the Earth*, Thomas Berry states: "There is presently no other way for humans to educate themselves for either survival or fulfillment than through the instruction available through the natural world." (p.167). Some people make the case that our present educational system is anti-nature, others say it ignores nature. Certainly, most school education is very removed from nature, and this leads to the ignoring of, or hostility toward, nature. What are some ways to correct this?

First, it is widely held that nature education involves direct contact and experience with the natural world, that is, it involves a great deal of sensory experience: touching, smelling, seeing, hearing, tasting and more—feeling with the whole body rather than just understanding something with the mind. This demands that a lot more of school education take place out-of- doors, and a lot more of the out-of-doors get into the classroom. And to help save a planet this cannot be done at a peripheral level, but must become central to school education. Present priorities need to be shifted in favor of increased nature education in the out-of-doors.

Moreover, getting a nature education to help save a planet means a lot more than simply learning facts about nature. It means developing a relationship with nature that embodies respect and reverence—nurturing a special affinity with nature that our present society seems to lack. And the relationship cannot be one of dominance over nature since this is the root cause of our present dilemma. Incorporating "nature quests" or "vision quests" which entail spending days alone in the out-of-doors are proven ways of nurturing a close relationship with nature. In this we have much to learn from the Native American experience.

In terms of content, ecology must assume a pivotal position. It needs to be a required subject even in primary school and must be integrated in virtually all subjects: history, geography, reading, writing, art, all the sciences. The ecology of the local bioregion needs special treatment with emphasis on how local culture (housing, consumption, etc.) can promote the Earth community in a particular bioregion. (Housing in desert bioregions has different architecture than housing in forest bioregions.) In order to truly prepare students for life in an ecological society, education will have to be integrated with all aspects of the total society.

Such education has to be directed at all age groups in the population not merely those attending formal school. Moreover, it needs to be life-long. In short, it necessarily must be revolutionary in content and method and in its consequences since its purpose is to allow the development of humankind alongside of the development of the entire Earth community. Such education must fill its teachers and students with a resolute distaste for the lifestyles, economies, politics, religions, and cultures which foster destruction and disruptions of the natural ecosystems on planet Earth. Are we ready to support a revolution? Nothing else will save our endangered planet.

— **Frank Traina**, *from Editorial in* **Pollen: Journal of Bioregional Education**, *Vol. 1, No.1, Spring 1990.*

BUILDING A BIOREGIONAL, SUSTAINABLE ALTERNATIVE

Doug Aberley

What follows is a step-by-step process by which a bioregional approach to sustainable economic development could be implemented in the rural regions of British Columbia, or any other bioregion. These steps are:

1. Define the borders of a bioregion by charting areas denoted by the following biophysical or cultural phenomena:
   - plant and animal communities
   - watersheds
   - physiographic regions
   - aboriginal territories
   - historic and current land use patterns
   - psychophysical sites
   - cognitive homelands
   - climate, etc.

2. Overlay the above boundary demarcations to show a composite border of the bioregion. Group discussion will evolve the logical biocultural limits of a life-place. Borders can be either hard, as a well-defined watershed height of land, or soft, where a less definable area may be jointly shared by two bioregions.

3. Compile a huge and incredibly detailed atlas of the natural and human elements which act and/or reside within your bioregion. This atlas will be the work of many people, and over a succession of years will be the accumulated wisdom by which means ecological and cultural regulation of human activity will evolve.

4. Compile a history which describes the evolution of biophysical and cultural environments within the bioregional. Special attention will be given to understanding how the bioregion environment has been used to increase or decrease the health and well-being of human populations.

5. Expand the bioregional history to include detailed understanding of the quantity and value of bioregion natural resources which have been harvested. This investigation will enable comparison of the contribution that the bioregion's economy has made to provincial and federal coffers to be measured against return services that have been received from central governments.

6. Complete a survey of how current structures of governance and development are organized and operate in your bioregion. This review should provide charts showing government and corporate organization, their theoretical rules of operation, and their actual performance. Special attention should be made to document the positive and negative effects which have resulted from outside control of local environments and economies.

7. From the above analysis a list should be compiled of any institutions, corporations, laws, or policies which are detrimental to the health of the bioregion. This list should be detailed and periodically updated for wide circulation.

8. Organize a sustained resistance against forces which are named as neglecting or destroying bioregion health. This activity would oppose large-scale export-based developments, centralized control of the bioregion economy, perpetual resource extraction tenures granted to corporations, ecosystem destruction, or any similar disregard of quality of life in rural regions. The suggested means by which this resistance may occur include individual and group efforts to lobby, letter write, take legal action, petition, protest, forming of alliances, and an array of other nonviolent actions.

9. Spend equal effort evolving alternatives to the structures of governance and development which neglect or destroy bioregions. This essential activity requires a sustained public education

process which never fails to take advantage of an opportunity to raise issues of bioregional identity and needs. It will be necessary to concurrently expand a bioregional perspective into all levels of community life by running for public office, writing letters to the editor, promoting cultural events, participating in small business enterprise, and other related activities.

10. The ultimate goal of the preceding steps will be to provide the means by which existing structures of governance and development will be reformed, and eventually replaced by those based on bioregional principles. Rear guard resistance, and forward-looking alternatives would combine to create a potent sustainability movement in any rural bioregion. Implementation of the bioregional

alternative can be completed through slow grafting of small parts of the alternative vision on to current institutions, or by creating what can be called a parallel society. Bioregional practice thus becomes a vital mix of changing the existing control structures wherever possible, while at the same time building alternatives independent of government support. The eventual result will be a growing public expectation that institutions should more quickly adopt bioregional configurations. Over an extended period of time there is every possibility that the bioregional alternative would predominate.

(From "Sustainable Development in Rural British Columbia: A Bioregional Context," 1989.)

...Ecotopia Emerging...

By early in the new year the relationships between the Ecotopian shadow government and the state governments in the Ecotopian territory had become very complex and delicate. After the Puget 1 disaster and recall election, Washington state had a de facto Survivalist government. Margaret Engstrom and her followers, however, knew that they could not exist long in isolation, and that the drama between the regional Survivalists and the federal government had only begun. They marked time, awaiting developments to the south. In Oregon, the state government had been a national leader in environmental matters for years, and there were many Survivalists in government departments on all levels. No confrontational issues had yet tested the relative loyalties of either the state apparatus or the citizenry at large. It was known to everyone, however, that the Survivalist Party was laying plans to contest all posts in the next election, and its support was solid and widespread; political observers predicted wholesale defections from both Democratic and Republican ranks.

It was in California, where the conflict over the Madera decision had been especially sharp, that the situation was most tense and problematic. Governor Clark's political base lay chiefly in the southern part of the state. He regarded the Survivalists as an insult to his federalist instincts and to his presidential ambitions, but he realized that their ideas were now deeply entrenched throughout the northern areas. He was not greatly worried by the direct electoral threat this constituted—he was confident that his solid southern backing could win him re- election. But the widening split between north and south on water and other questions seemed increasingly forbidding, and with this Bolinas nonsense, the prospect of actual civil disorder had begun to arise. Attempted secession from a county could be put down and laughed off. But the idea of secession from the nation was, he had been forced to admit, no longer merely a lunatic-fringe notion; and the idea of splitting the state had also developed a dangerous appeal in the north...

ORGANIZING A BIOREGIONAL CONGRESS

David Haenke

Step One: *DEFINE THE BIOREGION* In defining the region there are two main questions that you'll need to ask:

1. What is your effective organizing area?

Bioregional boundaries are never "hard." There is no bioregional map of North America or the world, but the closest thing available is the *World Biogeographical Provinces Map* by Miklos Udvardy and Ted Oberlander (available from *Coevolution Quarterly*). These provinces are huge, containing a number of bioregions which are not delineated. Many people use watersheds as ultimate definers, and if your group identifies strongly with a particular watershed, hydrologic survey maps may help you determine borders. Others feel that landforms, vegetation or other factors are the more significant determinants. Sit down with your core group, consult available hydrological, topographical, relief maps, etc., and discuss your feelings about the area you identify with.

Some natural bioregions are enormous, like the Great Plains or the Great Lakes drainage basin which covers much of seven states and part of Canada. A Great Lakes Bioregional Congress can bring together the essential energies of the vast area, then generate watershed organizing within the boundaries. The KAW (Kansas Area Watershed) Council organized a large watershed lying within the Great Plains bioregion. A smaller area offers the advantage of easier communications, familiarity with what is there, probability of a tighter organization, and a smaller number of participants. Organizing the entire Great Lakes Basin, however, can bring together more people, greater diversity, and can seed organizing in sub-bioregions for those who feel a need for more decentralization or a more local approach.

2. What and where are your resources and potential participants?

The concentration of potential congress attendees located in a particular area, sub-bioregion or watershed may be a natural factor of definition. Checking out the individuals and organizations representing sustainability may create an outline of the region you want to organize—bioregion, watershed, or even state. In the case of New York State, for example, the New York Congress on Sustainability was organized.

Step Two: *FORM A CONGRESS ORGANIZING COMMITTEE*

Ten people can organize and coordinate a congress. More may or may not be helpful. It is possible with fewer. To minimize concerns about concentrations of power in the organizing group, it can be stated in the invitation that the self-appointed authority of the convening group ends when the congress first assembles unless the congress chooses to affirm it.

Step Three: *IDENTIFY THE REPRESENTATIVES YOU ARE GOING TO INVITE FROM WITHIN THE REGION*

A congress needs some *a priori* level of consciousness and knowledge to exist among its participants, since it is a working body of fully participating equals, so common sense concerning invitations to appropriate individuals and organizations with fundamental roots in ecological

Sexism, Racism And The Land

Judith Plant defined ecofeminism as the coming together of ecology and feminism, and recognizing the interdependence of all life. This can be summed up as ecology being the recognition that "what we do to the web of life we do to ourselves" and feminism being the recognition that "what we do to ourselves we do to the web." In relation to the women's movement, ecofeminism is not just about rights, but about responsibilities as well. It is the understanding that not just women but men as well should take on the responsibility of caring for and nurturing the earth. She asked "how can we create ecologically sustainable communities that will thrive if we can't see that that tree is me?" Ecofeminism will help us to do that.

Dennis Jennings commented on a dangerous aspect of the bioregional movement, which is the failure to recognize that we are settlers, and lack a sense of history when we resettle the land.... It is very dangerous not to recognize your own "settler mentality" and deal with it. Dennis said that it is important to ask yourself, in relation to the land you inhabit, "Where are you from? How long have you been there?" and "How many generations have you buried your dead there?" It is critically important to "know the people who know the names of the places on the land."

Jacinta McKoy, in her introductory remarks, offered questions about how to create a new reality in regard to sexism and racism, asking the audience to embrace questions of power, race, and gender in their lives, and to look at the uses of power and privilege over people of color. She named racism and sexism as two "social diseases" which damage our lives and our human relations, commenting that "we won't go forward without dealing with this vicious cycle of domination and oppression." It is important to connect with people of color, who are not all the same; more action is needed. We must understand how the "isms" affect our lives, and we need to create and acknowledge diversity of peoples and cultures.

Gloria Yamato used a familiar metaphor in describing racism. Commenting on the need to "eliminate racism," she compared it to constipation. She explained that internalized racism is the "flip side" of racism, being the self- hatred felt by people of color for themselves and their people. She made the subject easy to understand by the use of phrases such as "mechanics of racism;" meaning take it apart, put it back together, leave out the funky pieces, and get another model of human relationships across racial lines. She also said racism "comes in several flavors," and is like a "booger on your face." If someone says you have a booger on your face, you thank them and wipe it off. Saying you don't have a booger on your face, or saying it is a mole and not a booger are forms of denial, analogous to denying that we are racists.

Gloria further explained that some of the various "flavors" of racism include overt racism, covert racism (which makes the subjects feel like they are nuts), unintentional racism, and self-righteous indignant racism. This latter form causes people to deny that they need to organize their own communities.

Margo Adair further commented that since nature is a basically harmonious force, it takes a great deal of energy to maintain an imbalance, such as racism. However, with the added power of mystification, it takes less overt force to keep it in place. In order to change this situation, we need to create relations of mutual respect rather than duplicate the oppressive relationships. It is hard for white people to examine their lives or behavior because "nobody wants to know how their privilege is paid for" and it is "taboo to discuss racism or sexism."

— **Milo Guthrie,** *report from the North American Bioregional Congress' workshop on "Sexism, Racism and the Land," first published in the* **Voice of the Turtle,** *Vol.3, Number 5, reprinted in* **NABC III Proceedings.**

awareness should be exercised. Ecological consciousness brings the same amazing, self-organizing quality to political gatherings as it does to ecosystems in nature. Suggested areas of sustainability from which to invite representatives include: feminists and green politics organizations, renewable resources, cooperative economics, safe energy, appropriate technology, permaculture/organic agriculture, sustainable forestry, agro-ecology, environmental/ecological groups, land trusts, conservation groups, environmentally-aware holistic health, education, media, arts, peace and social justice groups, ecologically-aware clergy and religious people, recycling groups, ecodefense, native people and people of color, environmentally-aware land-based people.

Step Four: *INVITATION/PRE-REGISTRATIONS*

Clearly set out the nature, philosophy, intent, logistics and purpose of the congress. List the organizations you are inviting, and highlight confirmations if you can get them in time. Even better, list sponsoring organizations if you are able. Make it plain this is a *congress* not a *conference*—a congress being a fully participatory event, not a conference where one sits and listens to speakers, workshop leaders and other entertainers. An effective attendance number is around 150 to 200. To get that many, approximately 1,500 to 2,000 forms should be sent at least three months before the event for 10% attendance.

Step Five: *CONVENE THE CONGRESS*

Suggestions on the nature of the event, which should be included in the invitation:

1. For a first congress, a four-day event (starting on Friday, ending on a holiday Monday afternoon is good, minimizing time off work). Two-day weekends are not long enough. Ideally, seven days should be allotted, but it is unlikely people will commit to that for a first congress.

2. Keep the costs low. Outdoor sites in beautiful places can be free or inexpensive. Church groups often rent retreat facilities. Serve simple nourishing foods from big pots, prepared on site by participants. As much as possible, use locally grown/processed organic foods. Try to charge a bit more than the expense to give a starting fund for the next congress.

3. At the first plenary of the Congress, agree on consensus procedures and whether or how to step out of consensus. Beforehand, invite an experienced consensus facilitator to the congress, and if consensus procedures are (hopefully) adopted, have her/him available to serve.

4. Plenary or full-group meeting time is important, as is committee or small group time. Plenary sessions are for making important announcements and presentations to the full group, with presentation time limited to 15 or 20 minutes maximum, and for the group to make decisions and consense, modify or reject proposals and resolutions brought by committees and individuals. In plenary a congress empowers itself, decides its future, adopts its founding principles and intentions. In committee, the productive heart of a congress, interested and informed smaller groups hammer out the nuts and bolts of issues for a swifter, clarified presentation to the larger whole. Suggestions for titles of committees can start with the categories used as bases for sending out invitations. Participants can suggest others, committees can merge, split or evaporate according to the energy and interest present. One things is certain: committees are the productive heart of the congress!

5. Don't over-schedule. Leave time for fun, walks, conversations and lightness. Emphasize participation among equals over events like workshops where a presenter/audience relationship exits. Workshops are important, but must not use up prime time priority.

6. Entertain yourselves; talent among your participants is more fun and less expensive than imported luminaries. The congress as a whole should include only full participants—equals. This pertains to media as well.

Step Six: *CONTINUE THE CONGRESS AS AN ON-GOING BODY*

If the event has been strong and inspiring, the plenary is most likely to come to basic agreements and will wish to continue to build on them. This will entail further convening, and decisions about frequency and dates and interim work must be made. One way to select a coordinating committee is to have each working committee choose a contact person and general focalizer who helps to maintain communication on activities the committee has chosen (if any) and agrees to come to, say, three planning meetings during the interim period before the next congress. Another is to allow a

One Town's All-Species Day

May 20, 1988: Santa Fe's 8th Annual All-Species Day: The theme: Why Wild?

Multicultural opening ceremonies

The day is kicked off by the San Juan Tewa Indian Buffalo Dancers. Next, in rustic harmonies, the De Colores Singers glorify the landscape of New Mexico in Spanish song. The crowd joins in, singing the beautiful 18th century hymn, "For the Beauty of the Earth."

All-Species Day Parade

Soon the parade starts up with rhythm sections leaping forth and the ecological floats moving slowly amongst the several thousand children, teens, parents and contingents of creatures. The masks, costumes, and other carried representations are the results of months of educational and artistic species studies in schools, church groups, girls clubs, scouts, etc. Roadrunners, rattlesnakes, piñon trees, coyotes, river otters, pumas, red-tailed hawks, western flickers, mosquito, antelope— the other creatures have come to town to remind us of their place in the world.

Pageant Puppetry Theater

The All-Species Parade of about 4000 people arrives at a large park for the year's giant puppetry pageant theater, "Aldo and the Wolf," dedicated to the naturalist author and wildlife biologist Aldo Leopold, who did so much to bring the science of ecology to the modern world. A quartet plays Pachelbel beautifully from their wheelchairs. A group of teenagers from a local drug abuse program come in as stilt-dancing performers in a crane dance. Wild serenity is invoked for a moment in the city. The wolf study group from a local school club JADE (Juveniles Against the Destruction of the Earth) makes their choreographed stalking moves in masks made from recycled materials as full-size buffalo puppets appear out of a cloud of smoke. The pageant has begun.

Ecological Sideshows

Later, during sideshow time, three elementary school classes have prepared their plays on wilderness topics so they can be presented today. The crowd moves from professional mimes and musicians to puppeteers, dance groups and speakers each with short repeated shows on ecological themes. Live buffalo, wolf, and raptors in the care of local ranchers and animal doctors arrive.

Images of nature in its glory and balance, scenes of family and community overcome oppressive forces of ignorance and destruction. The world for a moment seems turned right-side-up again. People are seen in the course of the day crying, laughing, thinking out loud with strangers and in a few paved hearts, seeds of appreciation are starting to germinate.

For a list of literature, audio tapes and videotapes available from the All-Species Project, send a stamped, self-addressed envelope to: 804 Apodaca Hill, Santa Fe, NM 87501, USA.

— Chris Wells, *from* **North American Bioregional Congress III Proceedings,** *1989.*

steering council with no numerical limit to self-select if they will commit to attend interim meetings and carry out the directives of the plenary. Emphasize sustained effort at comfortable levels to avoid burnout. The work is deep and vital, but it must be fun and non-stressful to be sustained.

(From **North American Bioregional Congress II Proceedings,** 1986.)

CONSENSUS

Caroline Estes

During the past 25 years, since I was first exposed to the use of consensus in Quaker meetings, I have been involved in some widely different situations in which consensus has been successfully used.

In 1965, at the time of the Free Speech Movement in Berkeley, I watched this process being used in both the small council that was the governing body and the large mass meetings of up to 5,000 persons. The council was made up of such diverse representatives as Goldwater Republicans, Marxists, Maoists, Democrats, Socialists, "Hippies" and simple activists. Mario Savio, leader of the movement, said that during the entire, tense, dramatic time, the group made only two strategic mistakes in carrying out the sit-ins, marches and confrontations, and these were the two times they came to a place where they weren't able to reach consensus, and so they voted. Both votes led them in the wrong direction. Similarly, in the large mass meetings, there was consistent agreement among those assembled, after much talking and discussion. There is no doubt it was a tense and exciting time—and that the unity in the group was very strong.

Since then I have worked with many groups that use this type of decision-making, whether in community gatherings, neighborhood meetings or family (Alpha) meetings. I have found that it works as more than just a decision-making technique, for the unity and understanding it fosters serve in many ways to advance the basic purposes of these groups.

The Basis

Consensus is based on the belief that each person has some part of the truth and no one has all of it, no matter how we would like to believe so, and on a respect for all persons involved in the decision that is being considered.

In our present day society the governing idea is that we can trust no one, and therefore we must protect ourselves if we are to have any security in our decisions. The most we will be willing to do is compromise. This means we are willing to settle for less than the very best—and that we will always have a sense of dissatisfaction with any of our decisions unless we can somehow maneuver others involved in the process. This leads to a skewing of honesty and forthrightness in our relationships.

In the consensus process, we start from a different basis. The assumption is that we are all trustworthy (or at least can become so). The process allows each person complete power over the group. The central idea for the Quakers was the complete elimination of majorities and minorities. If there were differences of view at a Quaker meeting, as there were likely to be in such a body, the consideration of the question at issue would proceed, with long periods of solemn hush and meditation, until slowly the lines of thought drew together towards a point of unity. Then the clerk would frame a minute of conclusion, expressing the "sense of the meeting."

Built into the consensual process is the belief that all persons have some part of the truth, or what in spiritual terms might be called "some part of God" in them, and that we will reach a better decision by putting all of the pieces of the truth together before proceeding. There are indeed times when it appears that two pieces of the truth are in contradiction to each other, but with clear thinking and attention, the whole may be perceived which includes both pieces, or many pieces. The either/or type of argument does not advance this process. Instead the process is a search for the very best solution to whatever is the problem. That does not mean that there is never room for error—but on the whole, in my experience, it is rare.

This process also makes a direct application of

the idea that all persons are equal. If we do indeed trust one another and do believe that we all have parts of the truth, then at any time one person may know more or have access to more information but at another time, others may know more or have more access or better understanding. Even when we have all the facts before us, it may be the spirit that is lacking and comes forth from another who sees the whole better than any of the persons who have some of the parts. All of these contributions are important.

Decisions which all have helped shape and in which all can feel united make the carrying out of the necessary action go forward with more efficiency, power and smoothness. This applies to persons, communities and nations. Given the enormous issues and problems before us, we need to us the ways that will best enable us to move forward together.

The Process

How does this process actually work? Consensus can be a powerful tool, yet like any tool, it needs to be used rightly. Its misuse can cause great frustration and disruption. To make the most of its possibilities we need to understand its parts and process.

Consensus needs four ingredients—a group of people willing to work together, a problem or issue that requires a decision by the group, trust that there is a solution, and perseverance to find the truth.

It is important to come to meetings with a clear and unmade-up mind. That is not to say that prior thinking should not have been done, but simply that the thinking must remain open throughout the discussion—or else there is no way to come to the full truth. This means everyone, not just some of the group. Ideas and solutions must be sought from all assembled, and all must be listened to with respect and trust. It is the practice of oneness for those who are committed to that idea—or it is the search for the best possible solution, for those who are more pragmatic.

The problems to be considered come in all sizes, from "who does the dishes" to "how to reach accord on de-escalating the arms race." The consensus process begins with a statement of the problem—as clear as possible, in language as simple as possible. It is important that the problem not be stated in such a way that an answer is built in, but that there be an openness to looking at all sides of

the issue—whatever it may be. It is also necessary to state it in the positive: "We need to wash the dishes so they are clean and sanitary," not, "The dishes are very dirty, and we are not washing them correctly." Stating the issues in the positive begins the process of looking for positive solutions and not a general discussion on everything that is bad, undesirable or awful.

The meeting needs a facilitator/clerk/convenor, a role whose importance cannot be too strongly emphasized. It is this person whose responsibility it is to see that all are heard, that all ideas are incorporated if they seem to be part of the truth and that the final decision is agreed upon by all assembled.

Traits that help the facilitator are patience, intuition, articulateness, ability to think on her/his feet and a sense of humor. It is important that the facilitator never show signs of impatience. The facilitator is the servant of the group, not its leader. As long as the group needs the clerk she/he will be there. It is important also for a facilitator to look within to see if there is something that is missing— a person who has been wanting to speak but has been too shy, an idea that was badly articulated but has the possibility to help with the solution, anything that seems of importance on the non-verbal level. This essence of intuition can often be of great service to the group by releasing some active but unseen deterrent to the continued development of a solution.

The facilitator must be able to constantly state and restate the position of the meeting and at the same time show that progress is being made. This helps the group to move ahead with some dispatch.

And last, but by no means least, a sense of humor. There is nothing like a small turn of phrase at a tense moment to lighten up the discussion and allow a little relaxation. Once you have found a good clerk or facilitator, don't let her/him go.

Often there are those who want to talk more than is necessary and others who don't speak enough. The facilitator needs to be able to keep the discussion from being dominated by a few and to encourage those who have not spoken to share their thoughts. There are a number of techniques for this. One is to suggest that no one speak more than once, until everyone has spoken; another is to have men and women speak alternately. This is particularly helpful for a short time if one gender seems to be dominating the discussion. However, it is not well to have any arbitrary technique used for too long. It is well to use these ways to bring a balance into the group, but these artificial guidelines should be abandoned as soon as possible. My experience is that a single two- or three-hour session with guidelines usually establishes a new pattern, and there is little need for the artificial guidelines to be continued.

No matter how well the discussion is carried forward, how good the facilitator and how much integrity there is in the group, there sometimes comes a point when all are in agreement but one

SUSTAINING BIOREGIONAL GROUPS: The KAW Experience

At a Kansas Area Watershed Council winter camp many years ago, we decided to have a sweat lodge in a cave half way up a cliff. The only place to heat the rocks was a long walk away, and the only way to transport them was to form a human chain around the cliff and pass a dutch oven hand over hand. Although the temperature by daylight was unusually warm for December, by the time the rocks were hot enough, winter had returned. Eventually, we filled the center of the cave with glowing rocks, undressed, and poured water on the rocks. Unfortunately, we didn't realize that the cave had a large opening that would suck all the steam out. Sitting naked in 30-degree weather in a central Kansas cave, we did the only thing we could—we laughed and howled!

Still, the experience brought us the gift of a story that gives our group a sense of its history and of the future. Hand over hand, we pass the weights, we distribute the work, we share the food, we hold each other. Bioregionalism, to become a more common reality for all, tells such a story. How we care for one another, child or adult, animal or plant or rock, is what determines what we learn about our lives here and of the future.

Starting bioregional organizations is the easy part. Sustaining them, like sustaining any good friendship or marriage, is what tries our souls.

We have made certain choices to come together—to work in community for the sake of community. Whether it be our interests in alternative agriculture, midwifery, prairie restoration, or insuring the rights of animals or

people, bioregionalism is the common book of the future we write together. And it's a book that hopefully will hold the names of our children and of their children. After all, bioregionalism is about sustainability above all else. This movement intricately links our lives to the rhythms of the ecosystems in which we live, and teaches us how to live as stewards of our homes, respectful of the environment to the point that we devote our works and words to preservation and restoration of the earth long after we're buried in it.

Luckily, the earth grants us endless opportunities to learn to live in our place while honoring the past and striving for a balanced future. Plants blossom and go dormant, animals hunt and hibernate, clouds form and disperse. All around us the earth is always moving, and through that motion, perpetuating itself in every aspect. Hopefully, the bioregional organizations we form and sustain are no different. Using the earth as a model, we continually learn to honor the processes of growth and change and the range of diversity within our groups. And in doing so, we perpetuate the human manifestation of a healthy ecosystem.

We cannot afford to ignore the issue of how to sustain ourselves as we proceed, and how to sustain the groups in which we work. This process is often the most tedious and heartbreaking because it requires us to open our private lives up to change and growth and to examine our behavior and response, our egos, our desires, our limitations.

We all need to be continually mindful of the importance of long meals and walks together, or two. At that point there are three courses open. One is to see whether the individuals are willing to "step aside." This means that they do not agree with the decision but do not feel it is wrong and are willing to have it go forward, but do not want to be part of carrying the action forward.

During the gathering of the sense of the meeting, if more than two or three persons start to step aside from a decision, then the facilitator should be alert to the fact that maybe the best decision has not yet been reached. This would depend on the size of the group, naturally. At Alpha it is OK for

---

of recognizing the value of unscheduled time at events. Too often we get so involved in doing the "work" that our time together is like that of a parent who works 80 hours a week coming home to spend a few hours of "quality time" with his or her child. We cannot afford to offer each other only the scraps of our energy; indeed, we deserve the best of one another's love, a love rooted in community and commitment to deal as openly and patiently as we can possibly stand with each other.

Beyond our need to sustain each other, we must look to the future. Here the common link of our children (and I mean collectively more than individually) affords us the true opportunity of caring for the earth for the long run. We have learned the hard way at KAW: that we must incorporate children more into our events. At first we didn't place much of an emphasis on children; many adults avoided signing up for childcare, and either the kids ran wild (certainly appropriate at times) or had to learn excess patience with adults buried in meetings. We now focus on incorporating children's activities into the heart of the event (and, to be honest, we hire quality childcaretakers for the arteries of the events).

As the kids in KAW grow older, they're starting to take more interest in planning their own activities. In a few years, with many of them teenagers, perhaps they'll meet on their own and with us to plan more and more of the events we sponsor. Already at the camps, they usually have their own sweat. Sometimes we hear them singing school songs or KAW songs or just giggling. Whatever they do in their sacred spaces, although certainly influenced by us, is their business and our future. At best, we give them time and space to understand their vital role in caring for the earth as well as the direction and support for handling the responsibility of that understanding.

One of the triumphs of NABC III was the way the All-Species Projects involved and motivated children to take some ownership of the ideas of bioregionalism. If they can feel they own these ideas and ideals, they can find ways to act and speak and dream for a sustainable future for all of us. Through All-Species, children develop a life-long connection with an animal, a connection that brings them strength and pride and hope. In addition to working with this project, we've found that nature walks, preparing meals, building sweat lodges, dances, songs, skits, and craft workshops help children feel that bioregionalism isn't some adult distraction but a way of living that they also shape while it shapes them.

Our community is our family, and as with any family, we must find ways to come to terms with each member to be at peace with ourselves. Like camping in a seemingly hostile territory, we must find ways to live there despite the insects, brambles, nettles and sudden storms of human interaction. Community means commitment to live in a place (of land, weather, people, change) and successful community means living well and in balance within our respective places.

Perhaps it all comes down to the occasional moments when we can truly see ourselves and what we're doing. For me, such moments come at the KAW closing circles. One by one, adults and children step into the center and offer water from their region or prayers or songs or thanks or dance. Some of us in pain, some in joy, all in transition, the circle bonds us in care for each other that flourishes beyond the circle, and community that grows beyond our lives.

— *Caryn Mirriam-Goldberg* . *First published in* **North American Bioregional Congress III Proceedings**, *1989.*

one person to step aside, but as soon as another joins that one, the clerk begins to watch and to re-examine the decision. It might be that at that time the facilitator would ask for a few minutes of silence to see if there was another decision or an amendment that should be considered that had been overlooked that would ease the situation.

Another possibility is to lay aside the issue for another time. We need to have some perspective on what we are doing, and the need to make a decision now is often not as important as the need to come to unity around whatever decision is made. Personal experience has shown me that even the most crucial decisions, seemingly time-bound, can be laid aside for a while—and that the time, whether a few hours or days, is wisely allowed; when again assembled, we come to a better decision than was possible in the beginning.

The third possibility is that one or two people may be able to stop the group or meeting from moving forward. At that time there are several key ingredients to be considered. On the part of the meeting, it is important that the meeting see the person who is holding up the meeting as doing so out of that person's highest understanding and beliefs. The individual(s) who are holding the group from making a decision must also have examined themselves well to know that they are not doing so out of self-interest, bias, vengeance or any other emotion or idea except the very strong feeling and belief that the decision is wrong—and that they would be doing the group a great disservice by allowing it to go forward.

This is always one of those times when feelings can run high, and it is important for the meeting, or group, not to use pressure exerted to go against your examined reasons and deeply felt understandings.

In my personal experience of living with the consensus process full-time for 12 years, I need to say that I have seen the meetings held from going forward on only a handful of occasions, and in each case the person was correct—and the group would have made a mistake by moving forward.

There is another situation which does occur, though rarely, where one person is consistently at odds with everyone else. Depending on the type of group and its membership, it would be well to see if this person is in the right organization or group. If there is a consistent difference, the person cannot feel comfortable continuing, and the group needs to meet and work with that person.

Recently, I was privileged to facilitate the first North American Bioregional Congress, held in Missouri. Over 200 persons arrived from all over the continent, and some from abroad, and worked together for five days, making all decisions by consensus. Some of those present had used the process before or were currently using it in the groups they worked with at home; but many had not used it, and there was a high degree of scepticism when we began as to whether such a widely diverse group of people could work in that degree of harmony and unity. On the final day of the Congress, there were a very large number of resolutions, position papers and policies put forward from committees that had been working all week long. All decisions that were made that day were made by consensus—and the level of love and trust amongst participants was tangible. Much to the surprise of nearly everyone, we came away with a sense of unity and forward motion that was near-miraculous, but believable.

(First published in **The New Catalyst**, No.3, Spring 1986.)

To an observer from a distant planet, the earth hung in the night sky as it had for millions of years, unflickering and serene. The evolution or extinction of creatures upon its surface, even of those as remarkable as humans, were imperceptible on a cosmic scale. From a closer viewpoint, as from a satellite in high orbit, the fertile crescent of Ecotopia could be distinguished, green with trees, along the Pacific coast. Within its boundaries the human species had recognized that it too was a part of nature, which could not indefinitely be mocked.

If that idea spread sufficiently fast and far among the other nations of earth, the heedless rush of technological exploitation might be turned back and biological disaster averted. On the whole, destruction still reigned; surrounded by desolation, Ecotopia seemed a small, precarious island of hope. But its inhabitants had lit a beacon that might yet guide other travelers home.

— **Ernest Callenbach**, from **Ecotopia Emerging**, Banyan Tree, 1981.

WELCOME HOME!

A growing number of people are recognizing that in order to secure the clean air, water and food that we need to healthfully survive, we have to become guardians of the places where we live. People sense the loss in not knowing our neighbors and natural surroundings, and are discovering that the best way to take care of ourselves, and to get to know our neighbors, is to protect and restore our region.

Bioregionalism recognizes, nurtures, sustains and celebrates our local connections with:

Land
Plants and Animals
Springs, Rivers, Lakes, Groundwater & Oceans
Air
Families, Friends, Neighbors
Community
Native Traditions
Indigenous Systems of Production & Trade

It is taking the time to learn the possibilities of place. It is a mindfulness of local environment, history, and community aspirations that leads to a sustainable future. It relies on safe and renewable sources of food and energy. It ensures employment by supplying a rich diversity of services within the community, by recycling our resources, and by exchanging prudent surpluses with other regions. Bioregionalism is working to satisfy basic needs locally, such as education, health care and self- government.

The bioregional perspective recreates a widely-shared sense of regional identity founded upon a renewed critical awareness of and respect for the integrity of our ecological communities.

People are joining with neighbors to discuss ways we can work together to:

1. Learn what our special local resources are;
2. Plan how to best protect and use those natural and cultural resources;
3. Exchange our time and energy to best meet our daily and long- term needs;
4. Enrich our children's local and planetary knowledge.

Security begins by acting responsibly at home.

Welcome Home!

This statement was adopted by the first North American Bioregional Congress in 1984 and reaffirmed at NABC II and III.

— **The North American Bioregional Congress**, 1985.

RECOMMENDED READING, BIOREGIONAL DIRECTORY, BIOGRAPHIES

I. Recommended Reading

Van Andruss

The following is a deliberately short list of books selected to introduce the reader to the basic perspectives of bioregionalism. Related books and articles abound in such numbers as to be countless. Remember that all books, articles and reports pertaining to your home bioregion could be relevant. Abundance of materials depends on where you come from.

Background

Regarding the history and philosophy of bioregionalism, it would be a pleasure to mention a few that have personally brought me along the path.

I have Lewis Mumford to thank for exploding illusions about the advantages of grand-scale civilizations. His work characterizing the Megamachine since its beginnings in the Near East and Egypt educated me to the nature of Empire, even before Murray Bookchin, *The Fifth Estate* (an anarchist journal from Detroit) and the more recent array of feminist literature filled in the topic. The great humanist, Kropotkin drew my attention to the tyrannical methods of the State in whatever guise. He favored instead the small-scale, locally self-governing communities like the Russian village, or *mir*. His outstanding contribution was to put scientific knowledge and history in the service of the people. *Mutual Aid* is the essential book of that generous person's thought.

It is tempting to reach back into the 19th century and cite ancestors to a bioregional view. Kropotkin was one utopian thinker, and of course there were others, like the industrialist, Robert Owen, and the French theorist, Charles Fourier. Fourier had a big influence, incidentally, on those inspiring idealists at Brook Farm near Concord, Massachusetts, whose experiment in cooperative living enjoyed a brief but happy flowering. I'm referring to Sarah and George Ripley, Margaret Fuller and others. Not far away, Thoreau was penning his anarchist essay, "Civil Disobedience." No single book adequately covers the ferment around the Concord of that period, though many treat of it.

Kropotkin, friends at Brook Farm, the Transcendentalists, Owenites, Fourierists—all human-scale social romantics of the 19th century—led me in the direction of bioregionalism.

I cannot proceed without mentioning the utopian experiments of our time in North America during the late sixties, early seventies. A short shelf of communitarian literature came out of this period, the most inspiring from Vermont. Those youthful days are described in Ray Mungo's *Total Loss Farm*, and in the collectively written work about the same domestic commune, *Home Comfort*.

Of history books preparing the ground for bioregionalism, the following pop into mind: Lewis Mumford's *The Myth of The Machine* on the rise of patriarchal civilization; Edmund Wilson's *To the Finland Station* on the rise of socialism; E.H. Carr's *The New Society* on the antecedents to a "free enterprise" political setting; Murray Bookchin's *Ecology of Freedom* on the institutions of hierarchy; L.S. Stavrianos' *Global Rift* on the rise of the Third World; Leopold Kohr's *Breakdown of Nations*, on the small nation imperative; Howard Zinn's *A People's History of the United States* on Empire-building the American way.

For the great work ahead, the more one learns about the earth/life sciences the better. An ecological perspective was brought home to me by Lynn Margulis' *Microcosmos* and *Early Life*. Everywhere in her pages is the evidence that we live in a planetary interdependency, an all-species community of communities. Individualistic stances in nature are mistaken and maladaptive, while symbiosis (mutual benefit) is more properly the method of the new organic age.

Journals

Bioregional ways have been practiced by peoples since the beginning of human experience, but as a notion that figures in the popular mind, as an "ism," it is new. The literature of the movement is to be discovered mainly in a variety of green alternative journals, with names like *Coyote, Columbiana, North Country Anvil, The New Catalyst*. Some of these publications have passed out of existence, others have survived. All speak eloquently and in a familiar manner about the life in their regions.

Journals appealing to a wider audience have played important parts in formulating the philosophy and generally spreading the word. I have in mind, for example, *Coevolution Quarterly, Synthesis* (now known as *Green Synthesis*), *RAIN* (no longer published), *In Context* and *Raise the Stakes*. *Raise the Stakes*, the voice of Planet Drum Foundation in San Francisco, has been a principal source during the whole life of the movement. This com-

pany of poets and social thinkers gave bioregionalism its original inspiration and is still going strong. Planet Drum Foundation has made available reprints of basic articles, mainly from *Raise The Stakes*, in their new *Catalogue of Bioregional Primary Sources*.

Early on, *CoEvolution Quarterly* put out an excellent issue introducing bioregionalism, called "Bioregions" (Winter, 1981). Here the reader will find a series of illuminating articles back when the vision was fresh on the horizon. The Jim Dodge article, "Living by Life," first woke me up to the active values of this view. Also in "Bioregions," find a fundamental treatment of "The Concept of Social Ecology" by Murray Bookchin; and be encouraged to make community in a rural, hometown setting by "The Kansas Experience."

More recently, *The New Catalyst*, Spring 1986, published a special issue on bioregionalism worth reading.

Along with journals, the bioregional literature includes a number of informally-printed booklets, papers and pamphlets like Paul Gilk's populist statement, *Nature's Unruly Mob* (*North Country Anvil Magazine*, 1986), Don Alexander's *Bioregionalism: Pseudo-science or Sensibility?* (Trent University, no date), and the plain-spoken pamphlet of David Haenke's called *Ecological Politics and Bioregionalism* (New Life Farm, 1984), certainly one of the historic rallying points of the movement. An early place-oriented volume is Gary Lawless' *The Gulf of Maine*, an issue of *The Blackberry Reader*.

The publications above may not be readily available in a local library, but can be acquired through connecting up with the bioregional network.

Books

Reinhabiting a Separate Country: A Bioregional Anthology of Northern California (Planet Drum Foundation, 1978) gave us our first outstanding example of a "bioregional presentation" in book form. It is an imaginative evocation of the character of a home region through poems, interviews, essays, maps and pictures. Here is a joyous celebration of the Shasta people, their special terrain of consciousness, including the work of Raymond Dasmann on the physical layout of Northern California, "I am Looking at a Picture of Home." This is a model discussion that could be applied to our own areas. The "Introduction" to *Reinhabiting a Separate Country* and the last essay called "Rein-habiting California" remain the most definitive statements around on the question, "What is Bioregionalism?"

Becoming in fact a separate country, dropping out of the nation- state, is the theme of Ernest Callenbach's two novels, *Ecotopia* (Banyan Tree Books, 1975) and *Ecotopia Emerging* (Banyan Tree Books, 1981). They form a compendium of ideas on alternative culture. In the story, Northern California, Oregon and Washington split off and shape their society according to an ecological politics. Though the books offer a dubious portrayal of human nature, they are fun and suggestive. A current utopian vision—highly recommended—is *Always Coming Home*, by Ursula LeGuin (Bantam, 1986).

Dwellers in the Land (Sierra Club, 1985) is a book that we've all had occasion to learn from. It was written by Kirkpatrick Sale to fill a gap. Until he undertook to do the work, no other formally-ordered book on bioregionalism existed. *Dwellers in the Land* is best used in a course of study. A good index is included as well as a rich "Bibliography and Notes" for further inquiry. All chapters are informative, but I especially recommend "Past Realities" for its short history of regionalism in the U.S. We are reminded here that bioregionalism is a form of regionalism. Interesting historians and planners are reviewed, namely Frederick Jackson Turner, Lewis Mumford and Howard Odum.

A new publication portraying a bioregional philosophy through interviews, *Turtle Talk: Voices for a Sustainable Future* (New Society Publishers, 1990), is the first of *The New Catalyst* magazine's "Bioregional Series." Including Gary Snyder, Peter Berg, Starhawk, Freeman House, Caroline Estes, with an excellent Forward by Kirkpatrick Sale, *Turtle Talk* offers a stimulating set of conversations about key aspects of bioregionalism.

*

The books that follow are not wholly about bioregionalism but contain elements belonging to it.

A familiar work, and one close to my heart, is Brian Tokar's *The Green Alternative: Creating an Ecological Future* (R. & E. Miles, 1987). The special value of *The Green Alternative* is in its summary description of the global green movement, which provides an appropriate background to bioregionalism. Both the movement in Europe and the U.S. are covered, offering a wealth of events and actions by which the term "green" is defined. The book as a whole sees bioregionalism as a preferred strategy within the wider green movement. An intelligent book you wouldn't hesitate to hand over to friends or relatives, even those likely to disagree. Exceptionally complete "Notes on Sources" are a treasure for the avid reader.

No Foreign Land (Pantheon Books, 1973) by Wilfred Pelletier and Ted Poole is another book with an essential place in a bioregional picture. This is the story of Wilf Pelletier, an Ojibway from Manitoulin Island on Lake Huron, in Ontario, who finds the personal meaning of community in his home village after travelling deep in the territory of competitive white society. Knowing both the native and the non-native worlds, Wilf is able to bring out the differences with great accuracy. The experience is a revelation to those brought up in the psychology of individualism. Despite the spineyness of the topic, the beauty of this book is in its accessibility and warm friendliness. See especially the chapter, "Home is Here."

Basic Call to Consciousness (Akwesasne Notes, 1978) is without doubt one of the most powerful books on our shelves. Again, it is written from the point of view of native North Americans. It stands as a critique of Western Civilization through the eyes of a tribal people, the Haudenosaunee (or Iroquois). This is the story of the twenty-one delegates who travelled with passports issued by their own nation to Geneva where they pleaded their case for survival before a United Nations assembly. For its expressiveness as a cultural view, its approach to governance and to life on the land, this book should be an inspiration to all bioregionalists. It is profoundly philosophical and might easily change your life.

A related book comes to mind, entitled *Healing the Wounds: The Promise of Ecofeminism* (New Society Publishers, 1988), edited by Judith Plant. This includes a feminist critique of His-story as well as asserting our connectedness with all life forms on the planet. It is not far from a native perspective itself. Feminism is one of the strong elements of a bioregional approach, which builds on the fundamental desire to care for all things. The editor is herself a bioregionalist and a partner in compiling *Home!*

Three other basic books presenting a feminist perspective are Susan Griffin's *Woman and Nature: The Roaring Inside Her* (Harper, 1978); Carolyn

Merchant's *Death of Nature: Women, Ecology and the Scientific Revolution* (Harper, 1980); and Starhawk's *Truth or Dare: Encounters with Power, Authority and Mystery* (Harper, 1987).

The problem of racism remains poorly understood in the bioregional movement as elsewhere. Several books have helped me along the way. Wendell Berry's *The Hidden Wound* (Houghton-Mifflin, 1970), which is one American's attempt to come to terms with a racist heritage; and Vincent Harding's *There Is A River* (Random House, 1981), a magnificent account of the black struggle in the U.S. from the colonial period to the end of the Civil War.

Permaculture is another strand of the green movement and is practically one with bioregionalism. Its focus is on effective methods of reinhabiting the land. Its great advocate is Bill Mollison who has been writing and lecturing on the subject for years. A big tome of a book, *Permaculture: A Designer's Manual* (Tagari Publications, 1988) has recently been published and looks indeed like an encyclopedic work on the subject. The permacultural view covers seemingly all aspects of alternative life—community organization, economics, agriculture and restoration.

An earlier work on planning and design is *Bioshelters, Ocean Arks, City Farming: Ecology as the Basis of Design* by Nancy Jack Todd and John Todd (Sierra Club Books, 1984). This is the fruit of a decade's experience in research at the New Alchemy Institute in Massachusetts. Also see the sourcebook produced by the people at Tilth called *The Future is Abundant: A Guide to Sustainable Agriculture* (Tilth, 1982) concerned with environmentally-sound approaches to forestry, farming and gardening in the Pacific Northwest. Another valuable book on reinhabiting North America is *Meeting the Expectations of the Land: Essays in Sustainable Agriculture and Stewardship* (North Point Press, 1984) edited by Wes Jackson, Wendell Berry and Bruce Coleman. And for a history of the corruption of agriculture in the U.S., a devastating account, see *The Unsettling of America* by Wendell Berry (Sierra Club/Avon, 1972).

For those seeking ideas concerning the reinhabitation of the city, an important work is *Knowing Home, Studies for a Possible Portland* (Rain Umbrella Inc., 1981). A more recent publication is *A Green City Program: for San Francisco Bay Area Cities and Towns*, written and edited by Peter Berg, Beryl Magilavy and Seth Zuckerman (Planet Drum, 1989).... There is a great deal of experimen-

tal inquiry to be done in this area. *A Green City Program* represents an informative, creative introduction to the task. Just published, see also *Green Cities: Ecologically Sound Approaches to Urban Space* by David Gordon (Black Rose Books, 1989).

Speaking of design and planning, I want to mention one more source: Doug Aberley's unpublished master's thesis, *Bioregionalism: A Territorial Approach to Governance and Development in Northwest British Columbia*, completed at the University of British Columbia in 1985. From this study, perhaps the only one of its kind, I have learned better what it means to do the real footwork of bioregionalism—gathering the data on the home region, marking out the boundaries, creating the maps and overlays, making up the charts, researching the history of the place and its people from the archaeological past, their adaptations, and the practices of civilized people in recent times, the facts on their economy, trade and industry. In a bioregional study like this, one literally becomes intimately familiar with a certain part of the earth and the activity that goes on there. Of course it is infinitely complex, but one starts somewhere, as the author has shown. This is a bioregional study of the land of the Skeena River in Northern British Columbia, showing how our special bias can be made presentable for public discussion. A valuable tool for regional organizing anywhere. *Bioregionalism: A Territorial Approach* is no doubt available to those, again, who go seeking in the network (see the Bioregional Directory).

North American Bioregional Congress Proceedings

The *Proceedings* from the three North American Bioregional Congresses, the first in 1984, offer the reader an inside view of bioregionalists at work and play. To us it seems all very interesting. The *Proceedings* are printed in book form, obtainable from the two "bioregional bookstores:" *The New Catalyst*, Box 189, Gabriola Island, B.C. V0R 1X0 Canada; and Planet Drum Foundation, Box 31251, San Francisco, CA 94131, U.S.A.: $10 each. These pages show us in our serious deliberations, our workshops and plenaries, our ceremonies and circles. This is our tribe. We are assembled from all over the continent. Songs, poems, presentations, resolutions, opinions and many photographs display the cultural beliefs of the people. An important resource for anyone interested in actually joining the movement.

Other Sources

A more extensive bibliography has been compiled by Kirkpatrick Sale and Steven Davison, and can be obtained from the Hudson Bioregional Council, c/o Sale, 113 W. 11th, New York, N.Y. 10011.

II. Bioregional Directory

Planet Drum Foundation publishes a special issue of *Raise The Stakes* as a directory of bioregional groups Turtle Island-wide. The first, entitled "Emerging States," appeared in Spring 1987, and they updated this in the Fall 1989 issue. The Directory costs US$4.00 and is available from either Planet Drum or *The New Catalyst*.

III. Biographies

Van Andruss, co-editor of *Home!*, lives among friends in the interior mountains of British Columbia. A student of Fred Brown's, in the 70's he dropped out of Civilization, returning to nature, and has only come back in order to participate in the "Turnaround Decade" of the 90's. Interested in regional organizing, forest defense, all aspects of grassroots democracy, he is also a writer, husband and father.

Christopher Plant is one of the editors of *The New Catalyst* magazine, a bioregional journal published in British Columbia. One of the editors of *Home!*, he also co-authored *Turtle Talk: Voices for a Sustainable Future*—a collection of interviews with key activists that explores the full breadth of the bioregional view and which is the first of *The New Catalyst*'s Bioregional Series of books. He also helped organize the third North American Bioregional Congress, held in British Columbia in 1988.

Judith Plant has raised three children, and lots of good food. She is also a co-editor of *Home!*, *The New Catalyst* magazine, and *Turtle Talk: Voices for A Sustainable Future*, and editor of *Healing The Wounds: The Promise of Ecofeminism*. An ecofeminist and practicing bioregionalist, she helped organize the third North American Bioregional Congress held in British Columbia.

Eleanor Wright, co-editor of *Home!*, has been learning to live-in-place beside a cool, clear mountain stream in the dry forested transition zone between the Coast Mountains and the interior plateau of British Columbia.

She and other members of her community share their homeplace with Douglas Fir, Ponderosa Pine & Juniper; Mule Deer & Mountain Goat; Cougar, Coyote & Bear; Pileated Woodpecker, Water Ouzel & Golden Eagle; and, of course, Salmon. Along with her community she is actively engaged in trying to preserve enough of the ecosystems in their 400- square-mile wilderness watershed that life as it is there now will be able to continue in spite of tremendous pressure from logging, mining and hunting interests from outside the valley. She was also a member of the Site Committee for the third North American Bioregional Congress.

*

Doug Aberley lives in Northwest British Columbia where he has been administrator/planner for the historic community of Hazelton since 1979. He became involved in the bioregional movement in the mid-1970s after training in traditional regional planning failed to link culture, environment and economy in an ecological context. His main bioregional interests include writing a bioregional mapping primer, researching the history of regionalism, and exploration of North Pacific coast bioregions via Zodiac.

David Abram is a native of Paumanok, the long, fish-shaped island poised at the mouth of the Hudson river, where he has lived as close neighbor to black-crowned night herons and the fiddler crabs of the salt marsh. A sleight-of-hand magician, he has traded magics with indigenous sorcerors in the ocean islands of Indonesia and the sky islands of the Himalayas, and has lived and worked in the coastal islands of western Canada, where he was tutored by harbor seals. Author of numerous articles on ecological philosophy, he is currently writing a book on the interdependence of land and language.

Akwesasne Notes: A Journal for Native and Natural People, is the official publication of the Mohawk Nation at Akwesasne, near Rooseveltown, N.Y. Beginning as a local newsletter about a bridge blockade 20 years ago, Notes has evolved into an important voice covering events and analyzing stories about Native Peoples from Malaysia to Montreal.

Luanne Armstrong was born and raised on the east shore of Kootenay Lake in south-eastern British Columbia. She spent twelve years there as an adult, farming and raising four children. Now she works in Merritt, B.C., teaching in a native college. She has been active in various peace, feminist and environmental groups.

Peter Berg is the founder and present director of Planet Drum Foundation, an educational and organizing group that publishes information, presents talks and workshops, creates forums, and pursues research about the relationship between human culture and the natural processes of bioregions. He edited *Reinhabiting a Separate Country: A Bioregional Anthology of Northern California* and co-authored *Eco-decentralist Design* and *A Green City Program for San Francisco Bay Area Cities and Towns*. Bioregional organizing trips have taken him throughout the U.S. and to Canada, Mexico and Europe to speak, hold workshops and (of late) perform eco-comedy.

Thomas Berry is an historian of cultures committed to the view that history is now being made primarily not within nations or cultures or between nations or cultures but between the humamn community and the life systems of the earth. His book *The Dream of the Earth* is concerned with this subject as are the various essays he has published. Presently he is Director of the River-dale Center of Religious Research in Riverdale, New York.

Murray Bookchin is a founder and director of the Institute for Social Ecology in Vermont, and is perhaps best known for his book, *Toward An Ecological Society* (Black Rose 1980). A historian, his view that human nature is essentially cooperative—what he terms "social ecology"—and that humankind, if freed from the tyrranny of centralized, hierarchical power structures, can be self-organizing, has had considerable impact upon the alternative movement. A bioregional sympathizer, he is mainly active with the Vermont Greens.

Kelly Booth is an erstwhile bioregional philosopher

and community accountant from British Columbia, whose current pre- occupations center around gardening and the eco-rock band, Zumak, for which he plays bass guitar. His head ached for many months following the third North American Bioregional Congress for which he acted as a succesful financial comptroller—one of the reasons for his having since given up the financial arts.

Ernest Callenbach grew up on ten acres in Appalachia, where he raised chickens, turkeys, and pigs, and learned that nature generally knows best. In 1954 he migrated west to Berkeley, where he has been on the staff of the University of California Press. He has a garden, a compost bin, and walks to work. Besides *Ecotopia Emerging*, he has written *Ecotopia, The Ecotopian Encyclopedia*, and (with his wife Christine Leefeldt) a children's book, *Humphrey the Wayward Whale*. With Michael Phillips, he wrote *A Citizen Legislature*: a proposal to end U.S. electoral corruption through choosing representatives by lot. He is associated with the Elmwood Institute.

Leonard Charles, Jim Dodge, Lynn Milliman, Victoria Stockley, the authors of the Bioregional Quiz, lived together for 17 years at Root Hog Ranch in the Alta Pacific bioregion. Collectively, they were the founding partners of an environmental consulting company. Kathryn Cholette, Ross Dobson, Kent Gerecke, Marcia Nozick, Roberta Simpson and Linda Williams are six Canadians who attended the Green Cities conference held in Chicago in 1989 and who are each active within Green and/or bioregional circles in different regions of Canada.

Gary Coates is Professor of Architecture at Kansas State University and the editor and author of *Resettling America: Energy, Ecology and Community*. He has published numerous articles on the topics of participatory design, organic and ecological architecture and the design of sustainable buildings, towns and cities. He frequently lectures and conducts workshops on these and related topics in America and Europe.

Julie Coates is Director of Information Services for Learning Resources Network, an international association of adult educators. In addition to her work in community education and development, she has been instrumental in developing a statewide awareness of the folklore and folk history of Kansas. She has published numerous articles on adult and community education and lectures frequently in the United States and Europe on topics related to the development of community education programs.

Michael Crofoot is from New Zealand where he actively promotes the permaculture movement "down under." He was an organizer of the Third International Permaculture Conference held in New Zealand in 1989, and has been wooing bioregionalists with offers of marriage since before the second North American Bioregional Congress, which he attended.

Raymond Dasmann has worked for the past forty and more years in the field of ecology and conservation with a particular interest in wildlife and wild country. His work with UNESCO, IUCN, and the World Wildlife Fund has taken him to many countries and developed an awareness of the need to protect cultural diversity as well as biological diversity. At present he is Professor Emeritus at the University of California, Santa Cruz.

Jim Dodge lives in the Coast Range of northern California, which he calls the Alta Pacific Bioregion. He is the author of *Fup* (a story), *Not Fade Away* (novel), *Palms to the Moon* (poems), and, most recently, *Stone Junction* (a novel). After fifteen years on an isolated homestead, where he worked in environmental restoration with the Cazadero Forest Workers' Cooperative and as a land use consultant for Leonard Charles and Associates, he's now teaching part-time at Humboldt State University.

Caroline Estes teaches consensus and facilitation out of long experience in Quaker meetings, plus facilitating large meetings that are run on consensus. She has facilitated all three North American Bioregional Congresses and several Green meetings, as well as sessions of the Fourth World Assembly and a bioregional gathering in Cascadia, where she lives at Alpha Farm, an intentional community she co-founded in 1972.

Pat Fleming has been involved for many years as a psychologist and social worker exploring alternatives to traditional psychiatry. She has also worked with peace, environment and women's groups internationally. She helped establish the Interhelp Network in Great Britain and Australia. For the past several years she has been conducting Council of All Beings workshops and other empowerment tools using voice and movement.

Helen Forsey has her roots on both the Québec and Ontario sides of the Ottawa River. Her love for the land led her to study agriculture, and she worked for a number of years in international development. Since 1984 she has made her home at Dandelion, a small ecofeminist intentional community in Eastern Ontario. As a writer and activist she tries to "think globally, act locally" to resist and reverse the patriarchal destruction of the planet.

Frisco Bay Mussel Group (FBMG) operated as a regularly meeting study group for the San Francisco Bay Area and Shasta Bioregion between 1975 and 1978. Members included natural scientists, political activists, community organizers, and artists who wanted to learn from each other about local natural systems and characteristics. As a result of information presented at FBMG meetings, the group was the first to oppose the Peripheral Canal scheme to divert Northern California's Sacramento River water to Southern California. Its full-page newspaper ad explaining the Canal's adverse effects on San Francisco Bay prompted established environmental groups such as the Sierra Club to also speak out which eventually led to ballot defeat of the proposal.

Jacqueline Froelich is an inspired bioregional artist and expert printer. Amon her many activities over the years, she has been involved with the Eureka Wate; Center's work in Arkansas, and has been central to local and North American Bioregional Congresses.

Jeremiah Gorsline has lived for the last 14 years in the Olympic Peninsula. He has worked as a tree-climber, dairy milker, landscaper and bookseller. In 1976 he began working with cooperatives, contracting reforestation work with State, Federal and Corporate forest-managers through the Pacific Northwest. For the past six years he has been part of the worker-owned Salal Café in Port Townsend. Active as a conservationist, especially in the area of plant-ecology and timber management issues, he is currently one of the directors of the Washington Native Plant Society and chairperson of the Olympic Peninsula Chapter. He is a contributing editor for Empty Bowl, a non-profit cooperative publisher, and is editing a volume in the Dalmo'ma series on Indian-White relations on the north Olympic Peninsula.

Tom Greco, Jr. is a freelance networker, writer, publisher, econimist and consultant whose work is focused upon social, economic and monetary restructuring. He has special interest in community economics, cooperative enterprise, local economic development, personal responsibility and growth, and natural and social ecology. His articles have appeared in *The Whole Earth Review*, *The Catholic Worker*, and *Green Revolution*. He is the author of *Money & Debt: A solution to the Global Crisis*

Milo Guthrie, also known as Milo Pyne, is still wondering what he will do when he "grows up." A biosexual bioregionalist, ecofeminist, and eclectic buddhist-pagan by inclination and necessity, and a botanical consultant by profession, Milo does a lot of idle speculative thinking on what kind of life the human species could live and wonders where we went wrong (and why so many people seem to think things are just fine). Milo assisted in the formation of the Short Mountain Sanctuary, a fairie (spiritual gay male) community in Tennessee, as well as the Cumberland-Green Council, a bioregional network in the upper mid-south. He is presently studying botany in North Carolina, and serves on the Board of Directors of the Piedmont Bioregional Institute, in Uwharria Province.

Gwaganad, also known as Diane Brown, is a member of the Haida Nation, ts'aalth clan. She has been married to Larry Brown, off and on, for twenty-four years. She has two children, Jud, 17, and Lauren, 15. For twenty years she been the Community Health Representative for Skidegate, in Haaida Gwaii (Queen Charlotte Islands).

David Haenke has been immersed in total systems ecological work since arriving in the Ozarks in 1971. He co-founded the Ozark Area Community Congress (OACC)—the first bioregional congress—in 1977, conceptualized and organized the North American Bioregional Congress from 1981 to 1984, was one of the five organizers and convenors of the U.S. Green Committees of Correspondence in 1984. He has been the Coordinator of the Bioregional Project of New Life Farm, Inc., since 1982, and also directs the Ecological Society Project of the Tides Foundation, while remaining active in OACC and ecological work on many levels in the Ozarks and around North America.

Freeman House practices watershed restoration and bioregional speculation near Petrolia, California. Born in California, and misinformed there about the nature of nature, he went home to the Coast Range after his perceptions were given a long bath in the pearly mists of Puget Sound, Ish River country. His early association with Planet Drum Foundation provided a context for the transition. He is a co-founder of the Mattole Watershed Salmon Support Group and the Mattole Restoration Council.

William Koethke has lived at Big Mountain on and off since 1980 and for periods of months in the Jila Forest with campfire and sleeping bag. He is completing a book on the planetary eco- crisis which features a complete social-permacultural proposal for the San Francisco watershed. This book is intended to answer the question "How Do We Live in Balance with Nature?"

Leopold Kohr, born in Austria in 1909, wrote *The Breakdown of Nations* in 1957, presenting the theory that bigness is the source of all social misery. His ideas had a most important effect on E.F. Schumacher, author of Small is Beautiful and consequently on the bioregional movement today.

Alison Lang has long experience of living in the dry Fraser bioregion, near Lillooet, British Columbia where she also practices Zen. An artist and drum-maker, she also helped to organize the third North American Bioregional Congress, held near Squamish in 1988.

Fraser Lang is a bioregional poet from the mountains of British Columbia; he also is a singer/songwriter/musician with the eco-rock band, Zumak, and was also a member of the site committee for the third North American Bioregional Congress.

Gary Lawless is a native of the Gulf of Maine bioregion. He lives on Damariscotta Lake. In 1977, he edited *The Gulf of Maine: A Bioregional Reader.* He is co-owner of Gulf of Maine Bookstore, and editor/publisher of Blackberry Books. He was one of the organizers of the Gulf of Maine Bioregional Congress, and was on the site committee for the fourth North American Bioregional Congress. His latest book of poems is First Sight of Land.

Jeffrey Lewis was involved with the 1986 and 1988 Cascadia Bioregional Congresses and lives in Portland, Oregon, where he works with young children. His interests include grassroots economics and reclaiming the cities. He has been active with the People of Color Committee of the North American Bioregional Congress.

Aldo Leopold is the author of the environmental "classic," *A Sand County Almanac*, first published in 1949. A collection of Leopold's essays on wilderness and the importance of land health and ecological diversity, the book remains key reading for bioregionalists and wilderness lovers everywhere; it concludes with his famous statement of the "land ethic."

Michael Linton is the originator of the LETS (Local Exchange Trading System) system, first begun in the town of Courtenay, British Columbia. Using "green" dollars in place of regular currency, LETS is an alternative economic system that facilitates exchange and trading of work and skills among people even when "the system" isn't working.

Joanna Macy, from Berkeley, is a teacher of world religions and an activist in movements for peace and justice. She is the author of *Despair and Personal Power in the Nuclear Age* and *Dharma and Development*, a book about the Sarvodaya self- help movement in Sri Lanka. She is co-founder of the international Interhelp Network, a global network of people from all walks of life who strive to integrate political, emotional, and spiritual dimensions of the work for peace and justice.

Lynn Margulis, along with her son, Dorian Sagan, has contributed greatly to making biological theory accessible to a wide audience. Their book *Micro-Cosmos*, a "saga of the life of the planet," helps greatly to replace the view of evolution as "chronic competition" with a cooperative view of life as being a product of networking.

Jerry Martien has lived in the Humboldt Bay region

of northern California for twenty years. In addition to cultural organizing—a term he finds silly and redundant—he has several times over-committed himself to the editing of bioregional publications, most recently *Upriver/Downriver*. He has published three poetry chapbooks, all of intense local interest. Despite a life-long obsession with economics, he somehow makes a living as a carpenter.

David McCloskey originated near the confluence of the McKenzie and Willamette rivers in Oregon and now lives with his family in the Snoqualmie watershed, in Ish River country, in Cascadia on the northeast rim. He teaches Sociology, Anthropology, Human Ecology, and Geography at Seattle University. He has been teaching and writing on the significance of place and bioregionalism for over a decade. He recently authored an "Environmental Bill of Rights" amendment to the Washington State Constitution.

Rob Messick was born in the piedmont of North Carolina, spent some time at The Farm in Tennessee, and is now co-editor, graphic artist and technician, photographer, and bookkeeper with Katuah Journal in North Carolina. He has learned much about the complexities, joys, and difficulties of sustaining a bioregional journal through working with his friends at Katuah and the growing network of people involved in environmental concerns throughout the region. He is a self-taught artist, along with being a naturalist, theoretical scientist and somewhat of a mystic.

Caryn Mirriam-Goldberg, besides editing Konza (Kansas Area Watershed—KAW—Council Newsletter) and organizing KAW Council events, is involved in planning the founding Congress of The Great Prairie Bioregional Congress. She teaches poetry and fiction writing at the University of Kansas and through local elementary school programs. She lives close to the Kaw River in Lawrence, Kansas with her husband, Ken Lassman, and son, Daniel. Her poetry has appeared in many literary journals and is forthcoming in several anthologies.

Bill Mollison, from Tasmania, received the 1981 Right Livelihood Award for his work in environmental design. He is Executive Director of the Permaculture Institute, which he established in 1979 to teach practical design of sustainable soil, water, plant and legal and economic systems to students the world over. In 1974, he and David Holmgren developed and refined the Permaculture Concept, leading to the publication of *Permaculture One* and *Permaculture Two*. His latest book, Permaculture: A Designer's Manual is a land-mark publication on building sustainable ecosystems.

Marnie Muller lives with her family in the Little Sandymush Creek watershed, near Asheville, North Carolina. She is a founder and co-editor of *Katuah Journal: Bioregional Journal* of the Southern Appalachians, a quarterly publication which explores sustainable human-Earth relations in that region. She served on the Coordinating Committee for the first North American Bioregional Congress in 1984, as well as NABC II in 1986. Currently, she is involved in designing programs and curriculum for conceptually and kinesthetically accessing what Thomas Berry refers to as "The Dream of the Earth."

Sue Nelson is a long-time resident of the center of Los Angeles and remembers it before the days of solid freeways and other "development." A committed community activist, much of her work involves perpetual struggle against continued "developments" that would further diminish the natural and human diversity of this city; she has also contributed much energy to the North American Bioregional Congresses.

John Papworth lives in London, England, and is an Anglican clergyman, economist, journalist, author, social critic, broadcaster, ecologist, futurist, husband and father. He was a founder and editor of Resurgence magazine and also founded and now edits *The Fourth World Review* as well as being an associate editor of *The Ecologist*. He was also founder of the Fourth World Assemblies, and author of Prerequisites of Peace and New Politics and the Economics of Humanism.

Geraldine Payton, from Chesaw in Washington state, is one of the editors of *Columbiana* magazine, as well as being an active bioregionalist.

Wilfred Pelletier, an Odawan elder from Manitoulin Island on Lake Huron, has been working as co-director of the Nishnawbe Institute, an Indian educational and cultural project in Toronto. Together with Ted Poole, he wrote *No Foreign Land: The Biography of a North American Indian*—an eloquent account of one man's belief in his people and their traditions.

Sheila Purcell was Planet Drum Foundation's first intern, doing work on the "Listening to the Earth" Conference in 1979; later, in 1981, she was the first Planet Drum networker. Since then she has practiced environmental law and mediation. Currently she is working on air quality by way of promoting carpooling/vanpooling and use of public transit in San Francisco.

Kirkpatrick Sale is a co-director of the E.F. Schumacher Society, co-founder of the Hudson Bioregional Council (and its Wetlands Restoration Project), and the author of *Human Scale*, and *Dwellers In The Land: The Bioregional Vision*. He divides his time between two homes in the Hudson estuary, upriver in Cold Spring, New York, and downriver in Manhattan.

Jamie Sayen is a coordinator of Preserve Appalachian Wilderness (PAW), a grassroots group working to restore future Old Growth throughout the Appalachians. PAW has made a proposal to create a Northern Appalachian Evolutionary Preserve on lands currently owned by out-of-region multinational timber and paper corporations (and suffering liquidation clearcuts and herbicide sprayings). He is also an editor of The Glacial Erratic, the radical environmental journal of the Northern Appalachian bioregion. He is also a wild raspberry farmer.

Lance Scott has been active in various movements for social change over the years, particularly the Green and bioregional movements. He has been editor of *RAIN* magazine and the *Portland Alliance*, and is currently editor of the *Seattle Community Catalyst*, a local activist monthly. Lance is a fifth-generation resident of the Seattle area.

Gary Snyder lives in eastern Shasta Nation in the Yuba river drainage. One of the west coast's most widely published poets, he is finishing up a prose book, *The Practice of the Wild*, dealing with bioregionalism and several other concepts, and their application to our times.

Starhawk is the author of *The Spiral Dance: A Rebirth of the Ancient Religion Of The Great Goddess, Dreaming The Dark: Magic, Sex, and Politics* and *Truth or Dare: Encounters with Power, Authority and Mystery*. A feminist and peace activist, she also teaches at several San Francisco Bay Area colleges. She travels widely lecturing and giving workshops, and in San Francisco works with the Reclaiming collective which offers classes, workshops and public rituals in the Old Religion of the Goddess, called Witchcraft. She is presently working on a novel.

Daniel Stolpe's work has appeared in several issues of Raise the Stakes. His art has evolved into symbolic language out of an extended living and working relationship with the Swinomish Indians of Puget Sound.

John Todd and Nancy Jack Todd have been actively pursuing their work in planetary ecology for over twenty years. In 1969, they co-founded, along with Bill McLarney, the New Alchemy Institute, which was dedicated to exploring the potential of alternative, ecologically designed technologies for providing basic human needs. In 1982, they created a new organization, Ocean Arks International, to disseminate the ideas and practice of ecological sustainability throughout the world. Together with The Lindisfarne Association, they publish "Annals of Earth", edited by Nancy Jack Todd.

Brian Tokar has been an activist in the peace, antinuclear, and environmental movements for eighteen years, and has been active in bioregional politics since 1985. He is the author of *The Green Alternative: Creating an Ecological Future*, and has written and lectured across the U.S. and Canada on Green politics, bioregionalism, and other emerging ecological movements. Brian lives on an organic vegetable farm in the upper Winooski River Valley, east of Vermont's Green Mountains.

Frank Traina is director of Sunrock Farm, an educational farm outside of Cincinnati, Ohio. About 25,000 school children visit Sunrock Farm each year to learn about and experience the Earth and the Ohio River Region. He publishes a local bioregional newsletter, Four Rivers Earthworks, and is committed to the Bioregional Education Committee of the North American Bioregional Congress. Frank also gives workshops and talks on developing a sense of kinship with the Earth and one's bioregion. year ttle piece of Earth. He publishes *Pollen: A Journal of Bioregional Education* on behalf of the Bioregional Education Committee of the North American Bioregional Congress.

Chris Wells is a many-talented artist and environmental educator from Santa Fe, New Mexico. He is also one of the co-founders of the All-Species Project, a cultural arts/education program working in schools and diverse communities culminating in a yearly event: an All-Species Day celebration of our connection to the Earth and all species.

Michael Zwerin has been jazz critic for *The Village Voice*, European editor for the same paper, and is now culture writer for the *International Herald Tribune*. He has also played trombone with Miles Davis, Earl Hines, Eric Dolphy and Mingus Dynasty. *Close Enough for Jazz* is his autobiography.

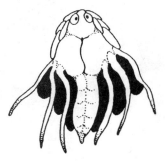

When the animals come to us,
asking for our help,
will we know what they are saying?
When the plants speak to us
in their delicate, beautiful language,
will we be able to answer them?
When the planet herself
sings to us in our dreams,
will we be able to wake ourselves, and act?

— Gary Lawless